The Catholic Church in the Twentieth Century

The Catholic Church in the Twentieth Century

Renewing and Reimaging the City of God

John Deedy, *editor*

Contributors:

John C. Cort
Sally Cunneen
John Deedy
James Finn
Gerald P. Fogarty, S.J.
Michael O. Garvey
Howard J. Gray, S.J.
Jeffrey Gros, F.S.C.
John C. Haughey, S.J.
Jeanne Knoerle, S.P.
Barbara Kraemer, O.S.F.
Catherine Lupori
Patricia M. McDonald, S.H.C.J.
Bishop Robert F. Morneau
David J. O'Brien
Mary Jo Richardson

A Michael Glazier Book

THE LITURGICAL PRESS
Collegeville, Minnesota
www.litpress.org

A Michael Glazier Book published by The Liturgical Press

Cover design by David Manahan, O.S.B. Photographs by Diane Towalski, courtesy of *Saint Cloud Visitor.*

1	2	3	4	5	6	7

Library of Congress Cataloging-in-Publication Data

The Catholic Church in the twentieth century : renewing and reimaging the city of God / John Deedy, editor ; contributors, John C. Cort ... [et al.].
    p. cm.
   Includes bibliographical references.
   ISBN 0-8146-5947-0 (alk. paper)
   1. Catholic Church—History—20th century. 2. Catholic Church—Doctrines—History—20th century. I. Deedy, John G. II. Cort, John C.

BX1389 .C33 2000
282'.09'04—dc21
                                                 00-035652

For Margaret and John Manship

Contents

Foreword: From Triumphal to Pilgrim Church   ix
> *John Deedy*

The Papacy: From Low Regard to High Esteem   1
> *Gerald P. Fogarty, S.J.*

Priestly Ministry: A Search for Identity and Purpose   21
> *Howard J. Gray, S.J.*

Sisters and Brothers: An Evolved and Evolving Religious Life   37
> *Barbara Kraemer, O.S.F.*

The American Catholic Family: Reality or Misnomer?   57
> *Sally Cunneen*

Women and the Church: Rooting Out Stereotypes   73
> *Catherine Lupori and Mary Jo Richardson*

Catholic Youth: The Presumed Become the Pursued   89
> *David J. O'Brien*

Catholic Education: Helping Shape Intellectual, Cultural, and Civic Life   101
> *Jeanne Knoerle, S.P.*

Biblical Scholarship: When Tradition Met Method   113
> *Patricia M. McDonald, S.H.C.J.*

Ecumenism: From Isolation to a Vision of Christian Unity   131
> *Jeffrey Gros, F.S.C.*

Social Justice: Catholic Teaching Goes Global   149
> *John C. Cort*

Money and the Faith: Is Mammon an Ogre Still?   169
    John C. Haughey, s.j.

Church and State: Large Issues Resolved, Large Issues Pending   183
    James Finn

Communications and the Arts: Lost: The Mind of the Church   203
    Michael O. Garvey

Spirituality: Five Twentieth-Century Witnesses of Discipleship   217
    Bishop Robert F. Morneau

Contributors   235

Selected Index   241

Foreword

From Triumphal to Pilgrim Church

John Deedy

Early in the twentieth century—in 1907 to be precise—the book *The Thirteenth, Greatest of Centuries* appeared under the quaint, lost imprint of the Catholic Summer School Press. Given the publisher, the book hardly seemed to need explication. It celebrated a time—and a Church. Written by James J. Walsh, a New York medical doctor and Fordham University professor, *The Thirteenth, Greatest of Centuries* was enormously successful, running through more than ten printings, including a large special edition sponsored by the Knights of Columbus. The book made Walsh a celebrity on the Catholic lecture circuit and helped lead to a number of honors, including papal knighthoods and the University of Notre Dame's Laetare Medal for 1916.

Walsh was on firm ground. The thirteenth was a remarkable century. How could it be otherwise, when the thirteenth century produced the Magna Carta, the document which established the foundation for constitutional law and basic civil liberties as much of the world knows them today? The Magna Carta is a landmark of civil history. Walsh was not unaware of that fact, though his treatment of the document was almost cursory. His essential interest laid elsewhere. *The Thirteenth, Greatest of Centuries* was basically a denominational tract, and perfectly suited for a triumphalist ecclesial period.

Walsh focused on the Catholic Church, its great popes, artists, scholars, saints of that century—individuals such as Innocent III, Francis of Assisi, Thomas Aquinas, Dante, Giotto, Dominic, Albertus Magnus, Bonaventure, Elizabeth of Hungary, Clare of Assisi. He detailed the great humanitarian and artistic innovations that were the Church's—organized charities, grand libraries, spectacular Gothic cathedrals, literary and artistic glories, universities that became the cornerstones for wondrous advances in knowledge and education. He pointed to hospitals and medical care, the thirteenth being the century when, under the aegis of the Church, hospitals departed from their original purpose of dispensing hospitality to travelers, the temporarily homeless, and strangers (hence the origin of the name hospital), and evolved into facilities caring for the chronically ill and seriously incapacitated. In Walsh's view, the thirteenth century represented "the highest stage in human accomplishment." (The lowest, in passing? In Walsh's 1907 estimate, the eighteenth century, because of its rejection of religious authority and its glorification of pure reason.)

The Catholic Church of the twentieth century, the subject matter of this book, may not rival personality by personality, event by event, advance by advance, high point by high point, every detail of Walsh's thirteenth. But it had defining moments—indeed, two generally accounted of seminal importance: the convoking of Vatican Council II in 1962 and the election in 1978 of John Paul II, a Pole, the first non-Italian pope since the Dutchman, Hadrian VI, back in 1522. Each of those occurrences was to set the Church on dramatic new courses—the council in terms of ecclesiastical reform and renewal; the election of the Polish pope in terms of an ideological quickening of Catholic presence in the wider world. It is a journey that the Church is about to this day, with a pilgrim people as passengers. The thirteenth century, incidentally, had eighteen popes and three councils—Lateran IV, Lyons I, and Lyons II—and considerable papal and ecclesial history has passed down to us from those times, notably the inspiration of Francis, the art of Giotto, Thomas Aquinas' *Summa Theologiae,* reforms of Innocent III (alas, however, the Fourth Crusade and the mandating of special dress for Jews and Muslims to render them objects of opprobrium), and the Lateran Council IV's defining of the Eucharist in terms of "transubstantiation," a concept that settled an ancient theological quandary.

Still, by whatever measurement, the twentieth century was a remarkable one. Two world wars tested the fiber of the Church and left their marks on it, some problematic. A pact with Italy—the Lateran Treaty of 1929—moved the Vatican out of the Middle Ages and into the modern family of nations. The Polish pope was instrumental in the eclipse and eventual downfall of Communism, a system many feared would lead to global atheism. In the household of the Church, meanwhile, the practice of the faith underwent extensive, dramatic changes, the full effects of which are likely still being assimilated.

Energizing this historic evolution were gifted, sometimes controversial popes (one already sainted, Pius X), artists, scholars, and numerous others of holiness and esteem, excusing inevitable human foibles. Among them were the wartime pontiffs Benedict XV and Pius XII, the paleontologist Pierre Teilhard de Chardin, John XXIII, Mother Teresa, Dorothy Day, Thomas Merton, John Courtney Murray, Padre Pio, Edith Stein, Georges

Rouault, Eric Gill, Graham Greene, G. K. Chesterton, Georges Bernanos, Jacques Maritain, François Mauriac, Karl Rahner, Barbara Ward, Paul VI, Yves Congar. The list goes on.

If the shade of James Walsh is protesting that the twentieth-century's cast of Catholics is notches below those of his thirteenth century, the obvious counter is that we are yet too close in time to events of the twentieth century and the personalities who shaped them to have their import fully gauged. History, like bread, must leaven. It needs space. For all we know, the twentieth century could prove one of the greatest for the Church since Christ walked the earth.

Certainly the century must be accounted of special significance in the annals of Catholic Christian history. There are many reasons why, even apart from the Vatican II and the Polish pope, and perhaps none more so than the historic breakthroughs that occurred on the gender issue. Women, historically Catholicism's second-class members, did not achieve full equality in the Church during the twentieth century, but there were very many advances. At long last the Church displayed signs, however reluctantly at times, of becoming an equal-status, gender-blind institution.

For one, the twentieth century saw the first females raised to the rank of doctors of the Church—persons, that is, honored in essential part for their scholarship and learning. St. Teresa of Avila was designated a doctor of the Church on September 27, 1970. (In 1930 a suggestion that she was worthy of the dignity was rejected with the flippancy, *obstat sexus*—"gender is an obstacle.") A week later, on October 4, 1970, St. Catherine of Siena joined her in the ranks of doctor, and twenty-seven years afterwards, in 1997, St. Thérèsè of Lisieux. There are now three women among the Church's thirty-two doctors. The balance is disproportionate still, and some might be inclined to discount the honoring of these three women as mere tokenism. On the other hand, their recognition is implicit concession that women merit a place intellectually alongside the best and the brightest of Catholic men. In Catholic historical context, that acknowledgment is near revolutionary.

The twentieth century also saw the first women, religious and lay, admitted into the proceedings of an ecumenical council. True, these women were but a handful and they entered only as auditors, and belatedly at that, not being invited in until 1964. (The council had been going on for two years, and was then in its penultimate session.) But the point remains that they were admitted into an ecclesiastical deliberation of the most exalted kind. Never before in Catholic Christian history had women been anywhere near the engine-room of power, when the fate of the Church was being decided. True, the conciliar roles of these women were circumscribed and their interaction was unofficial at best. But the female gender had achieved a presence, and that of itself spoke volumes. As much as anything else that happened in the century, the presence of women in the *aula* of St. Peter's at the Vatican Council II may have signaled the true beginning of the end of patriarchy in the Catholic Church.

Of course, the gender gap was not eliminated by those developments, and maybe not even significantly closed. The question of female ordination, for example, was broached, but encountered stern dismissal at the highest level. Nonetheless, a chasm was narrowed, and as the century wound to a close additional issues of gender were addressed with varying measures of success, such as the use of inclusive language in the liturgy and prayers of the Church, and the right of females to be present in church sanctuaries as lectors, cantors, eucharistic ministers, even as acolytes. By century's end there was what amounted to a near-wholesale admission of women into pastoral, ministerial, and administrative roles—although some might be tempted to wonder, in light of the shortage of male vocations and the need for more hands to get jobs done, whether this development was wholly altruistic. That same need, of course, combined with emphases of Vatican II to bring large numbers of laymen into direct service to the Church, including thousands as permanent deacons, an order of ministry restored in the Roman Rite two years after Vatican II, after having fallen into disuse in the fourth or fifth century.

Beyond gender, so much transpired in the century, and with such cumulative effect, as to alter the very entity of Catholicism. The net result is that the Church that arrives at the year 2000 is a quite different Church from that which entered the century in the final phase of the twenty-five year pontificate of Leo XIII. Today, in the waning years of another long pontificate, that of John Paul II, it is quite a different Church from the one presided over by Pius X from 1903 to 1914, Benedict XV from 1914 to 1922, Pius XI from 1922 to 1939, Pius XII from 1939 to 1958, John XXIII from 1958 to 1963, Paul VI from 1963 to 1978, John Paul I, the "late summer pope," from August 26 to September 28, 1978, and, since then and as this book is published, John Paul II.

Over those one hundred years numerous attitudes, some indefensible but seemingly fixed forever in the Catholic psyche, were faced and in many cases repudiated. The twentieth was the century, for instance, when the Church at last came to grips with ancient and scandalous anti-Semitic proclivities, most specifically at Vatican II when the Church Fathers repudiated the notion of Deicide, which had linked Jewish people without distinction to the death of Jesus and held their offspring across the ages, if not accursed of God, then *perfidii*—as the term of the old Good Friday liturgy had it until John XXIII ordered the word expunged. There was progress also in mending breaches with other churches and faiths—the Orthodox, Islam, and, of course, Protestantism.

A large factor in these ecumenical developments was the routing from the Catholic psyche of the notion that the Church never changes—indeed, never need change.

The Catholic Church—the same forever, yesterday, today, tomorrow. Permanency. It was what Catholicism was all about. The world could change, but not the Catholic Church. Whatever its shortcomings, whatever the frailties of its leaders, whatever the institutional misadventures, this Church was the perfect organism. Of course, Catholics of the first five or six decades of the twentieth century, as generations before them, were living in a kind of time capsule, one that was seriously misprogramed. The notion of "unchange" was a total misconception. The Catholic Church did change—in fact, had changed many times over the centuries, as history tried to remind those who would listen. It changed, for instance, on slavery, on the charging of interest on loans, on torture, on capital punishment, to limit oneself to the most obvious instances. To be sure, most change was gradual, and often so subtle as to be hardly noticed, taking place without the very need to explain anything to anyone. But change happened.

What made change in the twentieth century so exceptional is that Catholics saw it up close and in living color, so to speak. It was undeniable. Some of the changes were of small consequence, and as often as not had to do with the sweeping away of old legalisms. But in a time of greater reverence for tradition and established forms, the impact was huge. Those changes form a litany. Consider:

Entering the century, fish or some other "penitential" dish distinguished Catholics from others at table on Fridays; they abstained from meat (Spanish Catholics excepted, thanks to papal indult), else risked salvation itself; today Catholics can eat meat on Friday with nary a concern about suffering forever in hell or that place called purgatory. Entering the century, the priest said Mass with his back to the people and Latin was the universal language of the liturgy; today the altar is turned around, the priest faces the congregation, and the vernacular is in place everywhere in the world. Entering the century, cremation was held a pagan abomination; today cremains may be present in churches for funeral Masses. Entering the century, food or drink any time after midnight broke the eucharistic fast; today water disturbs the Eucharistic fast not the least and abstinence from food is reduced to one hour. (Anyway, who's holding a stopwatch?) Entering the century, Mass was strictly a morning ritual; today Mass might be celebrated at almost any hour of the day. Entering the century, women did not darken a church without head veiled, even if the covering was a silly Kleenex; today, forget it. Throughout most of the century, Sunday Mass was a dress-up occasion; today Sunday congregations resemble "dress-down Fridays" at the office. Sisters, brothers, and many priests, meanwhile, have commonly shed religious garb for secular clothing.

As indicated, these changes—and those cited hardly begin to exhaust them all—are mere accidentals of religious practice, changes such as might happen in any century, at any time, and of course over the centuries did in many categories of faith. Once upon a time, for instance, individuals might be required to do humiliating public penance for their sins and married couples might be forbidden conjugal privileges for transgressions of one sort or another. Today it is a challenge just to get Catholics into the confessional box for what is now called the sacrament of reconciliation. Once upon a time, there were so many holy days on the Church's calendar—the Decretals of Gregory IX (c. 1235) listed forty-five weekday feasts on which attendance at Mass was obligatory—that the pursuit of everyday commerce was a problem. Today holy days are few, their number varying not only from country to country, but within countries as well, including the United States (e.g., the feast of the Ascension).

On the other hand, the twentieth century saw changes on matters of large substance as well, changes so great as to put the Church on a different footing entirely with governments and all other religions. Much of this occurred as the Church shifted ground in its understanding of the relationship of Church and state, on religious freedom, and on the question of salvation outside the Catholic faith. Indeed, one might argue that nothing brought the Catholic Church more squarely into the modern world than changes in those three areas, and none more so than the change in the Church's position on salvation.

Historically, Catholic understanding was that in order to be saved, one *had to belong,* one *had to be a member* of the Catholic Church. From the third-century theology of St. Cyprian, through *Unam sanctam* (the 1302 bull of Pope Boniface VIII), through the profession of faith sworn to by the Fathers of Vatican Council I, the teaching was explicit: *Extra ecclesiam nulla salus:* "Outside the Church, no salvation." That meant belonging to the Catholic Church, none other. Early in the century, as the meaning of "church" became more nuanced, the Catholic Church began, albeit subtly, to move away from that teaching. The axiom itself, however, has never been formally repudiated—that is, not until November 21, 1964, when *Lumen gentium,* Vatican II's Dogmatic Constitution on the Church, was promulgated. With *Lumen gentium* came formal acknowledgment that the divine plan of salvation was far more generous than what Western

Catholics had ever been led to believe. The document conceded that God did indeed work through churches other than the Catholic Church alone, and with that allowance whole new ecumenical horizons were opened.

Much more happened in the Church's twentieth century: dramatic evolutions in Catholic education and programs of catechesis; *Humanae vitae,* Paul VI's birth-control encyclical, and the subsequent challenges to Church-teaching on matters of sexual morality; the exodus in the second part of the century of many priests and nuns from formal religious life; the precipitous decline in new religious vocations, male and female.

These and other developments of the century are probed in the essays of this book, and in contexts fuller than the quick itemization offered above. As such the book is intended as a counterpoint to those exploring the Church's challenges and prospects in the new millennium. It is not conceived as a crystal ball. Naturally it is tempting to look to the future and speculate on the Church's agenda in the years ahead. For instance, will the new century—indeed, the new millennium—see change in the Church's position on a non-celibate priesthood or its position on female ordination? Will it see walls of divisions between various faiths come tumbling down after centuries of division? Such speculation is seductive, especially since so much in the Church seems on the cusp of additional change. Not all the essayists in this book are immune to the temptation to peek ahead, but by and large they leave speculation to heaven—or at least to others. The book's essential purpose is to look back, to trace and to weigh the events and developments in the century just closed out. What took place? What went right? What went wrong? What was learned? What might have been learned? Where do we stand now? These questions are discussed with varying degrees of directness.

Such a book could sum to a tendentious agenda, but tendentiousness is not the purpose here, and I trust readers will find no more than necessary in these pages. The book's focus is essentially American, although not provincially so, I hope. In any instance, the designation "American" covers so much geography these days that much of the American experience has a resonance elsewhere in the world. Focus is also largely on the Western or Roman Rite, this being Catholicism's predominant rite.

That said, there are things this book does not attempt, and could not without growing to a tome or multi-volume production. It would have been interesting, for example, to employ a world vision, and explore the impact of certain Vatican II documents—*Dignitatis humanae* (Declaration on Religious Freedom), say, or *Unitatis redintegratio* (Decree on Ecumenism)— on Catholics in places such as Latin America or the Asian rim. What is the meaning of such documents for inculturation and the general state of affairs of the Catholic Church in those areas? Important as such questions are, they are matters for another book with a different audience from those expected to read this volume.

Inevitably there are overlaps in the essays that follow. Neither the Church nor history is so neatly compartmentalized that topics can be laid out and contained within strictly-defined parameters. So, if John Cort's essay on social justice spills over into Fr. John Haughey's essay on wages and the uses of money (or vice versa), or if Sally Cunneen's essay on the family brushes into that of Catherine Lupori and Mary Jo Richardson on women in the Church, or the same with David O'Brien and Sr. Jeanne Knoerle in the areas of youth and education, then so be it. Added texture hardly hurts the treatment of a subject. The editorial objective has been to allow the essayists a freedom of range—those essayists cited, as well as James Finn, Fr. Gerald Fogarty, Fr. Howard Gray, Sr. Barbara Kraemer, Br. Jeffrey Gros, Michael Garvey, Sr. Patricia McDonald. Bishop Robert Morneau's essay is placed last in the book, as it seems appropriate to conclude on the meditative note that he provides.

***

A few acknowledgments are in order, beginning with Michael Glazier, who helped refine the idea for this book and who stayed in touch throughout. Long-time Catholic-press colleague and friend Cornelius M. Buckley advised even as life ebbed. He is thanked posthumously. Edward R. F. Sheehan, Frs. Paul F. Bailey and Raymond A. Schroth, S.J., proved valuable consultants. So did several others.

The Papacy: From Low Regard to High Esteem

Gerald P. Fogarty, S.J.

There is an old adage in Rome that a "political" pope is followed by a "religious" one, that a pope who sought to relate the Church to the external political world tends to be succeeded by one who focuses on the interior life of the Church. Granted the limitations of such an adage, it is helpful for analyzing the popes of the twentieth century.

The century dawned with Leo XIII nearing the end of his pontificate, second in length only to that of his immediate predecessor, Pius IX (1846–78). His abiding intellectual legacy was the Thomistic revival, the theme of his first encyclical, *Aeterni patris* (1879), calling for Catholics to use the philosophy of the Angelic Doctor. The corpus of many of his encyclicals laid out a blueprint for relations between the Church and the modern state, which the later American theologian John Courtney Murray, S.J., would use in his reflections on religious liberty. But in *Rerum novarum* (1891), Leo XIII also addressed the social question then emerging in the industrialized European and American world. He had also issued the first encyclical on the biblical question that would not be settled until Vatican II. His approach was basically balanced, but toward the end of his pontificate he gave indications that he held suspect the new method of "historical criticism" of Scripture. Yet he also opened the Vatican archives to scholars, Catholic and non-Catholic alike.

In regard to external affairs, in 1878 Leo had inherited the Roman Question, the status of the pope in Rome which was now the capital of the kingdom of Italy, and the *Kulturkampf*. By 1887 he had settled relations with the German Empire and again began inserting the Church into modern affairs. But still the Roman Question overshadowed his pontificate. It provided at least part of the background to his condemnation of Americanism in 1899 and his begrudging toleration of the American praise for the separation of Church and state and religious liberty. In an effort to put pressure on the kingdom of Italy and preserve the sovereignty of the Holy

See guaranteed in international law, he attempted to reestablish rapport with France. This sacrificed the possibility of the election of Cardinal Mariano Rampolla del Tindaro, Leo's secretary of state and architect of the *ralliement* in France, as his successor.

Leo's death in 1903 brought to the fore some of the tensions latent in the latter part of his pontificate. The cardinals at the conclave, including James Gibbons of Baltimore, the sole American, were leaning toward Rampolla as the next pope when Cardinal Jan Puzyna of Krakow cast a veto against him in the name of the Austro-Hungarian emperor.[1] The conclave then turned to Cardinal Giuseppe Melchiore Sarto of Venice, a spiritual, though not learned, prelate. Taking the name Pius X, he immediately set about arresting what he saw as alarming tendencies among Catholic scholars. He named the thirty-eight-year-old Raffaele Merry del Val as his cardinal secretary of state and began an increasing campaign against scholars; Rampolla became secretary of the Holy Office, but played no role in the anti-Modernist crusade. Under Pius' direction, the Biblical Commission, originally established as a more progressive organ under Leo XIII, issued a series of restrictive instructions, upholding, among other things, the Mosaic authorship of the Pentateuch.[2] Pius' movement to curtail what he considered dangerous scholarship culminated with the condemnation of Modernism in *Pascendi Dominici gregis* on September 8, 1907. He then tolerated, if he did not actually sponsor, the integrist witch hunt against seminary and university professors.[3] In 1910 he issued an oath against Modernism to be taken by every candidate for ordination, by priests before becoming pastors or bishops, and, annually, by every member of seminary faculties.[4] On a devotional level, he reformed Church music and restored Gregorian chant, encouraged frequent Communion, and admitted children of the age of reason to the Eucharist.

Pius X considered Leo XIII's policy toward secular governments to be too irenic and asserted through Merry del Val the rights of the Church, as a result of which France broke diplomatic relations in 1904 and, the following year, confiscated Church property. But he also recognized the growing importance of the Church outside Europe. In 1911, for example,

[1]   Hubert Jedin and John Dolan, eds., *History of the Church,* vol. 9: *The Church in the Industrial Age* (New York: Crossroad, 1989) 382.

[2]   For the implications of these "responses" for American Catholic intellectual life see Gerald P. Fogarty, *American Catholic Biblical Scholarship: A History from the Early Republic to Vatican II* (San Francisco: Harper & Row, 1989) 96–198.

[3]   Émile Poulat, *Intégrisme et catholicisme intégral, un réseau secret international antimoderniste: La "Sapinière," 1909–1921* (Tournai: Casterman, 1969) 64–78.

[4]   DS, 3537–50.

he named two cardinals in the United States, William O'Connell of Boston and John Farley of New York. Pius X died on August 20, 1914, just as World War I was erupting.

The conclave of 1914 represented a shift back to the Rampolla party. Of the American cardinals only Farley, who had been in Europe and remained there when he learned of the pope's failing health, made it to the conclave. The conclave chose Giacomo della Chiesa, archbishop of Bologna, named a cardinal only the previous May. Having served as secretary to Rampolla, then nuncio to Spain, della Chiesa followed his mentor to the Secretariat of State in 1887 and became under secretary in 1901, a post he held under Merry del Val until being appointed to Bologna in 1903. Taking the name Benedict XV, he replaced Merry del Val as secretary of state with Cardinal Pietro Gasparri. His first encyclical, *Ad beatissimi* in November 1914, put an end to the integrist movement against Modernism, but *Spiritus Paraclitus* in 1920 warned biblical scholars against interpreting the New Testament to mean that there was development from the position of events in the life of Christ to their incorporation in the Gospels. In 1917 he promulgated the Code of Canon Law, the first such codification of Church law in history, a task that had been supervised by Gasparri. At the same time he established the Congregation of the Oriental Church for closer relations with Eastern-rite churches in union with Rome.

But Benedict XV's pontificate was largely occupied with the war in Europe. His overtures to the warring factions, unfortunately, met with rebuff especially from the Allies. A secret clause in the Treaty of London in 1915 excluded the Holy See from any peace conference due to Italian endeavors to prevent the discussion of the Roman Question. As a result, Benedict's efforts to work for a separate armistice with the Austro-Hungarian Empire were thwarted when the Italians convinced the Americans that the pope was simply trying to preserve the Catholic populations of the empire. In October 1918 the new German government joined Austria in making overtures to President Woodrow Wilson for an armistice. Archbishop Eugenio Pacelli, the nuncio to Bavaria and conveyor of Austrian responses to the pope, voiced his frustration to Cardinal Gasparri: "On this occasion I cannot hide from Your Eminence my sadness in seeing Germany turning directly to the President of the United States, rather than having had recourse to the good offices of the Holy Father."[5] When the war was over, however, Benedict took the first steps toward settling the Roman Question. He put out feelers to Italy through Gasparri as early as 1915 and through Archbishop Bonaventura Cerretti in Paris in 1919. In January 1919

[5] Ibid., 2: Pacelli to Gasparri, Munich, Oct. 16, 1918.

he also gave his approval to Don Luigi Sturzo's Partito Popolare and thus put an end to the *non expedit* prohibiting Italian Catholics from participating in Italian politics. A year and a half later, he lifted the ban against heads of Catholic states from paying visits to the Quirinal, the official residence of the kings of Italy.[6] Benedict died suddenly of pneumonia on January 22, 1922, at the age of sixty-seven.

The conclave to elect Benedict's successor found itself deadlocked between Gasparri and Merry del Val, who represented the old order of Pius X rejected in 1914. No Americans were present at this conclave. Farley had died in 1918 and Gibbons in 1921. O'Connell of Boston and Dennis J. Dougherty of Philadelphia, the only American named a cardinal by Benedict XV, arrived on February 6, 1922, only to learn that on the fourteenth ballot the cardinals chose a compromise candidate, Cardinal Ambrogio Damiano Achille Ratti, Archbishop of Milan, who took the name Pius XI. Like della Chiesa, Ratti had only recently been named a cardinal. Educated at the Gregorian University in Rome, Ratti first taught at the seminary in Padua before undertaking his lengthy career at the Ambrosian library in Milan from 1888 to 1911. A distinguished palaeographer, he was appointed to the Vatican Library in 1911 and became prefect in 1914. In 1918 Benedict XV named him apostolic visitor to the newly formed Poland and Lithuania and then elevated him to nuncio and archbishop of Lepanto in 1919. He was consecrated by Cardinal Alexander Kakowski, archbishop of Warsaw. He remained in the Polish capital during the siege by the Red Army, but then ran afoul of Polish nationalism, from which Benedict rescued him by naming him archbishop of Milan and a cardinal in June 1921.[7]

Pius XI retained Cardinal Gasparri as his secretary of state for the first eight years of his pontificate. He normalized relations with France, but his most outstanding diplomatic achievement was the Lateran Treaty on February 11, 1929, with Benito Mussolini, the Italian prime minister. The treaty established the Vatican City State to guarantee the spiritual sovereignty of the pope and thus ended the Roman Question; a separate concordat regulated the relations between the Church and the Italian government. Soon thereafter, Pius XI replaced Gasparri as secretary of state with Pacelli, whom he named a cardinal in 1929.

But Pius was soon distracted by growing international tensions. In the summer of 1931, after several Fascist violations of the concordat, he is-

---

[6] Jedin and Dolan, *History of the Church,* vol. 9: *The Church in the Industrial Age,* 488–92.

[7] Roberto Morozzo della Rocca, "Achille Ratti e la Polonia (1918–1921)," *Achille Ratti: Pape Pie XI* (Rome: École Française de Rome, 1996) 95–122.

sued *Non abbiamo bisogno* condemning Fascism. Because of restrictions on Church presses, however, the encyclical was smuggled out of Italy by Monsignor Francis Spellman to be published in Paris.[8] In 1933 Pius XI signed a concordat with the National Socialist government of Adolf Hitler in Germany, thereby unintentionally neutralizing Catholic opposition to the regime. Over the next three years, however, he addressed thirty-four notes of protest against Nazi violations of the concordat. Finally, on March 14, 1937, he issued *Mit brennender Sorge* condemning Nazism as anti-Christian and ordered it read from the pulpit in every German Catholic church. Five days later, he published *Divini Redemptoris* condemning atheistic Communism.

Elsewhere in the world the Church was also under attack. In 1936 the Mexican government ended almost twenty years of persecution of the Church in order not to embarrass President Franklin D. Roosevelt with his Catholic constituents. The pope then urged Mexican Catholics peacefully to promote Catholic Action, a major theme of his pontificate. On June 3, 1933, shortly before concluding his concordat with Germany, he denounced the separation of Church and state in republican Spain. He then supported General Francisco Franco when civil war broke out in 1936.

Although Pius XI seemed more to respond to situations than initiate diplomatic endeavors, he was more proactive in regard to the interior life of the Church. He set the tone in his first encyclical, *Ubi arcano,* on December 23, 1922, calling for Catholic Action, the collaboration of the laity with the clergy in the Church's mission. Although the movement spread to many countries, he demanded that Catholic Action be under the direction of the hierarchy.[9] This may have been the reason why in 1923 Sturzo resigned from the Partito Popolare, which comprised most Italian Catholics but avowed independence of religion in the political sphere. In 1926 a royal decree banned the party and removed one of the strongest potential opponents to the Fascists. At the same time Pius XI condemned l'Action Française, a movement that, among other things, called for the restoration of monarchy.[10] In 1930 he issued *Casti connubii,* condemning contraception. The following year he commemorated the fortieth anniversary of Leo XIII's *Rerum novarum* with *Quadragesimo anno,* which developed his predecessor's thought particularly

---

[8] Gerald P. Fogarty, *The Vatican and the American Hierarchy from 1870 to 1965* (Stuttgart: Anton Hiersemann Verlag, 1982; Wilmington, Del.: Michael Glazier, 1985) 240.

[9] Pierre Barral, "Le magistère de Pie XI sur l'Action catholique," *Achille Ratti: Pape Pie XI,* 591–603, and Mario Casella, "Pio XI e l'Azione cattolica italiana," *Achille Ratti: Pape Pie XI,* 605–40.

[10] Jacques Prévotat, "La condamnation de l'Action française par Pie XI," *Achille Ratti: Pape Pie XI,* 359–95.

in regard to the principle of subsidiarity, that is, that governments should not assume the responsibilities of lesser organizations. Although he hesitantly approved the Malines conversation between Catholics and Anglicans between 1921 and 1926, he remained adamant that there was only one true Church and forbade Catholic participation in the nascent non-Catholic ecumenical movement.

As Pius XI began his pontificate, he cast a pall over the American Church by allowing the Consistorial Congregation to issue a condemnation of the National Catholic Welfare Council (NCWC), a standing body of the American episcopate. Although the condemnation was largely the work of Cardinal O'Connell with his friends in Rome, it was rescinded with the provision, among other things, that the name "council" in the title be changed to "conference" and that episcopal membership be voluntary.[11] The NCWC was the only episcopal conference in the world that comprised all the bishops. Pius XI, intent on centralization, may well have been suspicious of such a large organization. Yet in 1924 he did indicate the growing importance of the American Church by naming two more American cardinals, George Mundelein of Chicago and Patrick Hayes of New York, bringing the total number to three.

Pius XI's death on February 10, 1939, left little doubt as to his successor. On March 2, 1939, on the third ballot, the cardinals elected Eugenio Pacelli, who took the name Pius XII. Born in Rome and educated at the Gregorian University, the Capranica College, and the S. Apollinare Institute, he was ordained in 1899 and entered papal service two years later. In 1917 he was named nuncio to Bavaria and archbishop of Sardes. In that capacity, as was seen, he attempted to negotiate with the German Empire and Austro-Hungarian Empire about Benedict XV's peace initiatives. As secretary of state he not only was responsible for the concordats signed under Pius XI but also undertook travel to Britain, Argentina, France, Hungary, and the United States. He immediately appointed Cardinal Luigi Maglione as his secretary of state, with Giovanni Battista Montini and Domenico Tardini as assistants.

From the outset of his pontificate Pius XII was preoccupied with World War II then looming on the horizon. In 1939 he accepted Roosevelt's appointment of Myron C. Taylor as his "personal representative," a substitute for full diplomatic relations, and, together with the United States, sought unsuccessfully to prevent Mussolini's alliance with Hitler in

---

[11] See Fogarty, *The Vatican and the American Hierarchy,* 214–28. The most recent study of this is Douglas J. Slawson, *The Foundation and First Decade of the National Catholic Welfare Council* (Washington, D.C.: The Catholic University of America Press, 1992).

1940. In his Christmas allocution of 1939, he laid down five principles for a just and lasting peace, including disarmament, recognition of minority rights, and the right of each nation to independence. But still the charge is made that he was "silent" in regard to the Holocaust. The answer to the charge is complicated. On the one hand, while he opposed Communism, Pius XII did not support Germany's invasion of the Soviet Union in 1941. On the other, after some hesitation, he did support the American extension of "Lend-Lease" of armaments to Russia by distinguishing between cooperation with Communism and assistance to the beleaguered Russian people. He also insisted that the American bishops support the U.S. declaration of war against the Axis, which entailed an alliance with the Soviet Union. Yet he challenged the Casablanca Conference's declaration in 1943 that the Allies would accept only "unconditional surrender." His relations were also strained with the British over the incarceration of Italian missionaries in North Africa. From his experience during World War I, when Benedict XV's peace initiatives were rejected, he sought to maintain the Holy See's "impartiality" while still trying to work for peace. He also had a sense of the continuing binding force of papal statements. In his mind, for him to issue a new statement would seem to imply that Pius XI's condemnation of Nazism in *Mit brennender Sorge,* in which he himself played a role, was no longer in effect. After Cardinal Maglione died in 1944, he offered the position of secretary of state to Archbishop Spellman of New York, but then retained the position himself. With the end of the war, he turned his attention to combating Communism.[12]

Although Pius XII's role during the war remains controversial, he did set about to reform the internal life of the Church. In 1943 he issued two encyclicals, *Mystici Corporis* and *Divino afflante Spiritu.* The former focused on the Church as the Mystical Body of Christ, with gradients of membership, rather than the "perfect society" motif of Vatican I. The latter was the magna carta for biblical scholarship as it called for exegetes to use the historical criticism held so suspect during the anti-Modernist crusade. On an issue that had a more immediate impact on the laity, Pius XII issued *Mediator Dei* in 1947 calling for more active participation in the liturgy. He then made the first reforms in the liturgy itself by restoring the Easter Vigil in 1953 and took the first steps toward relaxing the eucharistic fast. Personally devoted to the Virgin Mary, in 1950 he defined that Mary was bodily assumed into heaven—only the second time a pope had exercised his infallible prerogative. He also declared 1954 to be the Marian Year and called for celebrations throughout the Catholic world.

[12] I have developed some of these themes more in my *The Vatican and the American Hierarchy,* 279–345.

But the last eight years of Pius XII's pontificate were characterized by a growing conservatism. In 1950 he issued *Humani generis,* which challenged the methods of the "Nouvelle theologie," called into question how polygenism could be reconciled with the doctrine of original sin inherited from a historical Adam and Eve, and criticized what he considered extremes among some biblical scholars. Leading proponents of the new methods, such as Yves Congar, o.p., and Henri de Lubac, s.j., were silenced. In the United States, John Courtney Murray, in the face of Roman and American opposition, ceased writing about religious liberty.[13]

But Pius XII also sought to internationalize the college of cardinals by appointing more men from non-European nations. In 1946 he held his first consistory, delayed as a sign of mourning until after the war, and named thirty-two cardinals, including Francis Spellman of New York, Samuel Stritch of Chicago, Edward Mooney of Detroit, and John Glennon of St. Louis, Glennon dying before returning to his see. In 1953 he named twenty-four more, including James McIntyre, archbishop of Los Angeles. Despite reduction of the Italian contingent to one third, Pius XII's declining health during the last years of his pontificate left many decisions in the hands of a conservative inner circle. When he died on October 9, 1958, the choice of his successor was by no means certain.

On October 28, 1958, the cardinals cast eleven ballots before settling on Cardinal Angelo Giuseppe Roncalli, the seventy-seven-year-old Patriarch of Venice. Widely regarded as a compromise and a caretaker pope, he took the name John XXIII—as a historian he might have wanted to settle the debate of whether the Pisan John XXIII was legitimate. He brought to his office a background widely different from his predecessor. Born of a peasant family in Sotto il Monte, near Bergamo, he attended the seminary in Bergamo before studying at the S. Apollinare Institute in Rome from which he received a doctorate in theology in 1904. After serving as the secretary to the bishop of Bergamo from 1905 to 1914 and teaching Church history in the seminary, he served in the Italian army, first as a hospital orderly and then as chaplain. In 1921 Benedict XV named him the national director of the Society for the Propagation of the Faith, but he still found time to write on diocesan history and the biography of St. Charles Borromeo, the fifth and final volume of which he completed in 1958. His researches brought him frequently to the Ambrosian Library and into contact with Achille Ratti, the librarian who, as Pius XI, launched Roncalli's diplo-

---

[13] Joseph A. Komonchak, "Catholic Principle and the American Experiment: The Silencing of John Courtney Murray," *U.S. Catholic Historian* 17 (Winter 1999) 28–44; Donald E. Pelotte, *John Courtney Murray: Theologian in Conflict* (New York: Paulist Press, 1975) 370–82.

matic career by naming him titular archbishop of Areopolis in 1925 and apostolic visitor to Bulgaria (he become apostolic delegate in 1931). In 1934 he became apostolic delegate to Greece and Turkey, a post he would hold for ten years, during which he established friendly relations with Orthodox and government officials. In December 1944 he was named nuncio to France, where he had to deal with the situation of those French bishops accused of collaborating with the Vichy government, set up theological courses for those German seminarians who were prisoners of war, and supported the priest-worker movement. Paradoxically in light of later events, his patron/protector at the Vatican especially during the latter part of his diplomatic career was Giovanni Battista Montini, under-secretary of state. In June 1953 he was named cardinal and Patriarch of Venice, where he was known for his pastoral sensitivity and resistance to the Communists.[14]

A caretaker pope may have been the conclave's plan for John XXIII, but his pontificate proved to be a turning point for the Church. At his coronation on November 4, 1958, the feast of St. Charles Borromeo, he announced his intention of being before all else a pastor. Rotund and approachable, he stood in contrast to his ascetic-looking predecessor. He lost no time in holding his first consistory to name new cardinals. Among the first was Montini, the archbishop of Milan. In the United States he named Richard Cushing of Boston, John O'Hara of Philadelphia, and Amleto Cicognani, the apostolic delegate for twenty-five years, whom he subsequently appointed secretary of state. He also abolished the rule established by Sixtus V in 1586 limiting the number of cardinals to seventy. In 1959 he held his second consistory and named Albert Meyer of Chicago and Aloysius Muench, former bishop of Fargo and nuncio to Germany. In 1961 he named yet more, including Joseph Ritter of St. Louis. By 1962 the college numbered eighty-seven. On January 25, 1959, the feast of the Conversion of St. Paul, moreover, he electrified the world by proposing a diocesan synod for Rome, a revision of the code of canon law, and especially the convocation of an ecumenical council.

John XXIII envisioned the council as a means of reuniting separated Christians of the East and West. In preparation for it, he established the Secretariat for Promoting Christian Unity under Cardinal Augustin Bea, s.j., a biblical scholar. He instructed the new body to carve out its own territory.[15] In the meantime, he established other preparatory commissions to

[14] Peter Hebblethwaite, *Pope John XXIII: Shepherd of the Modern World* (Garden City, N.Y.: Doubleday, 1985) 91–269.

[15] Thomas F. Stransky, "The Foundation of the Secretariat for Promoting Christian Unity," *Vatican II Revisited by Those Who Were There*, ed. Alberic Stacpoole (Minneapolis: Winston Press, 1986) 64–8.

draft documents for the council. Unfortunately, he left much of this preparation to the curia officials he had inherited from Pius XII. Cardinal Alfredo Ottaviani, the secretary of the Holy Office, was named chairman of the theological preparatory commission, which produced documents with a decidedly conservative cast. Tension between the curia and fathers of the council broke out on the opening day, October 11, 1962. During the first session, only the document on the liturgy was thoroughly discussed. One schema, "On the Sources of Revelation," was rejected only at the pope's personal intervention after the bishops failed to reach the two-thirds majority necessary.

But ecumenism remained one of John XXIII's personal projects. In December 1960 he received in audience Archbishop Geoffrey Fisher of Canterbury. In June 1961 he sent personal envoys to greet Ecumenical Patriarch Athenagoras I in Istanbul. He also sent greetings to Patriarch Alexis of Moscow. When the council opened, representatives of eighteen other denominations were present as observers. Of the Orthodox, however, only the Russians were present, due to division in the rest of the Orthodox world.

Independent of the council, John XXIII made other contributions to the interior life of the Church. *Mater et magistra* in 1961 updated the teaching of Leo XIII and Pius XI and introduced the obligations of rich nations toward poorer ones. *Pacem in terris* in 1963 was the first encyclical addressed to all humanity and not merely to Catholics. Drafted during the aftermath of the Cuban Missile Crisis, it focused on the dignity of the human person, recognized human rights and duties as the basis for a just peace, and stated that the purpose of government was "to safeguard the inviolable rights of the human person."[16] Such language was a marked advance over the thought of Leo XIII. He also called for peaceful coexistence between East and West, and for distinguishing between Marxist ideology and legitimate social aspirations of Communist states.

On other issues, John XXIII was ambiguous. On the one hand, he took the initiative to insert the name of Joseph into the Roman Canon and to omit from the Good Friday liturgy the old prayer for the "perfidious Jews." On the other, he displayed a conservative mind set. In 1961 he warned New Testament scholars to use caution in their exegesis and was responsible for prohibiting Stanislaus Lyonnet, S.J., and Max Zerwick, S.J., of the Pontifical Biblical Institute from teaching seminarians.[17] In 1962 he also warned against the theories of evolution of Pierre Teilhard de Chardin.

---

[16] John XXIII, *Pacem in terris* (Washington, D.C.: U.S. Catholic Conference, 1963) no. 60.

[17] Fogarty, *American Catholic Biblical Scholarship,* 323, 327, 331.

One of John XXIII's major contributions was the first steps toward a Vatican *Ostpolitik.* In Italy he urged the Christian Democratic Party to move to the left to address some of the social problems that had wooed so many people to the Communist Party. This won him favorable acclaim from Soviet Premier Nikita Khrushchev. On John XXIII's eightieth birthday, November 25, 1961, Khrushchev sent him greetings. Against the advice of his curia, the pope responded in a letter delivered by hand to the Soviet embassy to Italy.[18] His relationship with the premier grew closer during the Cuban Missile Crisis. No sooner had the council convened than the world came to the brink of atomic war. Both the United States and the Soviet Union agreed to accept a papal intervention. On October 25, 1962, John XXIII gave a radio address calling "on all men of good will" to negotiate. The *New York Times* carried the papal address on its front page, and TASS, the Soviet news service, distributed excerpts that had been published in *Pravda.* When the crisis was ended, John began *Pacem in terris.* At Christmas of 1962 Khrushchev sent him a message through Norman Cousins, an American editor. It stated: "On the occasion of the Holy Days of Christmas, please accept these greetings and congratulations from a man who wishes you good health and strength for your abiding quest for the peace and happiness of all mankind."[19] As a further sign of gratitude, Khrushchev released from prison Metropolitan Josef Slipyi of Lviv who then went to Rome to attend the council and remain in the curia. Subsequently, John received Khrushchev's daughter and son-in-law, Rada and Alexie Adzhubei, in a private audience and gave her a rosary together with other presents.[20] John had planted the first seeds of a new relationship with the Soviet Union that would bear fruit thirty years later.

For some time John XXIII had suffered from stomach cancer. His death on June 3, 1963, brought almost universal mourning from non-Catholics and Catholics alike. Symbolic of his rapprochement with Khrushchev and the eastern bloc, the Soviet navy ships in Genoa harbor flew their flags at half mast.[21]

Eighty cardinals were in attendance at the conclave to elect John XXIII's successor, the largest number in history. On June 21, 1963, on the fifth ballot, they chose Cardinal Giovanni Battista Montini, archbishop of

---

[18] Loris Francesco Capovilla, *Giovanni XXIII: Lettere, 1958–1963* (Roma: Edizioni di storia e letteratura, 1978) 336–7.

[19] Ibid., 53–7; a facsimile of Khrushchev's message to John XXIII with an English translation is given opposite p. 78. An Italian translation is given in Capovilla, *Giovanni XXIII,* 439.

[20] Hebblethwaite, *Pope John XIII,* 480–3.

[21] *New York Times,* June 6, 1963, 18.

Milan, who took the name Paul VI. To some, the selection of the shy, lean former member of the curia symbolized a return to Pius XII. To others, the choice represented not only continuity with some Johannine policies, but also the election of a man who well understood the workings of the curia and had represented progressive element under Pius XII. Born in Concesio, near Brescia, he was the son of a lawyer and leader in Sturzo's Partito Popolare. Frail in health, but bookish, he remained at home while attending the seminary in Brescia, where he was ordained in 1920. After graduate work in Rome he began his career in the secretariat of state, interrupted only by a five-month stint in Warsaw in 1923. An assistant to Cardinal Pacelli, then secretary of state, in 1937, he continued to have charge of the internal affairs of the Church when Pacelli became Pius XII. He was also chaplain to the federation of Catholic university students, from whom would come many of the future leaders of the Christian Democratic Party. Although he supposedly refused a red hat at Pius XII's second consistory in December 1953, a year later he was named archbishop of Milan, an appointment that has been variously interpreted as a sign of Pius' disfavor or of the pope's desire to get his protégé off the scene of the increasingly conservative curia. In Milan, Montini won a reputation for winning over the workers in the war-torn diocese and took the first steps toward ecumenism by entertaining a group of visiting Anglican clergymen in 1956.[22] During the first session of the council he spoke only twice, but on both occasions voiced his support for the more progressive wing of the council represented by Cardinal Josef Suenens of Malines-Brussels and Cardinal Giacomo Lercaro of Bologna. He also sent back a series of letters to his diocesan newspaper complaining of the poor management of the council and the mountain of undigested schemata presented to the fathers.[23] In addition, he frequently spent time with John XXIII. At the time of his election he had traveled more than any other pope up to that time. As pope, he set the precedent for papal traveling.

To expedite the work of the council, Paul VI appointed four cardinal moderators who would meet with him weekly. He also admitted lay auditors to the discussions, and subsequently he admitted women, lay and religious, as auditors. By the end of the second session in December 1963 the

---

[22] Peter Hebblethwaite, *Paul VI: The First Modern Pope* (New York: Paulist Press, 1993) 242–79. See also Giorgio Rumi, "L'arcivescovo Montini e la società del suo tempo," *Giovanni Battista Montini: Arcivescovo di Milano e il Concilio Ecumenico Vaticano II preparazione e primo periodo* (Brescia: Istituto Paolo VI, 1985) 17–33; and Enrico Manfredini, "Le scelte pastorali dell'arcivescovo Montini," *Giovanni Battista Montini*, 46–155.

[23] "Lettere dal Concilio," *Discorsi e scritti sul Concilio (1959–1963),* Quaderni dell'Istituto 3 (Brescia: Istituto Paolo VI; Rome: Edizioni Studium, 1983) 178–220.

council promulgated the Constitution on the Liturgy and the Decree on Mass Media. During the third session in 1964 Paul VI began to display either hesitancy or a desire to placate the conservatives. On November 21 the council issued the Dogmatic Constitution on the Church, with a *nota praevia* added at the pope's explicit command that explained that episcopal collegiality did not derogate from a pope's exercise of infallibility on his own authority. He also removed from the council's discussion at that session the draft document on religious liberty. The document's supporters mustered over eight hundred signatures, so he guaranteed that the topic would be first on the agenda during the fourth and final session. As a further sign of ambiguity at the end of the session, against opposition, he declared the Virgin Mary to be "Mother of the Church."

Despite signs of hesitancy, Paul VI personally continued the thrust toward ecumenism begun by John XXIII. On January 4–6, 1964, he went to the Holy Land, where he met Patriarch Athenagoras in Jerusalem. During the recess between the third and fourth sessions he flew to Bombay for the International Eucharistic Congress on December 2–5, 1964. On October 4, 1965, during the fourth session, he flew to New York to address the United Nations to plea for world peace. Accompanied by several cardinals, he made the journey and his speech official acts of the council. During that session he approved the council's Constitution on Divine Revelation, the Pastoral Constitution on the Church in the Modern World, and the Declaration on Religious Liberty, now strengthened beyond the original focus on the limitations of the state over religion to ground religious liberty on the dignity of the human person. As the session ended on December 7, 1965, he read a declaration from Athenagoras removing the excommunication cast against the pope in 1054. Simultaneously in Istanbul, Lawrence Shehan of Baltimore, the only American named a cardinal earlier that year, delivered a similar declaration from the pope removing the excommunication of Patriarch Michael Cerularius.

Although Paul VI sought to implement the council, especially in regard to ecumenism, his pontificate was fraught with controversy. On the one hand, in 1967 he issued his encyclical *Populorum progressio* on social justice especially in the third world. On the other, in 1968 he promulgated his last encyclical, *Humanae vitae,* which upheld the traditional ban on artificial contraception, contrary to the position taken by the special commission he had appointed to examine the question. Controversy soon ensued and cast a cloud over the remainder of his pontificate. At times he seemed to withdraw into himself, besieged not only by dissent over birth control but also by the resistance to liturgical and other conciliar reforms led by Archbishop Marcel Lefebvre, who was later excommunicated by

John Paul II. He was also deeply disturbed by the brutal murder of former Italian premier and Christian Democratic Party leader Aldo Moro, his close friend from the days when he was chaplain of Catholic university students. His last public appearance was presiding over Moro's funeral in May 1978. Nevertheless, he continued his overtures for ecumenism, especially to the Orthodox and Anglicans, and made several more trips abroad, including one to the Philippines, where he narrowly escaped assassination late in 1970.

But Paul VI also continued John XXIII's *Ostpolitik* and, in the process, sometimes alienated the United States. In 1968 Paul VI played an instrumental role, at the request of President Lyndon Johnson, in arranging for the Paris peace talks between the United States and North Vietnam.[24] But because the negotiations dragged on for several years, the pope may have grown frustrated with President Richard M. Nixon. On March 2, 1870, Nixon visited Paul VI.[25] This led to the president's reinstituting the office of personal representative in July, when he appointed Henry Cabot Lodge, former ambassador to South Vietnam and Nixon's running mate against Kennedy and Johnson in 1960.[26] In September 1970 Nixon paid another visit to the pope, one that seems to have been fraught with controversy.[27] With Vietnam as a backdrop, both superpowers in the Cold War were vying with one another to woo the Holy See. In November Andrei Gromyko, the Soviet Foreign Minister, had an eighty-minute audience with the pope, the duration of which prompted *Il Tempo* to chide the pope for treating Gromyko more warmly than he had Nixon.[28]

Paul VI also sought to continue his predecessor's policy in dealing with other Communist nations. In 1962 John began making preliminary overtures to the Hungarian government through Archbishop Agostino Casaroli about Cardinal Joseph Mindszenty, who had been convicted of treason and sentenced to prison in 1948. Released during the Hungarian revolution of 1956, the cardinal took up asylum in the United States embassy after the revolution failed. Now he was an obstacle to both the Vatican and American desires to lessen East-West tensions. In 1971, with the approval of the Hungarian government, Paul VI summoned Cardinal

---

[24] Joseph A. Califano, *The Triumph and Tragedy of Lyndon Johnson: The White House Years* (New York: Simon and Shuster, 1991) 326–7.

[25] *New York Times,* February 7, 1969, 1:8; March 2, 1969, 19:1; March 3, 1969, 14:1; March 28, 1969, 37:1.

[26] *New York Times,* July 4, 1970, 18:3.

[27] *New York Times,* September 16, 1970, 1:5; September 27, 1970, 4:1; September 29, 1970, 1:4 and 19:2.

[28] *New York Times,* November 13, 1970, 7:1; November 16, 1970, 6:4.

Mindszenty to Rome. For three years he retained the title of archbishop of Etzergom, but his outspoken criticism of the pope's policy toward Communism led to his forced resignation. But the Vatican was now able to regularize the situation of the Church in Hungary.[29]

Paul VI had left his mark on the Church. He had enlarged the college of cardinals from the 80 members at the time of his election to 138, but he also decreed that cardinals over the age of eighty were no longer to vote in papal election and that bishops should submit their resignations at the age of seventy-five. In addition to Shehan, he had named twelve American cardinals: in 1967, Francis Brennan of the curia, John Cody of Chicago, John Krol of Philadelphia, and Patrick O'Boyle of Washington; in 1969, John Carberry of St. Louis, Terence Cooke of New York, John Dearden of Detroit, and John Wright of Pittsburgh, transferred to Rome; in 1973, Luis Aponte Martinez of San Juan, Timothy Manning of Los Angeles, and Humberto Medeiros of Boston; and in 1976, William Baum of Washington. Paul VI died on August 6, 1978, at the papal villa of Castel Gandolfo.

When the cardinals assembled for the ensuing conclave, the majority favored a change, a pope without close ties to the curia. On the third ballot, on August 26, they elected Albino Luciani, the Patriarch of Venice, born sixty-five years before of working-class parents. Little known outside Italy, he had been engaged in pastoral work, teaching in the seminary at Belluno and engaging in diocesan administration before being named bishop of Vittorio Veneto in 1958. In 1969 he became Patriarch of Venice and was named a cardinal in 1973. Although he had earlier established friendly relations with the Communists, as patriarch he condemned them as incompatible with Christianity. His book *Illustrissimi* was a collection of whimsical letters to famous characters, both real and fictional, and illustrated his warmth and sense of humor. He chose the name John Paul I to show his continuity with the two popes of the council. On September 3 he replaced the pomp of previous papal coronations with the simple imposition of the pallium, the symbol of metropolitan authority. Only three weeks later, on September 28, he was found dead of a heart attack. His short pontificate had made little mark on the Church, but unfounded rumors abounded that he was about to make some dramatic changes and, for that reason, was actually murdered.

The second 1978 conclave in little more than a month illustrated the division among the cardinals. By this time, of course, they were better acquainted with one another. They could not, however, agree on an Italian candidate, but looked for a vigorous one who understood Euro-Communism.

---

[29] Hebblethwaite, *Paul VI,* 579–87.

On the eighth ballot, on October 16, they elected the fifty-eight-year-old Cardinal Karol Wojtyla, archbishop of Krakow, the first non-Italian pope since Adrian VI (1522–23) and the first Polish pope. He chose the name John Paul II and, like his predecessor, chose a simple inauguration ceremony.

John Paul II brought to the papacy a background vastly different from his predecessors. Born in 1920 at Wadowice, near Krakow, to a family of modest means, he attended local schools until 1938 when he and his widowed father moved to Krakow. There he enrolled at the Jagiellonian University to study Polish literature and acted in amateur dramatic productions. With the Nazi invasion of Poland in September 1939 the university was closed, but he continued to study in an underground network. He worked in a limestone quarry and later in a factory, but, in 1942, began clandestine study for the priesthood. With the Russian liberation of Poland in January 1945 the Jagiellonian University reopened, and he completed his studies and was ordained in November 1946. He then went to the Angelicum University in Rome, where he received a doctorate in philosophy in 1948 for a dissertation on the concept of faith in John of the Cross. From 1948 to 1951 he served as a parish priest before returning to the Jagiellonian to obtain a doctorate in theology with a dissertation on Max Scheler. He taught social ethics at the Krakow seminary and, in 1956, was appointed professor of ethics at Lublin. In 1958 he was named auxiliary bishop of Krakow and, in 1963, archbishop of Krakow. There he established himself as a staunch foe to the Communist government. In 1960 he published *Love and Responsibility,* a pastoral treatise on sexuality, which later influenced Paul VI in drafting *Humanae vitae.* He was thrust onto the international stage at Vatican II. A member of the preparatory commission, he attended all four sessions, during which he contributed to the discussion in favor of religious liberty. Named a cardinal in 1967, he traveled extensively, including several trips to the United States, where he became known to the Polish-American community. In 1976 he was invited by Paul VI to give the lenten addresses to the papal household, later published in English as *Sign of Contradiction.*

John Paul II set a tone far different from his predecessors. Early in his pontificate he was known for the virtually unprecedented papal exercise of hiking and skiing in the Alps. But on May 13, 1981, he was shot and seriously wounded by a young Turk, Mehmet Ali Agca, whom rumors tried to make an agent for the Bulgarians or even the Soviet KGB. While this may have contributed to John Paul's later debility with Parkinson's disease, it hardly curtailed his activity. In the first twenty-one years of his pontificate, the longest of any pope elected in the twentieth century, he issued thirteen encyclicals, twenty-nine apostolic letters, and nine constitutions. More indicative of his approach to being "universal pastor" were his travels. By the time he returned from his visit to the Holy Land in March 2000, he had made some ninety trips outside Italy. More than any other pope of the twentieth century, he put his own personal mark on the Church and had a profound impact on the world at large.

John Paul II's encyclicals reveal his mindset. His first, *Redemptor hominis,* issued in March 1979, treated Christian humanism and stated that true freedom and human dignity are best preserved in the Church. Three encyclicals treat social issues, *Laborem exercens* (1981), *Sollicitudo rei socialis* (1987), and *Centesimus annus* (1991). In each he argued that a just economic order could be based neither on Marxism nor on capitalism, but on the recognition of the dignity of work. In *Centesimus* he forcefully declared that the collapse of Communism in Europe did not mean the victory of Capitalism, and reminded the developed world that in some developing nations the same conditions existed that Leo XIII had addressed in *Rerum novarum.* Two encyclicals addressed the relationship between faith and reason and the objectivity of truth: *Veritatis splendor* (1993) and *Fides et ratio* (1999). In *Evangelium vitae* (1995) he presented the Catholic teaching on the sanctity of life and expressed strong doubts about whether capital punishment could be justified in the contemporary world, a theme he also enunciated during his pastoral journey to St. Louis in 1999, when he persuaded authorities to commute the sentence of a condemned man.

But John Paul II not only spoke to the Church; he also acted. Early in his pontificate he appointed Cardinal Joseph Ratzinger to head the Congregation for the Doctrine of the Faith. Together they sought to end dissent among theologians and to prevent the spread of liberation theology, which for the pope seemed to flirt dangerously with Marxism. In Europe they cracked down on theologians, most famous among whom was Hans Küng, a Swiss professor at Tübingen. John Paul II feared that Jesuits in Latin America were becoming too radical. After their general, Pedro Arrupe, suffered a stroke in 1981, he suspended the order's constitutions and appointed Paolo Dezza, S.J., as his delegate to govern the Jesuits in place of Vincent O'Keefe, S.J., whom Arrupe had appointed vicar general. Only in 1983 did he allow the Jesuits to hold a general congregation to elect a successor to Arrupe, who died in 1991. During a trip to Nicaragua in 1983 John Paul publicly chastised a priest who held office under the Sandinistas. In 1980 he ordered Robert Drinan, S.J., a Massachusetts congressman for ten years, not to run for office again.

In regard to the internal life of the Church, John Paul II has canonized or beatified more people than any pope in history—over one hundred were beatified or canonized during his 1999 trip to Poland alone. But some of the people he has so honored indicate a certain eclecticism. On the one hand, he beatified Cardinal Andrea Carlo Ferrari (+1921) of Milan who resisted the anti-Modernist witch hunt and was himself suspect of heresy. On the other, he beatified Monsignor Josemaria Escriva (+1975), founder of Opus Dei, whose members are widely regarded as staunch adherents to orthodoxy and, like the pope himself, opponents to Communism. John Paul is fond of using symbols, such as beatifications and canonizations, to express his ecclesiology. One symbol is fraught with significance for his desire for centralization in the Church. He introduced a new ceremony for the bestowal of the pallium, the sign of an archbishop's authority. Previously archbishops received the pallium in their own cathedrals; now they all travel to Rome to receive it personally from the pope in a single ceremony on June 29, the feast of Sts. Peter and Paul.

John Paul II is not afraid of controversy or opposition. To the laity he has taken a strong stance against birth control, but did not go beyond the official teaching of Paul VI's *Humanae vitae.* His prohibition of theological discussion of the question of ordination of women in a document following upon *Ordinatio sacerdotalis* (1994) alienated many women, particularly in the West. Yet his stance has to be seen in light of his efforts to win reunion with the Orthodox at the dawn of the new millennium. His encyclical *Ut unum sint* (1995) called for a reflection on the exercise of the papal office especially during the first one thousand years of the history of the Church when both East and West were united. He has, moreover, maintained cordial relations with the Ecumenical Patriarch in Istanbul whom he visited in 1979, but has been unsuccessful in arranging a meeting with Patriarch Alexis of Moscow.

But if John Paul II has been controversial within the Church, his achievement in the broader world has been immeasurable. Having a pope from Poland, a Communist country, emboldened the Polish people, led by Lech Walensa, to oppose and then overthrow the government. This first chink in the armor of the Eastern bloc led to tearing down the Berlin wall in 1989 and the collapse of the Soviet Union a year later. The pope had become a major player on the world scene. He received in audience not only President Ronald Reagan in 1982, but also Premier Gorbachev of the Soviet Union in 1989. He not only negotiated a new concordat with Italy in 1984 that provided for a separation of Church and state and removed government support for clergy, but he also established full diplomatic relations with the United States the same year.

In general, John Paul II seems to have had an ambiguous relationship with the United States, perhaps stemming from his earlier contacts with the Polish-American community. He nevertheless has recognized the importance of the American Church by appointing eleven cardinals: in 1983, Joseph Bernardin of Chicago; in 1985, Bernard Law of Boston and John J. O'Connor of New York; in 1988, James Hickey of Washington and Edmund Szoka of Detroit, later transferred to the curia; in 1991, Anthony J. Bevilacqua of Philadelphia and Roger Mahony of Los Angeles; in 1994, William Keeler of Baltimore and Adam Maida of Detroit; and in 1998, J. Francis Stafford of the curia and Francis George, O.M.I., of Chicago.

Much of John Paul's success in world affairs stems from his policy of carrying his message directly to the people in his many pastoral visits across the globe. While some Catholics might resent what they consider to be his autocratic style, many more turn out personally to greet him during his journeys. His early days as an actor in Nazi occupied Poland serve him in good stead as he makes mass appeals especially to youth. Although now physically impaired with Parkinson's disease, his mind remains clear. He will most probably lead the Church well into the twenty-first century. One of his greatest achievements is difficult to evaluate—his direct role in the overthrow of Communism.

During the century surveyed, the papacy has dramatically changed. The century dawned with Leo XIII, a self-imposed "prisoner" in the Vatican, a situation that remained until 1929. During World War I Benedict XV was virtually ignored by the warring powers, especially the Allies, and this may have made Pius XII overly cautious during World War II. The popes at the beginning of the century were obsessed with the issue of Modernism and, in the process, silenced many theologians, especially biblical scholars. Only Vatican II, called by the charismatic John XXIII, would settle many of those issues. From the low regard in which the papacy was held by the world in the early 1900s, it would have been hard to foresee the role that the popes, John XXIII, Paul VI, and particularly John Paul II, would play during and after the Cold War. But each pope brought to his office his own background and training that would shape his pontificate. Only Pius X and John Paul I were what would be called pastors. From the curia, sometimes with a brief tenure as bishop, came Benedict XV, Pius XII, and Paul VI. From the diplomatic corps came John XXIII. Pius XI and John Paul II each had academic backgrounds. Each pope would rely on his previous experience as well as the guidance of the Holy Spirit to meet the challenges of the Church in his particular age.

Priestly Ministry: A Search for Identity and Purpose

Howard J. Gray, S.J.

The issues surrounding priestly life and ministry in the twentieth century focus on priestly identity, the relationship of the priest to the other members of the Church, and the role of the priest in an increasingly secularized society. The catalyst for contemporary priestly life and ministry was the Vatican Council II.

Prior to Vatican II not much had been written about the theology of priesthood. As I approached ordination in 1961, I wanted to assemble some material on the nature of priesthood. After much consultation with a seminary faculty that was well informed and well published, I ended up doing an analysis of the scriptural letter to the Hebrews. Most of the reflective material that dealt with the priesthood seemed to be limited either to canonical considerations or to devotional and ascetical literature.

My experience was not an uncommon one.[1] But with the advent of Vatican II a new era of research, theological reflection, and pastoral expectations emerged. Despite some early misgivings that Vatican II had downplayed ministerial priesthood and emphasized the role of bishops and laity, the council had, in fact, initiated a shift in the model of priesthood. Daniel Donovan believes that the history of the principal decree on priesthood, *Presbyterorum ordinis* (On the Ministry and Life of Priests), indicates what this shift entailed.

> The bishops wanted to emphasize that the priesthood is not in the first place a state of life but rather a function, a service, a ministry. The kind of human and spiritual life that priests are called to embrace flows from, and has to be seen in relation to, what they are called to do. Here was a new way of understanding the unity of the priestly life and the distinctive form of its spirituality.[2]

---

[1] Edward G. Pfnausch, "The Conciliar Documents and the 1983 Code," *The Spirituality of the Diocesan Priest,* ed. Donald B. Cozzens (Collegeville: The Liturgical Press, 1997) 156–9.

[2] Daniel Donovan, *What Are They Saying about the Ministerial Priesthood?* (New York/Mahwah, N.J.: Paulist Press, 1992) 3–4.

While *Presbyterorum ordinis* emphasized that the foundation for ministerial priesthood rested on the threefold ministry of Christ as prophet, priest, and king, these titles do not exhaust either the New Testament data or the continuing theological reflection on priestly identity. These two influences, Scripture and theological reflection, continued to enrich and to challenge the way priests identified themselves or the ways others identified them.

Priestly Identity

Today there is no one, dominant, and finally persuasive theology of Roman Catholic priesthood.[3] Christ's example and teaching continue to invite a variety of models for imitation beyond those of prophet, priest, and king. Christ the Servant,[4] Christ the Host,[5] Christ the Teacher,[6] Christ the Liberator,[7] for example, offer powerful models for anyone who functions in ordained ministry in the Church. What these various titles have in common is their reliance on Christ as the ultimate model for priestly life and ministry.

This Vatican II–inspired return to the imitation of Christ, as found in Scripture, effected, or could have effected, a profound change in the way priests defined themselves and their ministry. Many priests found it a personal difficulty to linger over the gospel as a story of God's way to be human and not to question those institutional constraints that had sometimes made Christ seem remote or even harsh. The way that many priests began to interpret their life and their style of service led them to preach and to teach an ethics of love, service, and social justice. Probably many priests could not specify what had given a more humane and approachable style to their presence among God's people. But this renewed interest in the gospel as a narrative text for life, as distinct from the use of the gospel as a proof text for dogma or as a moment of inspiration, was a uniquely powerful influence on priesthood after Vatican II.

A second influence on the self-image of priests originated in the dialogue that they began to have with the people they served. Of course, priests had always spoken with the men, women, and children who lived

---

[3]   Ibid., 138.

[4]   Marinus de Jonge, *Jesus, the Servant-Messiah* (New Haven, Conn./London: Yale University Press, 1991).

[5]   Eugene Laverdière, *Dining in the Kingdom of God* (Chicago: Liturgy Training Publications, 1994).

[6]   Ben Witherington III, *Jesus the Sage: The Pilgrimage of Wisdom* (Minneapolis: Fortress Press, 1994).

[7]   Albert Nolan, *Jesus Before Christianity* (Maryknoll, N.Y.: Orbis Books, 1985).

in their parishes, attended their schools, or came to their retreat centers. But Vatican II had initiated a sense of partnership and participation between priests and people that moved the culture of the Church in the United States toward wider consultation and communal decision-making. Parish councils, school boards, retreat-house consultants included articulate, informed, and committed lay colleagues. These lay associates became for the priest with whom they worked "signs of the times." Their struggles in raising families, in business and the professions, in living in racially changing neighborhoods influenced profoundly how the priest defined his presence in a neighborhood or school community or retreat program. The growing belief among lay people that they were called to holiness prompted a new level of self-revelation from their pastor about how he also tried to pray, how he found God, and how he made practical decisions consonant with the values of the gospel.

The return to the gospel and the heightened conversations with lay people about Church life and practice had a profound impact on the way priests looked on their lives and structured their ministries. Some priests were threatened by the very liberty that the example of Christ offered them. For if Christ offers a variety of ways to follow him, how does someone choose the way that is right for him? Or if the person and mission of Christ can be so widely interpreted, what does a parish or school or retreat center choose as its particular mission?

Faced with questions about how priestly life and ministry reflected the values of the gospel and met the needs of the people of God, some priests retreated to the institutional assurances and canonical clarity of a pre–Vatican II Church. Frequently, these priests felt abandoned by the Church that had emerged since Vatican II and began to wait for the return of a more congenial ecclesial climate. But many priests found a new liberty of spirit and challenge for pastoral and social renovation. The 1971 Synod united reflections on ministerial priesthood with the call to justice as a constitutive element in the gospel.[8] The Synod symbolized a radical consensus that to be a priest in the contemporary world fractured by economic injustice, racial hatreds, and oppressive structures demanded a reassessment of how one preached, how one taught the values of the gospel, and where one worked to achieve a society more just and more genuinely loving.

Consequently, the call to effect social justice represented a third influence on priestly identity and ministry. Some felt that they could be truly priests only if their presence was among the poor and the marginalized or,

[8] Synod of Bishops, "Justice in the World" (November 30, 1971), *Liberation Theology: A Documentary History,* ed. Alfred T. Hennelly (Maryknoll, N.Y.: Orbis Books, 1990) 137–42.

at least, if their work directly confronted economic, racial, and gender injustices. Others concentrated their energies on raising the consciousness of an increasingly affluent Catholic population. But the message was clear. No priest could be deaf to the Church's summons that the gospel demands social justice and solidarity.

This combination of influences—gospel renewal, collaboration with the laity, and the call to justice as a constitutive part of the gospel—confronted a priest with a prophetic option: either to reexamine how he saw himself and his mission or to reject the significance of all or any one of these influences. When priests and the seminary faculties and staffs wrestled with these issues of gospel values, lay collaboration, and social justice, they carved out a sense of personal call and identity that transformed priestly ministry.

In the latter years of the century there developed a strong assertion of a more conservative priesthood, one that defined itself less in terms of self-discovery through dialogue with Scripture, lay people, and victims of injustice, and more in terms of the New Code of Canon Law and the *New Catechism*. These two styles of priesthood—one of self-discovery through dialogue with Scripture, lay people, and the poor and the marginalized, and one of adherence to the norms of Code and Catechism—are not mutually exclusive. But they each represent an emphasis, a style of self-identification and pastoral presence that co-exist in some tension. However the priest reaches self-definition, he has to face an overriding challenge confronting the Church in the United States.

Despite the continuing increase in the number of Catholics in the United States, from 49,000,000 in 1975 to 61,000,000 in 1998, the number of priests has decreased, from 59,000 in 1975 to 48,000 in 1997.[9] In August 1998 Cardinal Danneels, Archbishop of Mechelen-Brussels, told the delegates at the International Consultation on Priestly Formation that the first challenge confronting priestly formation is "the scarcity of vocations."[10] While the reasons offered for this decline in priestly vocations are varied, the reality of the decline effects every area of Church life. The Eucharist remains central to the faith life of the ordinary Catholic. Catholics hear the word of God at the Eucharistic celebration, identify themselves as a community of faith in that assembly, and find strength and consolation in the reception of the body and blood of Christ. Consequently, the decline in priestly vocations touches at the core of this Catholic practice. This phenomenon also touches at the core of priestly identity and mission.

---

[9] "Significant Issues and Trends Influencing the Church in the United States," *Seminary Journal* (Winter 1998) 79.

[10] Godfried Cardinal Danneels, "Training Candidates for the Priesthood," *Seminary Journal* (Winter 1998) 10.

A final consideration in this overview of priestly identity and mission involves the distinction between diocesan priesthood and religious life priesthood. In other words, does being a priest from the Archdiocese of Chicago and a priest from the Order of St. Dominic represent the same set of realities? An acknowledged authority in this area, John W. O'Malley, S.J., has pointed out that three key documents dealing with priestly identity and mission life—*Christus Dominus* (On the Pastoral Office of Bishops in the Church), *Optatam totius* (On the Training of Priests), and *Presbyterorum ordinis* (On the Ministry and Life of Priests)—"suggest that the specific difference between religious and diocesan priests lies in the fact that the former take vows of poverty, chastity, and obedience, whereas the latter do not."[11]

O'Malley's careful study argues that rather than one tradition of priesthood in which both the diocesan and religious clergy participate, we should more accurately speak of two traditions:

> Although there has been considerable and healthy overlap, a practical division of labor has in fact prevailed between diocesan and regular (i.e., religious) clergy through the ages. The "local," or diocesan, clergy have ministered primarily to the faithful according to time-honored rhythms of word and, especially, sacrament in parishes. They are the backbone of the Church's ministry to its own. Religious, when they ministered to the faithful, did so in similar ways but particularly in other ways that new circumstances seemed to require. This division of labor has taken the religious even farther afield, away from the faithful, in order to minister in some fashion or other to heretics, schismatics, infidels, pagans, and public sinners.[12]

This double tradition of priesthood is a particular richness within Roman Catholicism. As O'Malley concludes, "It is the genius of the Catholic Church up to the present . . . to contain them both."[13]

In concluding this section on priestly identity, then, we can describe ordained ministry within the Catholic Church as the continuation of the work of Jesus through individuals whose call to serve has been confirmed and empowered by the Church. The priestly mission involves a man in the work of preaching and teaching the kingdom of Christ, a kingdom of peace, justice, and love. It asks him to pray in the name of the entire community for its needs, particularly in the celebration of the Eucharist. The ordination of a man to the priesthood of the Church involves him in a process

---

[11] John W. O'Malley, "One Priesthood: Two Traditions," *A Concert of Charisms, Ordained Ministry in Religious Life,* ed. Paul K. Hennessey (New York/Mahwah, N.J.: Paulist Press 1997) 12.

[12] Ibid., 22.

[13] Ibid.

of personal and shared holiness, a process that only God will fulfill in the eternity of his final grace.

Relationships

Nothing is more important than relationship, the ability to stand in mutual openness and donation before another reality.[14] Relationship best describes the most intense exchange of God as Father, Son, and Holy Spirit. Relationship best describes the way God, in turn, communicates to us humans as Creator, Redeemer, and Sanctifier. Therefore, how priests relate to the world of the believer represents a privileged expression of divine activity adapted to human reality. The sacraments, the preaching of the word, and the celebration of the Eucharist represent intense moments of priestly relationship to the People of God. But the way a priest leads his community, shares his wisdom, prays with them, consoles them, and challenges them—all these are moments in which a priest relates the people of God to their God. The priest's primary task is to relate with people in ways that meet their needs to come before God. The priest is not the only one who does this, but his is a privileged moment of doing it.

A wise and devoted priest once told me that when he broke open the word of God to the people, he experienced two realities. As he spoke about God, he was conscious that the truth and holiness he uttered made him God's priest. But when he understood the fragility, wonder, struggles, and hopes of the people, he was most truly the people's priest. To mediate is to bring God and the human together, neither impeding this communication nor controlling it, but, simply and humbly, allowing God to deal with the people and to let the people deal with their God.

This mediation between God and the human always takes place within a culture, a particular set of human values, symbols, stories, and wisdom. What people cherish, how they ritualize or represent these values, the narratives that they honor as illustrations of their worth and hopes, and the reflective and organized ways in which they make sense of this reality— these represent a culture.[15] The priest, therefore, is both within and outside the culture of the People of God. He is within because he is the brother of these people, formed with them and for them. He is without because he is the priest of the eternal Christ, the Lord, and, as such, speaks

---

[14] Denis Edwards, "Personal Symbol of Communion," *The Spirituality of the Diocesan Priest,* 73–84.

[15] Robert Wuthnow, *Producing the Sacred* (Urbana and Chicago: University of Illinois Press, 1994).

a truth not in his possession and of a holiness beyond his control. As the representative of the people, the priest is bordered by the limitations of the human. As a representative of God, the priest is liberated for the continued mission of Christ. The rhetoric of priestly presence demands, then, ongoing conversation with the human and the divine.

The priests of the post—Vatican II Church touch the demands and ambiguity of this mediation daily. To represent the people today means to carry the quest of women for full participation in the life of the Church, including, for many women, priestly ordination. To represent the people today means to represent those who seek to redefine the sexual ethics of the Church as gays, as divorced and remarried, as couples who feel that they cannot have any more children but desperately need one another's love and support. To represent the people of God today is to represent the new Americans who push into a society often reluctant, sometime even hostile, to the person of color, to the person whose language and customs do not fit easily into Anglo culture. The priest does not create these concerns and these demands. They are there in the hearts and minds of the people he serves.

But to represent Christ's Church today is to labor to explain the Church's understanding of ordination as an exclusively male calling, to explain the Church's directives about sexual orientation, conduct, and integrity, and to articulate the Church's identification with the refugee, the migrant, the new Americans. The call to represent these teachings of the Church burdens every contemporary priest. It is one thing to issue doctrinal decrees and disciplinary directives; it is another to adapt these to the people who sit before you. Consequently, to explore the meaning of the priest's relationship to the People of God and to his bishop or superior is to explore a mystery being worked out in the struggles of this age and culture. Any review of the priesthood in the twentieth century has to lay out the grandeur of the grace of mediation and the sometimes painful tensions of what this means in the concrete realities of everyday living.

Women's ordination, sexual identity and intimacy, the economic and social assimilation of minorities into U.S. society—these kinds of tensions frequently touch most bishops only remotely; but they involve the priest, especially the parish priest, daily. While increasingly some priests find clarity and certitude in simply identifying Christ's will with the Church's directives, many other priests find agony and torment, trying to explain teachings and discipline which alienate or simply disinterest many. This pastoral tension is real and pervasive. As a recent document on priestly formation has noted, the heterogeneity of the Catholic population, the extreme ideological diversity and intolerance among many Church members, and the acute ministerial needs of today make the relationship between priest and people frequently problematic and painful.[16]

In another wholly distinct area, the increased involvement of competent, trained, and highly motivated lay personnel in all areas of Church life and ministry challenge both the presence and the style of priestly leadership. Somewhere between a totally consensus form of leadership (e.g., running the parish by equal vote on all issues; we define the mission of the school totally independent of the founding community's intention; we structure the activities of the retreat house toward only these participants) and a totally directive form of leadership (e.g., Father tells the parish council what to approve; the Fathers will interpret how the school mission is to be implemented; Father gives the final okay on all retreats), priests have to develop a new style of leadership. Priestly leadership must consult, must listen to and accept advice, must work to achieve credibility and support, must involve lay people in the plans for which they have to pay.

Unfortunately, few seminaries train seminarians for leadership in a new era of the Church's mission. Simply repeating the official decisions of the Church—whether local, regional or universal—about women's ordination, about the sexual asceticism required for gay people, about divorce and remarriage, about birth control and family planning, and about accepting immigrants and refugees into mainstream economic and social life will not be enough. Good causes, fidelity to the magisterium, loyalty to a pope, cardinal, or bishop are not convincing arguments to an increasing number of Catholics. There is a crisis of leadership in a Church that seems too often to espouse consultation when this is convenient and to demand blind obedience when discussion threatens authority. While priests, especially parish priests, most directly face these kinds of tension, they are woefully ill trained in crisis management. Whatever the beauty and vigor of the image of the priest as a mediator, mediation with the angry, the indifferent, and the wounded is a tough assignment, even when one has been trained for it.

The consolation of the contemporary priest is that he can rely upon a generous, well-trained and genuinely good-willed body of lay people who want to work with him. This has always been true, but in this post–Vatican II Church lay people are a gift even more finely honed and more urgently needed. On the other hand, the desolation of the contemporary priest is that on many issues that influence the quality and quantity of lay membership and active participation, Church authorities offer him the rhetoric of ultimatums and denial. Therefore, the contemporary priest can

---

[16] Timothy Reker, "Priests for the Next Millennium," *Origins* (April 29, 1999) 776–81.

find himself living in a kind of pastoral schism, helping people alienated from parts of the official Church to find a way to remain in the Church. No person of integrity wants to be in that position. But many priests find that this kind of accommodation is the only way that they can be at home with the Christ of the gospel and the authority of the Church. An even greater problem is that many priests cannot talk openly about this dilemma. Perhaps one of the greatest developing problems, especially among those more recently ordained, is that many priests see no problem, feel no tension, in trying to help people locate their place in the Church. For these priests the Church's magisterium is clear, definite, and direct. As one young priest said to me in a discussion, "If people want to remain in the Church, then they obey the laws. If they find this too burdensome, then they can leave. What is important is that people be truthful about their allegiance to the Church." What "Church" means is important in this discussion. For many conservative priests it can seem that whatever any Vatican spokesman says takes on an authority reserved to the pope or to the communion of the bishops. With such a mentality loyalty can become a fairly narrowly defined virtue.

At the opening of a new century we are living in a Church that largely avoids or suppresses conversation about those internal issues that dramatize differences in approaches or interpretations. I do not mean that the central government of the Church says nothing; I mean that the central government of the Church declares and does not discuss. There is seemingly little or no willingness to talk about women's desire for greater involvement in Church service or simply to listen respectfully to what gay people claim as their experience or to process the pain and confusion that many struggling Catholics have about sexuality, the use of authority, their need for parishes in which community is cherished. When there is free and open discussion, then it is usually the parish priest who is involved in this. The more open he is, the more a priest experiences the frustrations and dismissals of Catholics. "Recovering Catholics"—i.e., those lay people who have resigned from active Church membership but retain psyches and spirits seemingly enduringly stamped by their Catholic histories—populate the universities and cultural centers of our country. Any priest called to labor in these areas meets them and hears their narratives, but usually has no way to process with Church authorities what these people have shared with him. Consequently, a significant mission of the contemporary priest is finding ways to relate with those who have a lover's quarrel with the Church; it is a mission that is demanding and has little guidelines. I believe that it is a mission that will increase in importance in the years ahead.

As one century ends and another begins, the Church in the United States has a magnificent opportunity to engage all its people in the work of the kingdom, to emphasize what unites us, and to seek ways in which we can attain a common ground for dialogue and decision. But this reconciliation demands trained, sensitive mediators. It is also a mediation that can be accomplished only by priests and their bishops and their lay colleagues working together as a team.

The Priest's Role in Secular Society

Priests live in this world even while spending a great deal of time talking about the values of the kingdom of God. The relationship between the secular and the sacred is a timeless topic. Michael Crosby has assembled some criteria which lay out the various ways in which the world can be approached.

> The sacred and secular, religious and political, faith and justice dimensions of life are not opposite poles; rather they represent alternative dimensions of reality that interrelate and actually interpenetrate in varying degrees of sophistication and complexity. However, this approach has not always been predominant; in fact, it seems to be the third alternative to two other approaches that have dominated thinking in the past centuries.[17]

Crosby describes the first of these two approaches as "the withdrawal tactic," that is, Christians are pilgrims who are trying to make their way in a world that is radically corrupt and evil. He identifies this as the code of many fundamentalist sects. He criticizes this approach as un-Christian because it denies the ramifications of the incarnation.[18] Crosby describes the second of these approaches as "the accommodationalist tactic," that is, Christians try to fit into the culture and the governmental structures of their times, acting as model citizens of their society and full participants of their culture. He identifies this as the failure of the churches in Nazi Germany. He criticizes this approach as a retreat from the prophetic demands of Scripture and surrender to the state as the "controlling ideology for the life of faith."[19] Crosby adds a third model, "the Christendom model," where the Church becomes "the ultimate arbitrator of social values and institutional life." He identifies this with the Middle Ages under Pope Innocent III.[20] His

---

[17] Michael H. Crosby, "Relationship of Sacred and Secular," *The New Dictionary of Catholic Social Thought,* ed. Judith A. Dwyer and Elizabeth L. Montgomery (Collegeville: The Liturgical Press, 1994) 857.

[18] Ibid., 857–8.

[19] Ibid., 858.

[20] Ibid.

fourth model sees the sacred and the secular in a variety of tensions; tensions, which arise, from the reality of the incarnation.

Crosby's analysis is helpful in defining the world that the contemporary priest has to inhabit and in which he has to labor for the kingdom. It is a world where the secular and the sacred are in tension. On the one hand, the priest remembers what Jesus said, "For God so loved the world that he gave his only Son, so that everyone who believes in him may not perish but may have eternal life" (John 3:16). On the other hand, he also recalls that this same Jesus warned, "If you belonged to the world, the world would love you as its own. Because you do not belong to the world, but I have chosen you out of the world—therefore, the world hates you" (John 15:19). Both sayings guide the life of the priest. He must love the world as the place in which Christ's Spirit labors to bring all to the peace of Christ; he must distrust that world that resists the gospel and enfeebles its mission. Vatican II called on all Catholics to discern the signs of the times in the light of the gospel. What did this come to mean for the priest in his own life and in his ministry?

First of all, the spirituality of the priest represents the context out of which he makes his decisions about how to live, how to exercise his ministry, how to spend his time, where to place his resources. In the latter quarter of the twentieth century the term "spirituality" gathered a number of definitions and descriptions.[21] However, there is general agreement that spirituality focuses on how a man or a woman makes decisions about his or her ultimate values. For Christians God as revealed in the life and mission of Jesus constitutes the ultimate value. To follow Christ as that ultimate value is to live in discipleship. The priest joins his sisters and brothers in this journey, walking the road of life in the companionship of Christ and one another. The contemporary journey is not easy for priest or people. Christian discernment means following Christ in this world.

Second, this world is a wounded reality, which the Christian Good Samaritan must be willing to see with a compassionate eye and to work to heal with a practical involvement. To withdraw from this call to be contemplative before the reality of the world is to ignore the first half of the parable. To ignore the need for personal involvement in the healing of the world is to ignore the second half of the parable. Priests and people are supposed to take to heart the command that Jesus issues at the conclusion of the parable: "Go and do likewise" (Luke 10:37).

Third, in order to discern the priest has to do some kind of inventory on the moral and religious climate of the times. For example, in *The Clash*

---

[21] Michael Downey, *Understanding Christian Spirituality* (New York/Mahwah, N.J.: Paulist Press, 1997).

of Civilizations and the Remaking of the World, Samuel P. Huntington identifies five manifestations of moral decline:

1. Increase in antisocial behavior, such as crime, drug use and violence generally;
2. Family decay, including increased rates of divorce, illegitimacy, teen-age pregnancy and single-parent families;
3. At least in the United States, a decline in "social capital," that is, membership in voluntary associations and the interpersonal trust associated with such membership;
4. General weakening of the "work ethic" and the rise of a cult of personal indulgence;
5. Decreasing commitment to learning and intellectual activity manifested in the United States in lower levels of scholastic achievement.

The future health of the West and its influence on other societies depends in considerable measure on its success in coping with these trends, which, of course, give rise to the assertions of moral superiority by Muslims and Asians.[22]

To relate the gospel to the people of this time and within this culture means that the priest has to recognize the dual task of citing disorder and of supporting people who have to live with and through the disorder. How he preaches the gospel in this kind of context and how he teaches the ramifications of the gospel against this kind of social background have become increasingly daunting. Much of his time is spent trying to cope with the disorders that threaten the society in which he lives and labors. The call to ethical and religious reform is difficult. It cannot be a simplistic moralizing about how bad things are. It cannot be a fundamentalist retreat from life. It cannot be an escape into some piety that creates a world unrealistically removed from the terror and demands of modern culture. One of the major tasks that confront the priest today is to find ways to bring gospel and culture into dialogue.

Other challenges to the contemporary priest arise from within the subculture of the priesthood and of Catholicism. Of course, one of the major trials has been the incidence of pedophilia among diocesan priests and religious. This has been a heavy burden for the Church: the bishops, the priests, the people. It has contributed both to a severe weakening of trust in priests and to a heaviness of heart among priests themselves. Today most dioceses and religious congregations have in place clear directives on how incidents of pedophilia are to be handled, with genuine

---

[22] Samuel P. Huntington, *The Clash of Civilizations and the Remaking of World Order* (New York: Touchstone of Simon and Schuster, 1997) 304.

and professional care for the victims and their families and with decisive procedures for the addict. But these procedures came slowly and at great cost, financially, psychologically, and spiritually.

As more and more lay Catholics became better educated, rose on the economic ladder, and assumed national leadership in business, the professions, and public life, priesthood diminished as a significant career choice. There was a grace in this because it purified the motives for a man's choice of the priesthood and emphasized the servant character of his choice. But it also meant that fewer and fewer parents encouraged their sons to think of becoming a priest. Moreover, the rise of lay leadership and the development of highly competent lay ministers diminished, to some extent, the sense of uniqueness of the role of the priest within a parish, a school, or a retreat center. Finally, as U.S. Catholics had smaller families, parents were reluctant to see a son become a priest and thus lose the promise of grandchildren.

Another cultural phenomenon that had an impact on contemporary priests was the Church's strong assertion that ordination was restricted by the will of Christ to men. For many women this decision caused them great pain, both because they felt a genuine call to priesthood within the Church and because they felt it was simply one more instance of the Church's reluctance to admit them into real partnership in Church leadership and governance. Other women simply interpreted this denial as the final validation that the Church had nothing for them. The response of women to an exclusively male priesthood and to the dominantly male leadership within the Church has been varied. But what has been important is that priesthood became a target for feminine anger, hurt, and, frequently, rejection.[23]

Finally, the acceptances of priests from the Anglican Church and from other Protestant denominations and their subsequent assimilation into the ranks of Catholic priesthood have met with some ambivalence among priests. Of course, many welcomed these new priests as brothers in the ministry. But there was among many priests a concern that the Church had become a haven for some converts whose major agenda was to keep conservative, even reactionary, Christianity alive.

As one reviews the various social forces that have shaped both the Church and secular culture, one realizes that the priesthood is changing in ways that the Church cannot wholly control. Priestless parishes have created a new kind of liturgical life and encouraged a new kind of lay leadership. Some dioceses have recognized this and instituted sophisticated

---

[23] Literature here is extensive, but an excellent survey of the issues can be found in Mary Jo Weaver, "New Catholic Women Ten Years Later," *New Catholic Women: A Contemporary Challenge to Traditional Religious Authority* (Bloomington: Indiana University Press, 1995) ix–xxvi.

programs designed to educate and to form lay leaders closely identified with the bishop and, frequently, with a more conservative interpretation of Church doctrine and practice. All this has also called renewed attention to the role of the ordained deacon in parish life.

A review of the literature on priestly spirituality, diocesan and religious, reveals an emerging sense of living in an ambiguity that only God can resolve.[24] Weakness and power, loneliness and solidarity, identity and function, sacred and secular—the listing of the contrasts could go on and on. The experience of ambiguity is not a sign of disintegration or of diminishment. It is an invitation to love more deeply within the mystery of the human as a radical orientation toward God. Reconciliation has far more profound significance than "making up." It is rather a "bringing together," an ability to surrender to what I for one do not fully understand but totally trust. It is what makes great literature and music and art. It is the power of the parables of Jesus, insisting that the reign of God is both like and unlike everything we see and touch and hear. This mystery that invites priests to a new level of intimacy with God is not theirs alone. It is the gift Christ gives to all Christians to help them "to wait with joyful hope." In the midst of intense secularity the priest finds both identity and his deepest relationships not in fleeing the struggle between the sacred and the secular but by embracing it.

Conclusion

In attempting to give an overview of where U.S. priests, diocesan and religious, stood at the close of the twentieth century, we have centered on three areas of their life and ministry: their identity, their relationships, and their culture. In each of these areas we have noted patterns of response, ways priests have dealt with these realities. Priests have located their identity in the meaning that Christ has for them, in the expectations of the people of God, and, especially in the last quarter of this century, in the justice that embraces the poor and the marginal. Priests have defined their relationships, consciously or unconsciously, as spokespersons and interpreters, guides and companions, moving between the values of the kingdom as enunciated by the Church and the priorities and demands of the world in which they and the people they serve have to live and work.

Priesthood in the new millennium will be different. Questions of identity will remain as parish structures change. The decline in the number of active priests will influence how bishops manage the present Church infra-

---

[24] A collection that illustrates this point can be found in *The Spirituality of the Diocesan Priest.*

structure. The growing emphasis in Catholic universities and colleges, hospitals and medical centers on defining and integrating others into their mission comes out of a concern that as religious personnel diminish in these institutions, someone has to assume responsibility for the traditions that made them distinctive. What has been happening in Catholic universities and colleges and in hospitals and medical centers, namely, the gradual creation of a new culture of leadership and management, is going to happen in parishes across the United States. Even if there were a leveling off of the active priest population, even if there were a sudden surge in vocations to religious life and to the priesthood, the parish structure would have to change. As lay people assume more responsibility for the community life and the apostolic work of the parish, the priest will become more and more part of a working team and not the sole leader or even the chief administrator. Numerical decline influences the way priests function; and while function does not equate identity, function structures the way identity emerges. One or two priests staffing a large metropolitan parish cannot hope to have oversight much less direct involvement in every area of parish life. Micro management is no management. Delegation, subsidiary, teamwork—these have to be the mode of operating the parish of the future.[25]

Relationships will only become more influential in the ministry of the priests. As their work becomes more dependent on lay leadership and partnership, priests will have to rely not on presumptions of competency, authority, or power, but rather on the recognition from lay people that they are competent, effective, and important to the life of the parish, the school, the hospital, the retreat center. This heightened reliance on partnership rather than ownership will create tensions, especially if seminaries do not train their candidates in team ministry and the array of skills needed to effect team ministry. Even more important than skills is formation in a spirituality that liberates priests and people for genuine communion in all areas of Church life.

Discerning how to deal with a secular culture is not a modern phenomenon. What is new is the pervasive power and influence of secularity and the diminishment of religious values in the ways that governments, industry and business, education and professions, business and mass media make decisions. How to confront, how to negotiate, how to cooperate, and when to do any or all of these involves the pastoral strategy of the Church. For example, the Church's stand on the death penalty or economic justice

---

[25] Archbishop Daniel Pilarczyk, "What Will and Won't Change in the Future Parish," *Origins* (April 29, 1999) 773–6. Archbishop Pilarczyk offers an alternate projection for the Church of the future.

for all or peace and war are frequently at odds with the economic and social pragmatism of those who most influence our culture and society. In those instances where government and big business support the Church, it is usually in the area of private morality and with the expectation that this maintains good order and, ultimately, will promote a conservative agenda.

The riches of the priesthood lie deep within the mystery of Christ's decision to empower his community to preach and to teach, to heal and to confront, to nourish and to make holy—all in his name and through the power of his Spirit. This is the vital center of the priest's life and mission. This constitutes his most enduring identity, his most intimate relationship, and his most effective presence to his culture. But it is a gift that dies unless it is shared with the priestly people of God.

Sisters and Brothers: An Evolved and Evolving Religious Life

Barbara Kraemer, O.S.F.

As we bridge the centuries, looking back and looking forward, what can we learn about religious life in the United States for sisters and brothers? At the close of the nineteenth century, the experience of people in the Western world, including the United States, was one of change and dislocation because of industrialization and urbanization. The United States was coming out of the Spanish-American War (1898) and establishing itself as a world power. On the domestic scene, a progressive philosophy affected politics, education, and social life.

Institutionalized Approach to Life and Ministry

Many religious communities were founded during the 1800s and experienced a period of growth and stabilization in the early years of the twentieth century. Though these new congregations were apostolic in orientation, their lifestyle tended to follow a monastic pattern. The Code of Canon Law, promulgated in 1918, led to uniformity of structure and lifestyle for religious congregations of different traditions.[1] This stable way of living and working operated effectively, in tune with the spirit of organization and order in industrial U.S. society. A theology of separation from the world and religious life as a "higher state" prevailed, both in religious congregations and in the Catholic Church, though this theology was not necessarily that envisioned by the founders of these congregations.

The missionary activity of the Catholic Church developed within this environment. Missionary congregations were present in the United States

---

[1] Apostolic religious have an active ministry. They comprise over 90 percent of the women's congregations in the United States today. Contemplatives devote their lives to prayer and live in cloistered groups. Monastic communities were established for prayer and work, mostly within the monastery walls, but their monks and nuns can have an active ministry outside their monasteries.

before the twentieth century, but the first U.S.–founded overseas mission societies were Maryknoll—the Catholic Foreign Mission Society of America (1911) of the brothers and priests, and the Foreign Mission Sisters of St. Dominic (1920). Other mission-sending congregations began during the same period, their call strengthened by papal documents on mission promulgated in 1919 and 1926.[2] It was the Society of Catholic Medical Missionaries, established as a pious society in 1925, that became "the first Roman Catholic congregation of women to work as surgeons, obstetricians, and physicians,"[3] but not until the ban on religious sisters being doctors was lifted. This congregation led the way in providing professional preparation for religious women to become doctors.

Between 1920 and 1953, missionary groups focused their efforts in Asia, especially China, most serving among the poor. Their missionary goal was conversion to the Catholic faith. Religious congregations that were not founded as mission-sending groups also sent missionaries, often volunteers, respecting that the missionary vocation was not for everyone. Men and women had different approaches to mission, which was affected by their status in the Church. Priests had a definite sacramental and liturgical role in building the church and fostering the spiritual life of the people. Sisters functioned in supporting roles, meeting tangible and immediate needs. As they worked among the people, sisters were the first to engage in interreligious dialogue. "Brothers had access to the lives of the people in some of the same ways" as sisters, but sometimes they were not understood, because they were not priests or sisters. For example, The Irish Christian Brothers, who were educators, returned from China in the 1930s.[4]

During the next three decades, awareness of the "missions" and financial support for the work of evangelization grew in the U.S. church, primarily due to the influence of teaching sisters. Young men and women were inspired to follow in the footsteps of the first missionaries, both in the United States and in China. Chinese religious continued to support the Catholic population in their country, working underground after the American missionaries were forced to leave.[5]

Until mid-century the lifestyle of all religious—apostolic, missionary, monastic, contemplative—was highly structured, all activities circumscribed by the horarium. Religious separated themselves from the world and interacted with the world through schools, hospitals, and parishes.

---

[2] *Maximum illud* (1919) and *Rerum ecclesiae* (1926).

[3] Angelyn Dries, *The Missionary Movement in American Catholic History* (Maryknoll, N.Y.: Orbis Books, 1998) 105.

[4] Ibid., 262–4, and interview by author, 31 January 1999.

[5] Ibid., 114–48.

Their lives reflected the Church of that era, a Church that operated as a closed system with clear boundaries, preserving its members from the evils of the world and helping them protect their faith from the "perils" of Protestantism.

Americans born between 1925 and 1942 were known as the "Silent Generation," people who "largely conformed to the world built for them"[6] by the previous generation. They were loyal to the institutional Church and, for those in religious life, to their religious community. The Catholic population of this generation was served through the parish structure, including parish schools. Many Catholics were from immigrant families and appreciated the freedom of religion in the United States and the ability to maintain ties with their religious cultural heritage through the Catholic Church. They valued religious life, because religious were the "professional" Catholics who furthered the mission of the Church and functioned as its work force. It was the religious who built the Catholic school system in the United States and educated each new generation of Catholics.[7]

After World War II and later during the Cold War, these Americans were concerned with enemies outside the country. They welcomed the respite of peace in the mid-1940s, and, because of the GI bill, veterans had opportunities to return to school. Many Americans sought to advance themselves through education, and religious both provided this education and became better educated themselves.

Many religious brothers were engaged in teaching, especially in their own high schools and colleges. Others dedicated themselves to physical work on church properties, agriculture, nursing, printing, and bookbinding, both at home and at missions overseas. They were support staff to the priests, taking as their model the role of St. Joseph in the Holy Family. This distinction between "teachers and those in overalls" reflected the division in U.S. society between those who received advanced education for professional roles and others who worked in the trades after completing high school.[8] Brothers were not as well known as priests, and the "hiddenness" of their vocation did not help them attract new members. At Mission Secretariat conferences in the 1950s brothers first met together to

---

[6] Patricia Wittberg and Bryan Froehle, "Generation X and Religious Life: New Findings from CARA Studies," *Horizon* (Spring 1998) 3f.

[7] According to Robert Schreiter, many people believe that "the reason for the vitality of the U.S. church, which is not matched in any other industrialized nation, comes from the socialization—and we would add, evangelization—carried on through this school system." "The New Evangelization," *Word Remembered, Word Proclaimed,* ed. Stephen Bevans and Roger Schroeder (Nettetal: Steyler Verlag, 1997) 52.

[8] Dries, *Missionary Movement,* 156–7.

discuss their way of life. In 1958 they began publishing a *Brothers' Newsletter* for non-teaching brothers, and by the end of the decade brothers working overseas had developed a greater self-consciousness of their role as missionaries, not only mission helpers.[9]

Sister Formation Movement

Religious congregations of women with colleges had emphasized liberal arts education and graduate education for their members long before the Sister Formation Movement began.[10] Many sisters who were already engaged in teaching and nursing had to attend evening and summer classes to complete their college degrees. At meetings of the National Catholic Education Association, discussions took place about the necessity of sisters completing a bachelor's degree before beginning to work. In 1950, to ensure the quality of Catholic educational and health care institutions, Pope Pius XII insisted that religious teachers receive professional training. This led to the establishment of the Regina Mundi Institute (1954) in Rome and the Sister Formation Conference in the United States (1956). Congregations of sisters throughout the country took action. The *Sister Formation Bulletin* assisted the planning of spiritual, intellectual, cultural, and religious life formation for U.S. sisters. An Overseas Project was launched to invite sisters in developing countries to attend U.S. colleges.[11]

Higher education for religious led to other changes. Sisters studied new disciplines, dialogued with persons of different perspectives, and were influenced by the mass media.[12] For some, advanced education meant new options, and they left religious life to pursue a career. For many others, education led to new thinking about religious life, and a readiness to participate in making changes once the Vatican II renewal began.

It was also during Pius XII's pontificate that conferences of major superiors were established in the United States (1956), the Conference of Major Superiors of Men and the Conference of Major Superiors of Women (which in 1968 took the name Leadership Conference of Women Reli-

---

[9] Ibid., 157.

[10] Katarina Schuth, "The Intellectual Life as a Value for Women Religious in the United States," *Women Religious and the Intellectual Life: The North American Achievement,* ed. Bridget Puzon (San Francisco: International Scholars Publications, 1996) 18.

[11] Dries, *Missionary Movement,* 205.

[12] Sandra Schneiders, "Leadership and Spirituality in Postmodern Religious Congregations," paper presented at the annual meeting of the Leadership Conference of Women Religious, Rochester, New York, 23 August 1997, 7.

gious).[13] These conferences assisted their members in carrying out their leadership and management responsibilities within their congregations, with other institutes, and with the Church and society. Because the conferences were in place at the time of the Second Vatican Council, there was a mechanism for interaction and common implementation of new directions.

Changes of Course in the 1960s

At the beginning of the 1960s, Pope John XXIII urged U.S. religious superiors to send 10 percent of their members as missionaries to Latin America. Many U.S. religious were already there, and now other congregations began to send personnel. They also enlisted lay volunteers to help in their work. Church concern for Latin America paralleled action at the national level in the United States. To promote social and economic development, John F. Kennedy initiated the Alliance for Progress and established the Peace Corps. This was the beginning of a decade of development in Latin America, promoted by the U.S. government and supported by the Church's understanding of mission as development.

The decade of the 1960s in the United States was also a decade of controversy and revolution in thinking and acting because of two movements: civil rights and protest of the Vietnam War. People looked critically at their society, saw that some things were radically wrong, and insisted on changes. Religious participated in civil rights marches, demanding respect for the rights of all Americans. They demonstrated the prophetic dimension of their vocation at a time when the official Catholic Church was not speaking out. The lack of official Church witness led some religious to leave their congregations. Similarly, religious participated in protesting the Vietnam War and accepted the consequences of civil disobedience for challenging the misguided authority of the federal government.

Call to Renewal of Religious Life

This was the context within which religious received the call to renew their institutes and become part of the modern world. The mandate from the

---

[13] The major superiors of some congregations of women who were not in agreement with the Leadership Conference of Women Religious formed their own organization, Consortium Perfectae Caritatis, in 1970. This later became the Council of Major Superiors of Women Religious (C.M.S.W.R.), an organization which currently represents the superiors of 10 percent of women religious in the United States.

The Association of Contemplative Sisters, founded in 1969, has served members of cloistered communities; it is not a conference of major superiors officially approved by Rome.

Second Vatican Council was taken seriously. Sisters and brothers had already imbibed Cardinal Suenens' message in *The Nun in the Modern World* (1961) and Pope John XXIII's announcement of *aggiornamento,* his reason for calling the council in 1962. Religious studied the documents and sought to apply them to their lives, especially *Lumen gentium* (Dogmatic Constitution on the Church, 1964), *Gaudium et spes* (Pastoral Constitution on the Church in the Modern World, 1965), and *Perfectae caritatis* (Decree on the Renewal of Religious Life, 1965). Msgr. John Hillenbrand, in his presentations to religious after the council, described the revolution that these documents represented by explaining that the Catholic Church was no longer up on the mountain looking down at the people in the stream below. The Church was now present alongside the people in the stream. Thus, religious as part of the Church were to be there as well; they were asked to read the signs of the times and respond according to their charism and founding purpose.

The work of renewal required the participation of all members, and a process of ongoing formation took place as religious studied theology and Church documents, as well as their own constitutions and history, seeking to learn how to reclaim their founding charism and express it in making a response to modern needs. Throughout the century, the lives of religious had been determined by the external structure of rules and customs, horarium, decisions of superiors, and assignments. Now religious were invited to participate in developing and guiding their lives by an inner structure, based on a deep personal spirituality and a charism shared with others in their religious communities. They were called to carry out their mission in collaboration with others, working in solidarity to bring the Church and society into conformity with Gospel values.

To understand the readiness for change among women religious, the leaders of women's congregations in 1965 commissioned Sr. Marie Augusta Neal, S.N.D. de Namur, to conduct a sisters' survey based on the council documents. With the assistance of sister sociologists all over the country, she collected data from 139,000 women religious. (The survey was updated with samples in 1979–80 and 1989–90, to show the change in thinking over the decades.)[14] Each congregation received a report, comparing the congregation to the national profile. This data was a valuable planning tool for the congregations and was used by special general chapters called to determine the content of renewal and later to update their constitutions.[15]

[14] An analysis of the results of the 1979–80 survey can be found in Marie Augusta Neal, *Catholic Sisters in Transition: From the 1960s to the 1980s* (Wilmington, Del.: Glazier, 1984).

[15] Marie Augusta Neal, *From Nuns to Sisters: An Expanding Vocation* (Mystic, Conn.: Twenty-Third Publications, 1990) 56f.

Personal Development and Choices

Two significant areas of renewal for all religious congregations in the post–Vatican II era were personal development and relationships between individuals and the community (i.e., a renewed understanding of the vow of obedience). The challenge was to establish a balance between the dignity of the human person and promotion of the common good, the two poles of Catholic social teaching. Religious congregations could not foresee the consequences of embarking on this path of renewal, even though they knew they must proceed. Religious had lived structured lives, with all decisions made about them, generally without consulting them. A commitment to personal development of the members was based on a recognition of each one's vocation and talents. This meant that religious men and women began to be involved in making the decisions about their education[16] and formation, their apostolic service and religious dress, which led to greater personal responsibility and commitment in religious life.

In many congregations, especially women's congregations, religious were encouraged to make individual choices in relation to their life and work. They could choose members of their living groups and where to live, thus forming small intentional communities. They could make decisions about their ministry, which often led to collaboration with the laity and the growth of new ministries in response to human needs of the times. These decisions also led to choices for work outside of institutions belonging to the congregation or the diocese. These new opportunities to make choices about their lives led some sisters to leave their communities, because they did not see religious life as different from the life of a dedicated single lay person.

Changed Understandings of Authority

Through study and discussion religious came to new understandings of the vows, especially the vow of obedience. They became attentive to the Holy Spirit speaking in each community member, not only in the superior. Living the vow of obedience meant that each one assumed personal responsibility within the community and participated in governance. There were meetings and small group discussions, as sisters and brothers developed new ways of working together. A team approach to leadership replaced

---

[16] Schuth points out that placing decisions about continuing education in the hands of members, including younger members, means that the choices will not be guided by a structured plan to accomplish "a clearly articulated mission." As a consequence, the congregation may be jeopardizing its "intellectual vitality" and ability to face the serious intellectual questions of the future. "The Intellectual Life," 17.

the single superior who consulted with the council. Chapters incorporated democratic principles in their functioning, and met more frequently to address all areas of renewal. Religious were developing a new form for the organization of religious life.

At the local level, community life meant more than living in the same building; it required learning how to share authority and responsibility, how to make decisions together about prayer, meals, transportation, house budget, expectations of one another, and group activities. There were house meetings and goal setting sessions. Common life issues were different for large groups with more space and privacy for individuals, versus small groups where there was a lack of personal space. Some formed healthy intentional communities; some left their communities; some chose to live alone.

Women and men religious embraced these changes in relation to obedience differently, because they had dissimilar experiences of authority prior to the Second Vatican Council. Men already had more latitude for action and more individual responsibility than women. Many women welcomed the changes because of the authoritarianism that had governed their lives. Some religious men and women went to the extreme of not accepting as legitimate any authority outside of themselves. This led to difficulties when sisters or brothers were given leadership responsibilities by the community but did not have the authority from the members to act. With hindsight one can recognize that communities faced the serious limitation of being unable to see the consequences of their actions as they made changes in elements of a system that had worked effectively over a long period of time. Difficulties were compounded when religious leaders counted on the good will of the members to make the new system work, but were confronted with criticism and lack of trust.

What occurred in religious life was an echo of the challenge to authority in the country during this decade. The U.S. government had once functioned as a unified system, with the patriotic support of citizens taken for granted; now the government was questioned about civil rights, the Vietnam War and Watergate, and C.I.A. activities in Latin America. There was no turning back.

Religious and U.S. Culture

The Baby Boomers had come of age, with their questions about the meaning of life and the value of institutions. Religious of this generation tended to mirror the wider U.S. culture. As they became part of U.S. society in order to incarnate Gospel values in it, they risked being affected by secularization and becoming too much a part of the culture with its materialism, consumerism, and individualism. Some left religious life because of its seemingly secular character, a perceived loss of religious dimension. There were other departures from religious life as an institution, in the same way people in the society at large were separating themselves from other institutions; for example, living in communes rather than nuclear families, not accepting societal norms or government policies that deprived people of their civil rights. For some, religious life could never change enough; for others, changes were too fast. And just as individualism characterized U.S. society during this period, so it left an imprint on religious life.

Confusion about the identity of religious in the Catholic Church also affected membership in U.S. communities during this decade and the ones to follow. Who are we? What do we have to offer the society? Why would we invite young people to join us? These questions exemplified the confusion that often accompanies sudden change. Attempts at answers led to frequent revisions of formation programs and, in some cases, to a moratorium on men and women being admitted to congregations. The loss of a generation of new members left a generation gap in many communities and made the entry of young persons into a group without peers difficult.

Although, during the first half of the twentieth century, congregations of religious grew through the addition of new members, that trend changed during the 1960s. For brothers, the number joining was stable at the beginning of the century, gradually increasing in the 1920s, significantly increasing in the 1930s, and peaked in 1966. Sisters represented a larger portion of the Catholic population throughout the century, and their numbers increased until the peak was reached in 1965. Figures 1 and 2 report the membership data for brothers and sisters during the twentieth century, and Figure 3 graphs the number of Catholics in the United States.

The civil rights movement highlighted the importance of respect for the human dignity of all persons and led to a rising self-consciousness of one's racial and ethnic origin. Among religious, new organizations came into being to respond to the concerns of numerical minorities in religious life—the National Black Catholic Clergy Conference (for priests and brothers) and the National Black Sisters Conference, both in 1968; Padres in 1969; and Las Hermanas in 1971.

The civil rights movement also led to awareness of discrimination in other areas of society, and challenges to sexism and clericalism. The women's movement (beginning with the suffragette movement in the early years of the century, coming to the fore with the civil rights movement) and feminism[17] have led to significant changes in the United States, but not

---

[17] Common to all forms of feminism, according to Maria Riley, is the "assertion of women's subordinate role in a patriarchal world and the commitment to change that reality."

Figure 1
Religious Sisters in the United States

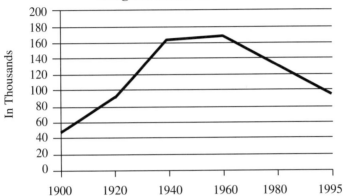

Source: *The Official Catholic Directory* (New Providence, N.J.: P.J. Kenedy and Sons, 1960, 1980, 1995); and George C. Stewart Jr., *Marvel of Charity: History of American Sisters and Nuns* (Huntington, Ind.: Our Sunday Visitor Press, 1994) 564–5.

Figure 2
Religious Brothers in the United States

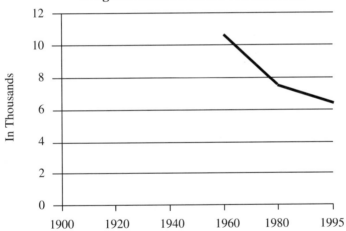

Source: *The Official Catholic Directory* (New Providence, N.J.: P.J. Kenedy and Sons, 1960, 1980, 1995).

*Date for brothers separate from priests was not available for the years 1900, 1920, and 1940. The category in these years was "religious men."

Figure 3
Catholic Population in the United States

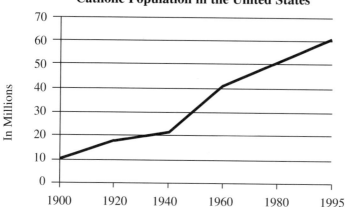

Source: *The Official Catholic Directory* (New Providence, N.J.: P.J. Kenedy and Sons, 1900, 1920, 1940, 1960, 1980, 1995).

*Catholics are identified from baptismal records and not by parish registration. Therefore, some Catholics will not be included in the number because they were baptized in another country, and others who do not identify themselves as Catholics will be included if they were baptized in the United States.

****

without serious conflicts in society, in the Catholic Church, and in religious life. Greater participation of women in society threatened those who could lose privileged positions and decision-making power; therefore, there was resistance and reaction. Religious women and men were challenged to incorporate the positive values of feminism into their way of life, working for greater inclusivity and mutuality in Church roles and relationships, however difficult these would be to achieve.

New Questions of Ministry and Membership

In response to the needs in American society, sisters and brothers initiated new ministries—adult literacy programs, health clinics and schools in poor areas, parish religious education programs and pastoral ministry, counseling centers for women, jail ministry, community organizing, social

---

The goal is equality of persons and/or transformation of the society. "The Significance of Feminism for the Intellectual Life of Women," *Women Religious and the Intellectual Life,* ed. Bridget Puzon (San Francisco: International Scholars Publications, 1996) 74.

and legal services for immigrants. More entered retreat work and became spiritual directors. Congregations of women formed Network, a national Catholic social justice lobby (1971), and with men's groups they established justice and peace centers and organizations for socially responsible investments. They participated in Project Equality, the National Conference for Christians and Jews, and other organizations working for racial justice.

Sisters and brothers in Latin America and other developing countries contributed to the local church's development of a global perspective and solidarity with people in other lands. When missioners returned home, either permanently or for a short period of time, they participated in mission education efforts in schools and parishes. This "reverse mission" activity made American Catholics aware of conditions in other countries and led to support for change of government policies or structures that impacted negatively on other peoples, including immigrants and refugees in the United States.

Religious were coming to understand "what it means to serve in a changed and changing world,"[18] and this generated new vitality and a new sense of mission. At the same time, the new individual ministries and corporate commitments meant that fewer resources were available for the institutions that religious had built and staffed. Fewer religious now taught in Catholic elementary and secondary schools, or in Catholic colleges and universities; fewer served in congregational health care institutions. In some cases, decisions had to be made to transfer ownership or close schools and hospitals. When this occurred, religious who had identified religious life with institutional service felt that their congregation no longer had a mission.

Congregations searched for ways to ensure that the mission of the institution would continue when they could not guarantee religious personnel to staff it. The laity have taken the leadership in Catholic schools, continuing the work religious had begun. Missionary congregations established volunteer programs to prepare the laity to take over work they had initiated.

Internally, religious congregations were concerned about the increasing proportion of older members and the problems of providing personnel and money for their future care when fewer women and men were choosing religious life. During the 1970s, planning for retirement needs, acceptance of religious into the federal social security program, and (in the 1980s) the National Conference of Catholic Bishops' decision to have an annual collection for retired religious helped to ameliorate these concerns. Sr. Marie Augusta

---

[18] Schreiter, "The New Evangelization," 52.

Neal has observed that these problems deflected "public attention from the more profound and compelling drama of a religious calling that seeks and suggests radical changes in the very structure of modern society."[19]

Associate Membership

Collaboration with the laity in mission led to a new mode of thinking about the relationships between religious and laity. Beginning in the 1970s, religious congregations developed a formal process for inviting lay women and men to share in their charism and mission. They invited them to become associate members, but did not require that the laity follow the way of life defined by the vows of poverty, chastity, and obedience. In a number of congregations, the first associates were former members who found a way "to belong and not belong," as one associate expressed her relationship to the community at that time. Although Third Orders for the laity date back to the Middle Ages, association is distinct in its inclusion of lay women and men as individuals participating in the life of the congregation, without canonical obligations. For religious, matters related to community life, ministry, authority and leadership, voting, and money are governed by the vows. Associates do not profess these vows; they have established their primary identity in another way of life.

Initially, members of some congregations believed that association could become a new form of religious life, replacing the previous form of vowed membership, though this has not happened. In 1988 the National Religious Vocation Conference, the Religious Formation Conference, and the Lilly Endowment funded a national survey of congregations with associate programs, in order to examine (1) the effect of associate membership on commitment to religious life, (2) the nature of recent programs, and (3) reasons motivating the growth of these programs. The survey, sent to 1,064 congregations, had a response rate of 68.2 percent (590 women's groups, 135 men's groups).[20] The study found that associates reflect the dominant age group in religious life—educated white women over fifty. Perhaps the most significant finding of this study, and also of a later study of the Sisters of Mercy,[21] was the fact that, as increasing numbers of lay women and men choose to become associates, their relationship to a religious congregation calls the congregation to more clearly define its identity.[22] What defines a religious congregation? Who is a member? Is association an alternative form

---

[19] Neal, *From Nuns to Sisters,* 7.

[20] Rosemary Jeffries, "Associate Membership Survey," *Horizon* (Winter 1991) 65.

[21] Rosemary Jeffries, "The Associate Movement: An Update," *Horizon* (Fall 1993).

[22] Ibid., 13, and Jeffries, "Associate Membership Survey," 64.

of membership in a congregation that has different ways of belonging, or is association a complementary but auxiliary relationship to the congregation?[23] The questions are significant if one's commitment in religious life is linked to the congregation's definition of membership.[24]

Religious and the Postmodern Generation

The 1990s generation of young adult Catholics, known as Generation X or the Survivor Generation, experienced a "childhood marked by political corruption from Watergate to Whitewater, . . . a rising gap between the rich and the poor, . . . increasing rates of divorce among their parents. . . . Since they often had little or no systematic catechesis, they are unsure of what it means to be a Catholic."[25] Some say these young people are apathetic or reluctant to make commitments, whereas others characterize them as hungry for spirituality and communal ties.[26]

Tom Beaudoin, a member of this generation, says that Generation Xers above all want to belong.[27] They may be indifferent to institutions and suspicious of them, as many others in this postmodern society, but they are searching for persons who are authentic witnesses and can teach them to be authentic witnesses in their lives.[28] The hunger for spirituality may be for a privatized therapeutic version of spirituality, arising from the individualism in postmodern culture, a return to the pre-Vatican "Jesus and me" theology of separation from the world, but it can be deepened by coming in contact with a spirituality that is rooted in God's presence in tradition and social witness and responsibility.[29]

Youth in the United States today, living in an information age, in an increasingly multicultural society, lack both mentoring by "wisdom figures" and a solid education in their faith. Religious can be the mentors and educators who prepare these young people to live harmoniously with people of various cultures and to be leaders in the church.[30] Attention to the needs of the younger generation is essential if they are to carry forward

---

[23] Jeffries, "Associate Membership Survey," 72–4.

[24] Ibid., 75.

[25] Wittberg and Froehle, "Generation X," 4.

[26] Ibid.

[27] See Tom Beaudoin, *Virtual Faith: The Irreverent Spiritual Quest of Generation X* (San Francisco: Jossey-Bass Publishers, 1998).

[28] Ibid.

[29] Regina Bechtle, "Spirituality" (Toronto, Canada: Seventh InterAmerican Conference of Religious, 1999).

[30] Brett C. Hoover, "Youth and Young Adults" (Toronto, Canada: Seventh InterAmerican Conference of Religious, 1999).

the mission of the Church as lay Catholics, clerics, and future members of religious communities. Are sisters and brothers in a position to invite them to religious life?

Religious today are primarily from the older age groups in the U.S. population, those who came of age after World War II and the early Baby Boomers. There are fewer members in their twenties, thirties, and forties. In addition, religious often live alone or in small groups without space for a new member. Their dedication to their ministries leaves little time for interacting with those who might be interested in religious life. This description does not characterize all religious, but it raises questions for religious to consider, if they are truly interested in inviting men and women to join them.

Another question: can more religious communities invite persons of various cultural groups to join their communities? Religious are aware that their membership does not reflect the racial and ethnic composition of either U.S. society or the U.S. Catholic Church. Some congregations, especially those in contact with different cultural groups in their ministry, are becoming more multiracial and multicultural. They have learned how to live with young people different from themselves and be enriched both by the differences and the discovery of their common humanity. Many other congregations are and will remain monoracial and monocultural in both ministry and membership. In an increasingly global society, what does that mean for their mission and their future existence?

A Call for Evaluation

What is the future of religious life in the United States? In 1992 some members and staff of the two conferences of religious (Conference of Major Superiors of Men [C.M.S.M.] and the Leadership Conference of Women Religious [L.C.W.R.]) formed a think tank in Washington, D.C., to see what would help them answer the question. They examined the social science research studies of religious life then being published, especially the Religious Life Futures Project conducted by David Nygren, C.M., and Miriam Ukeritis, C.S.J. They proposed to the conferences the establishment of the Center for the Study of Religious Life, in order to promote reflection on religious life in the United States and to serve as a resource to religious leadership, as they implemented directions that would ensure a future for their congregations. Funds were contributed by the religious congregations to establish the center in 1998. Honest assessment of the strengths and weaknesses of religious life at the beginning of the millennium will be a first step to developing strategies to assist religious leaders to move from a vision of what religious life could be to the creation of its future.

A call to evaluation is a call to change, to conversion. Not all communities will continue to exist, but this is to be expected. No order has had more than two hundred years of growth before it declined.[31] The life cycles of religious institutes in the past include growth, decline, sometimes death, sometimes revitalizations. At this time in history, pruning is needed for the plant of religious life to flourish; not all that has become part of the expression of religious life today is useful or worthy of being taken into the future. Religious are called to be prophetic, to be countercultural, and in this way to give witness to Gospel values and a Gospel way of life.

A number of areas need to be addressed, and they can only be listed briefly here. They are questions for religious and for all in the Church who want to see this way of life continue.

(1) The *identity* of religious congregations: defining why the congregation exists as a group in the Church; what comprises its way of life, that is, its spirituality, charism, mission, and community life; and who its members are. Some new communities that have formed in the second half of this century are clear about their identity. The Fellowship of Emerging Religious Communities consists of about a hundred new groups in the Catholic Church that are united by a desire to be canonical communities that follow the 1983 Vatican document Essential Elements in the Church's Teaching on Religious Life. And there are non-canonical communities of sisters and brothers who simply want to live religious life without pursuing official Church recognition. Another group of intentional communities, only a few of which identify themselves as Catholic, continues to grow. The *Communities Directory*[32] lists 550 with various characteristics—ecumenical, residential, mixed gender, celibate or married, etc. All these groups are clear about their identity. Could the "downsizing" (to use a term from the corporate world) that many older religious congregations have experienced be a wake-up call for religious to clarify their identity and purpose?

(2) The meanings of *authority and obedience* in religious life: resolving the questions left over from the 1960s about the relationship of the individual to the community and to those with authority, namely, elected or appointed leaders. Religious women, more than men, have developed

[31] Raymond Hostie, *The Life and Death of Religious Orders: A Psycho-Sociological Approach* (Washington, D.C.: Center for Applied Research in the Apostolate, 1983) 92.

[32] Rutledge, Mo.: Fellowship for International Community, 1996.

participative modes of decision making through discernment, consensus building, and assemblies of the whole. At times these processes are effective; at other times, they are wearing because it takes longer to reach conclusions and move to action. Some decisions are better for being the result of shared wisdom; other decisions are watered down or made too late to be effective because of the process. There is a desire for a new model of leadership and management that utilizes the principles of subsidiarity and inclusion, but without sacrificing the authority of elected leadership. Although religious may be able to conceptualize this model, there is little evidence yet of its effective operation.

One of the findings of the Religious Life Futures Project was that, while men expressed having greater difficulty with the vow of celibacy, for women the greater difficulty was with the vow of obedience.[33] This finding may reflect a reaction to authority that has persisted because of the greater limitations placed on women religious by the Catholic Church (and consequently by their congregations) and their unwillingness today to submit to patriarchal authority as they did in the past. Men's communities have increased participation in decision making, but a number have retained a structured approach to mission assignments.

3. A *corporate mission:* a way of expressing unity of values and commitment to implement the Gospel vision for the world. What is the congregational mission? In the past, many congregations were identified by the institutions they directed. Some still are known for the service they provide through these institutions. Others, like the Daughters of Charity, are identified by their commitment to people who are poor, which they take as the most important criterion for choosing ministries and making decisions about institutional service. Some brothers, in identifying their mission, have spoken of the need to witness community in a world of broken relationships.[34] Congregations of women have taken as a focus to stand in solidarity with women, especially women who are poor and marginalized. Men's communities that include both priests and brothers may have found that the bishop's need for personnel or economic necessities have determined their mission for them, to serve in parishes according to diocesan needs.

How do religious in the United States stand corporately with people who are poor and those who experience discrimination? How do they work to change the conditions of poverty in a society that has one of the highest

[33] David Nygren and Miriam Ukeritis, *The Future of Religious Orders in the United States* (Westport, Conn.: Praeger, 1993).

[34] David Werthmann, "Brothers in Clerical Institutes: A Hidden Gift," *Blessed Ambiguity: Brothers in the Church,* ed. Michael F. Meister (Landover, Md.: Christian Brothers Publications, 1993) 94.

per capita gross domestic products in the world? In the United States, the distribution of income is woefully skewed: Nearly 37 million people live in poverty, 13.7 percent of the U.S. population, 20.5 percent of all children.[35] A first step in addressing the structural problems of poverty and racism is coming to know people personally, seeing the faces of poor women, children, immigrants, refugees, and members of racial minority groups.

Given the poverty, racism, and sexism of our society, the public witness of religious has two dimensions: (1) a deliberate choice of downward mobility in individual and community lifestyle, which is a countercultural choice in a society that promotes consumerism and personal satisfaction to an extreme; and, (2) decisions and actions taken in collaboration with others to change structures and open opportunities to those who do not benefit from the resources in our society, in order to minimize the gap between the privileged and the marginalized.[36] The provincial of one community that works with immigrants expressed his congregational mission well: our focus needs to change from integrating immigrants into a new society to changing the society so it welcomes immigrants.[37] This can be accomplished as religious in that congregation, in collaboration with others, make their voices heard and create institutions and methods that put their words into action.

(4) Effective *leaders* translate a congregation's vision into action. These leaders are both those who are elected or appointed and those who speak from within or from the margins of the congregation. One of the unique competencies of outstanding leaders of religious communities in the United States today, according to the study by Nygren and Ukeritis, is the ability to use "the authority of the leadership position to mobilize commitment, building consensus or helping members to 'own' projects and policies of the congregation and other agencies."[38] Those leaders not in a "position" of leadership can similarly act to merge disparate efforts into a common project, especially today as all members share responsibility for accomplishing the mission of the congregation.

Of great concern to the leaders of some religious congregations is the insufficiency of resources both to carry out apostolic works and to meet responsibilities for the care of members. For fifteen years the National Asso-

---

[35] Lynette Engelhardt, "Hunger in a Booming Economy" (Washington, D.C.: Bread for the World), Background Paper No. 142 (September 1998) 5.

[36] Fred Kammer, "Option for the Poor" (Toronto, Canada: Seventh InterAmerican Conference of Religious, 1999).

[37] Patrick Murphy, provincial of the Missionaries of St. Charles (Scalibrinians), interview by author, 25 January 1999, Chicago.

[38] Nygren and Ukeritis, *The Future of Religious Orders,* 95.

ciation of Religious Treasurers has provided financial consultations. Now they cooperate with the Leadership Conference of Women Religious and the National Religious Retirement Office to help religious congregations address questions of their future. Through this Collaborative Viability Project, some groups have considered mergers in order to move from decline to revitalization. Leaders in religious life are engaged in a challenging process today as they help their congregations clarify goals in accordance with the congregation's identity and purpose, and organize effectively to carry out the congregation's Gospel mission at this time in history.

In the 1990s religious studied the link between quantum physics and quantum theology,[39] learning that they live in relationship with all of creation, that their lives and histories are interconnected. How can the relationships in religious life be structured in a way that fosters life and facilitates mission? Mary Frohlich, H.M., suggests that what religious life needs at this time of bridging centuries is "a holistic explanation of how contemplation, work, and theory are integrally related within praxis."[40] Religious are arriving at new understandings of the purpose and essence of their lives. As they step across the threshold into this new century, it is an appropriate time for them to review their journey, crystallize their vision for the future, and strategize together, so that what they hope for comes into being. Then they will continue to accompany others in the Church in the new millennium.

[39] See, for example, Diarmud O'Murchu, *Quantum Theology* (New York: Crossroads, 1997), and Margaret Wheatley, *Leadership and the New Science: Learning about Organization from an Orderly Universe* (San Francisco: Berrett-Koehler, 1994).

[40] Mary Frohlich, "Toward a Theology of the Religious Life, North American Women, and the Intellectual Life," *Women Religious and the Intellectual Life: The North American Achievement,* ed. Bridget Puzon (San Francisco: International Scholars Publications, 1996) 108.

The American Catholic Family: Reality or Misnomer?

Sally Cunneen

Who We Are

Anyone who has been to church lately knows very well that there is no such thing as the American Catholic family. In my parish as we enter the twenty-first century, Haitians, Asians, and Latinos share the pews with older Irish and Italian families, and we are served by Sri Lankan and African as well as native-born clergy. The mix is different elsewhere—and in some places nuns are caring for "priestless parishes"—but the reality is similar.

Diversity has always characterized American Catholics. When I was growing up in Providence in the 1930s and 1940s, each ethnic group had separate churches, hoping to preserve its own cultural and religious customs. The custom continues among Albanians who have just built a new parish church in Westchester County, New York, where I live now. Germans and Poles peopled the midwest, Latinos the southwest, French Canadians crossed the northern border. Great differences of class, education, and occupation marked these immigrant families, and such differences remain today.

But they also had something in common. Their very diversity was characteristic of American family life as a whole, which from the beginning of European colonization (by English, Dutch, Swedes and Danes) included high born ladies and gentlemen, working people, indentured servants and slaves, as well as more than forty native tribes. The pervasive American desire to better oneself economically and socially seems to have cut across all differences and acted as the major influence on Catholic families throughout the century. Added to that has been the constantly increasing tendency in the wider culture toward individualism, always pulling against family cohesion and authority, seen as early as 1830 to be the characteristic American trait by the French observer Alexis de Tocqueville. Under constant and increasing pressure from the more established and homogenized Protestant and secular forces around them, Catholic families have engaged in a continuing struggle both to embrace American values and to preserve and pass on their core religious and cultural inheritance.

The Way We Were

On the whole, Catholic families were easily distinguished from others in the first half of the century because of the strict rules they followed (divorce and mixed marriage were not tolerated, and if you did marry a Jew or a Protestant there was no church wedding and the children were to be brought up Catholic) and because of the distinctive practices they observed (fish on Friday, fasting from midnight if receiving communion the next day). Pastors seemed to have jurisdiction even over the dead, for they could refuse Christian burial to suicides and morally dubious relatives.

Some older folks I meet seem almost nostalgic about the old days when the family trooped to Mass each week in their Sunday best, the women wearing hats or veils. There were compensating features to this life. You knew what was expected and felt related to a community; you located yourselves by parish—you were from St. Sebastian's or St. Gregory's. Parish priests were respected and needed. Despite legendary tales of harsh discipline in parochial schools, a number of people have told me they do not know where they would be today if it were not for the supportive push nuns gave them. One of the most moving of these testimonies was from an African American man who had been an orphan in a foundling home where the nuns had made him feel both loved and competent—they were his family.

In the days when we were largely a church of immigrants, we were discriminated against by the established culture and needed to stand together. People, clergy, and hierarchy worked heroically to build a remarkable network of churches, schools, and hospitals. Until the end of World War II, Catholic people and their priests responded to economic and social pressures to succeed and to conform with a largely united front. The advice of Archbishop John Ireland that it was the religious obligation of laymen to make a million dollars did not fall on unresponsive ears. Although a few prophetic voices like that of Dorothy Day reminded Catholics that Christ came to serve the poor, they did not challenge Church authority, but merely appealed by their words and witness to Christian social teaching and the counsels of perfection.

There is no reason, however, to idealize what was an overly rule-oriented Church that was narrow in its sympathies. Often one ethnic group would not even speak to another, let alone to Jews and Protestants. A French- or Italian-Irish union was often considered a mixed marriage, a source of shame to both branches of the family. Robert Orsi's *Madonna of 115th Street,* which gives a vivid picture of the enclosed intimacy of Italian family life in New York City from 1880–1950, also reveals the shocked reaction of the Irish ascendency to their "primitive" neighbors who seemed to think religion was expressed in family rituals and not in church.

But cultural differences were certainly not foremost in the minds of most Catholic parents struggling to survive in grimy, crowded cities where they took the lowest and dirtiest of jobs. If the American family ideal in the early part of the century was one of a working father and a mother who stayed home to manage both house and children, most immigrant families could not share it. Wives and children worked as well as men, the women taking in laundry, sewing, and cleaning, many running boarding houses to make ends meet and save enough to send one of their sons to the seminary.

When the Depression hit in the thirties, nearly 60 percent of American families were living at or below the basic subsistence level of $2,000. Many women had to work at the clerical and service jobs now open to them. There were, of course, a growing number of middle-class and even wealthy Catholics early in the century: merchants like F. Scott Fitzgerald's parents in St. Paul who sent their son to Princeton, entrepreneurs, industrialists, and financiers like Nicholas F. Brady, John J. Raskob, and Charles M. Schwab, as well as politicians like Al Smith in New York, John F. "Honey Fitz" Fitzgerald in Boston, and his son-in-law Joseph P. Kennedy, who sent his sons to Harvard. Kennedy's appointment as ambassador to the Court of St. James in 1939 was experienced as a vicarious social elevation for American Catholics in general.

But the Kennedys, like most Catholic families, had more children than the American average and kept a signed photograph of Pius XII on their grand piano at Hyannisport. Their wealth and status did not cause them to rebel against the strict teaching of the Church on divorce or birth control. Yet that teaching was rooted in an ancient understanding of marriage as a social and legal contract which increasingly set it apart from the American norm. Women's ability to own property, get an education, and choose their marriage partners had shifted the marital focus from law to an interpersonal act. The Depression made the need to limit families more obvious, but even in the nineteenth century the birth rate had begun to decline intentionally and substantially.

In the 1920s, along with bobbed hair and short skirts, the idea of "companionate marriages" rather than the older Life-with-Father model became popular in the United States. By 1922, over 84 percent of married women and men believed that sex was an expression of love, healthy and pleasurable in married life and certainly as important as procreation. Margaret

Sanger, who had been deeply disturbed by the poor health and misery caused by the unwanted pregnancies of the very poor, began the Birth Control Movement in 1913, and its humanistic arguments slowly gained the approval of doctors, scientists, sociologists, and economists. Birth control clinics began to proliferate, and by 1935 some two hundred devices, including diaphragms and condoms, were available despite laws and ordinances against their sale or use. The public as a whole began to accept contraception, and the birth control movement gradually overcame legal restrictions.

Opinion began to shift among religious leaders as well. At their Lambeth Conference in 1930 the Anglican bishops, who had earlier condemned birth control, issued a measured resolution putting the ultimate decision in the hands of married couples: "Where there is a morally sound reason for avoiding complete abstinence, the conference agrees that other methods may be used, provided that this is done in the light of . . . Christian principles."[1]

Catholic theologians were well aware of the pressures for a declaration on birth control by the Church. John A. Ryan, a well-known advocate of social justice and the first American theologian to write on contraception (in 1916), suggested the direction papal teaching would take. Although many American Catholics were practicing birth control in good faith, he felt sure that if they were told by their confessors that it was a mortal sin, they would stop.

In 1930 Pius XI clearly and authoritatively made the point in his encyclical *Casti connubii:*

> Assuredly no reason, even the most serious, can make congruent with nature and decent what is intrinsically against nature. Since the act of the spouses is by its own nature ordered to the generation of offspring, those who, exercising it, deliberately deprive it of its natural force and power, act against nature and effect what is base and intrinsically indecent.[2]

This encyclical recapitulated and sharpened past doctrinal statements with no attention to the historical contexts in which they had arisen. The immense publicity given to it made it almost impossible for Catholic men and women considering the use of artificial birth control to do so in ignorance of the official teaching that it was a mortal sin. The pope clearly advised confessors not to connive in the false opinions of the laity or to confirm them in their errors.

Nevertheless, *Casti connubii* made at least one concession to modern attitudes. For the first time in such an authoritative document the word

---

[1] In John T. Noonan Jr., *Contraception: A History of Its Treatment by the Catholic Theologians and Canonists* (Cambridge, Mass.: Harvard University Press, 1965) 409.

[2] Ibid., 427.

"love"—though not connected to physical sex—was mentioned in connection with marital fidelity. This authoritative teaching, of course, was the work of celibate male thinkers who had little if any knowledge of the reality of married life, the biological and scientific aspects of childbirth, or the increasingly expensive and difficult task of childrearing. It did not enter their heads that they should have.

Working with a sentimental and patriarchal metaphor, Pius XI described women as "the heart of the home" and men as "the head." Though economic and psychological reality would seem to have dictated the need for a more realistic understanding of both as persons facing complex and demanding situations in and out of the home, there was no open outcry among U.S. Catholics against the encyclical. The self-identification of people with Church authority was still too strong. Many felt compelled to use some form of birth control, often denial of sex itself. But as late as 1963, two-thirds of the alumnae of Mundelein College who responded to an extensive survey said that "the heart of the family" was the best possible description of "the satisfactorily married woman in her home."[3] As one retired pastor told me:

> There really was such a thing as the American Catholic family when I grew up: they practiced faithfully what the Church taught and lived very much within a circle composed only of Catholic people. They were loyal to America and the country of their ethnic origin, but the pope and the Church came first. I would say that such families no longer exist.

Critical Years of Growth (1945–1968)

Following World War II, the American economy was booming, jobs were plentiful, and government programs helped veterans get college degrees and move to newly affordable homes in the suburbs. The fifties were the high point of national family togetherness. Marriage and birth rates soared and divorce rates were stable. Only a quarter of American wives worked out of the home.

A more confident generation of Catholics was part of this newly mobile middle class. They no longer confined their social contacts to fellow Catholics; many chose public schools for their children even when Catholic schools were available. These families, often with professional fathers, helped to build and support the increasing numbers of suburban churches which they attended faithfully. But they also exercised their sense of Christian vocation through work in the community, serving on school

---

[3] From a Mundelein College Survey mentioned in my book *Sex: Female; Religion: Catholic* (New York: Holt, Rinehart and Winston, 1968) 24. It is instructive to note that only 47 percent of the husbands who responded believed the wife to be "the heart of the family."

boards or running for local office. Some, particularly educated women, began to realize that they could no longer depend on the clergy for moral and spiritual guidance.

Mothers who worked were at a particular disadvantage. One woman who converted to Catholicism in the late forties told me recently that she went to her confessor for help in the early 1950s in dealing with the unexpected anger she sometimes felt at her children. "Do you work?" the priest questioned. "Yes," she replied, and he instantly concluded the conversation by asking, "What else do you expect?" She did not leave the Church; like many others, she changed confessors.

Despite the conservatism of the era—marked by the accusatory anti-Communism of Senator Joseph McCarthy—some couples began to realize that they and their families had missions of their own in the world. Sparked by the methods of European Catholic action brought to the midwest by Belgian Canon Joseph Cardijn in the late 1940s, a number of pioneer couples began to develop the grassroots organization that would become the Christian Family Movement (CFM). (It called itself "Christian" from the beginning to signal the members' openness to those of other faiths.) It was distinctive not only in its inclusion of women as equals but in its insistence on a relationship with and responsibility to the wider community. Though their families were frequently large, often consisting (like that of Pat and Patty Crowley, the best-known and most active of the executive couples who coordinated the CFM) of adopted as well as natural children, the CFM opened its homes to thousands of exchange students. Later it extended its active work to resettle refugees from abroad and to challenge racial prejudice in housing and employment in their own communities, though at the time such activities could get you listed as potential Communists on local police blotters. Its explosive growth—by 1953 thousands of couples in 181 cities belonged to the CFM—made it a significant force within U.S. Catholicism.

The CFM also took steps that would eventually help to shatter the vague idealization of women which had marked their exclusion from leadership positions in the Church. Men and women met together, breaking the earlier custom of most church groups to assemble separately by gender. A number of the clergy disapproved of the new CFM approach which might, they believed, trivialize discussion of the 'more serious' men's agenda. But the committed priests who became CFM chaplains saw a mission in the world for Catholic lay people just as the married couples did.[4] And for women in particular, the CFM provided an education in criti-

---

[4] For a serious, detailed history of the CFM movement read Jeffrey M. Burns, *Disturbing the Peace: A History of the Christian Family Movement 1949–1974* (Notre Dame, Ind.: University of Notre Dame Press, 1999).

cal thinking and action as part of the Church which strengthened them and deepened their marriages.

The desire to be Church and to commit themselves to social justice and intellectual and spiritual growth inspired many married couples in the 1950s and 1960s; their passion served as a kind of yeast in the Catholicism of the time. In our neighborhood we had both the Catholic Interracial Council and Marycrest, a cooperative community based loosely on Catholic Worker and CFM principles. The latter was an exciting mix of medieval Catholic customs and modern political commitment. The families at Marycrest were quite large, some with nine or more children. The couples were advised by their chaplain to "trust in God" in such matters. Though it was difficult—some left and a few succumbed to alcoholism and breakdowns—the majority who survived say it was a wonderful experience. No authority was telling them what to do; they were doing it themselves. They felt the devotion and sacredness of family life without any saccharine clerical preaching. They built each other's houses, blessed the fields on Rogation Days, and shared the celebrations and festivals of the liturgical calendar. But these same families were well informed supporters of interracial housing and opponents of nuclear testing. Many of the children from this community, now with grown-up children of their own, look back nostalgically on their early days.

But the spirit of families even in Marycrest began to break down in the face of the increasing necessity to limit births. The arrival of the birth control pill (1953), which separated sex from reproduction by suppressing ovulation, fostered a sexual revolution in the country at large, offering new challenges to married Catholics and moral theologians. Many couples by now simply exercised their own judgment. Though Church authorities had long ignored the increasing gap between Church teaching and the practice of believers, even Pius XII became aware that conciliatory moves were necessary. In 1951 he approved the use of the rhythm method of birth control based on the woman's ovulation cycle. In 1958 he told a conference of doctors that use of the pill might be permissible for medical reasons, even if the "indirect" effects would prevent births. It was a way of thinking that infuriated many couples. "This argument for the pill reads like an income tax avoidance scheme! What we need is a Christian ethic with an emphasis on love and responsibility."[5] The emphasis, however, bothered married people even more: "Why is the Church so overboard on sex instead of the nuclear bomb, war, and the condition of the poor?"[6]

---

[5] A young mother responding to a survey I conducted in 1965; the results were printed in my *Sex: Female; Religion: Catholic,* 116.

[6] Ibid., 110.

When in 1958 the pastoral Pope John XXIII was elected to the throne of Peter, his unexpected call for an ecumenical council raised hopes that teaching on marriage and sexuality would benefit from the fresh air he wanted to let in to the Vatican. For four exciting years the world's bishops met in Rome (1962–1965) while news of liberal opinions expressed there—including some on marriage and birth control—trickled out. Although Schema 13, "The Church in the Modern World," linked love to intercourse and acknowledged that spouses had to act "with full and conscious responsibility" regarding procreation, no specific teaching on contraception emerged from the council. Pope Paul VI had reserved the matter to himself. The schema appealed to specialists and to unnamed "experienced and virtuous couples" to explore the topic more fully in collaboration with theologians.

A great many took on the challenge, embracing what they felt was a new freedom ratified by the bishops at the council. In 1965 John T. Noonan Jr., then director of the Natural Law Institute at Notre Dame, published his highly influential *Contraception,* a comprehensive history of Catholic teaching on birth control from its roots in the ancient world to the conflicting arguments of the mid-1960s. His conclusion summed up the core of Church teaching over the ages: "Procreation is good. Procreation of offspring reaches its completion only in their education. Innocent life is sacred. The personal dignity of a spouse is to be respected. Marital love is holy."[7] All these traditional values could be preserved, he insisted, without implying the absolute sacral value of each coital act. What mattered was the quality of the relationship and the partner's commitment to these goals over the extended period of the marriage.

In the turbulent 1960s, public testimony from the laity began to appear alongside the revisioning of scholars and theologians. As Noonan pointed out, until 1963 no Catholic laymen had publicly criticized the ban on artificial birth control and no Catholic woman had ever written on contraception.[8] Now the floodgates were open, bringing to light the struggles of countless couples using rhythm with little success in the face of pressing physical, psychological, and economic problems.

Many made heroic efforts to live by rules that made no sense to them. Slowly they began to realize that they must consult their own circumstances and consciences:

> The sixth baby finished me. It took me so long to learn—twelve years—that I had to make my own decisions. Many of the serious emotional problems

---

[7] Noonan, *Contraception,* 533.
[8] Ibid., 489.

in our marriage were not necessary. How I wish that I had been taught that there were no simple answers, only the complex standard of generosity, and the personal freedom necessary to live up to it.[9]

In his first Catholic study for the National Opinion Research Center in Chicago (NORC) in 1963, Andrew Greeley discovered that 50 percent of American Catholics thought birth control and divorce were not wrong. The sense that a revision in Church teaching was inevitable was enhanced by the knowledge that in 1964 Paul VI had enlarged an international Birth Control Commission set up by John XXIII, adding women and married couples and reaffirming its mission. Both Noonan and the Crowleys served as members. When news was leaked to the *National Catholic Reporter* in 1966 that the majority of the commission accepted contraception, change seemed merely a matter of time.

In 1968 no word had yet come, and one of the best-known Catholic couples in the country, Philip and Sally Scharper, wrote a visionary article on the future of the family.[10] In it, they assumed that Pope Paul would continue to make no "binding pronouncement on the morality of means aimed at conception control." By 1975, they suggested, the effect of this non-action would serve to show "that the people within the church accepted and adopted what the 'world' had accepted long before: that two people entering marriage could choose, as equally moral options, a vocation to either procreative love or to creative love within the context of Christian marriage."

The Scharpers, parents of six children, were confident that enforced celibacy would be abrogated in a Third Vatican Council (in 1979) because the "sign-value of priestly celibacy as creative love and service to the community was now being more effectively realized through the husband and wife who had sacrificed parenthood in order better to serve the needs of the larger community." Advances in bio-chemical technology made it possible to separate sexuality from procreation, and theologians would realize that parenthood rested completely on choice. For a Christian couple in a densely populated world, they foresaw, parenthood would be seen as a charism based on a divine call that demanded "psychological maturity and the talents of educator and economist as well."

---

[9] Cunneen, *Sex: Female,* 79.

[10] All of the quotes by the Scharpers are from "The Futures of the Family," *Way: Catholic Viewpoints* 24:6 (July–August 1968). Both Sally and Philip made impressive contributions to the Church and mainstream culture—she on the stage and as a professor of drama as well as in many collaborations with her husband on television scripts and movies, he as a writer and editor at *Commonweal,* Sheed & Ward, and later at Orbis Books, where his committed ecumenical and Third-World interests created a prophetic new thrust in Catholic publishing.

In the Scharpers' vision of the future, couples would work in tandem with the declining number of priests presiding over small groups assembled for Sunday liturgies in apartment buildings or neighborhood shopping centers. By the year 2000, the Christian home would become "the living center of the Church, in much the same way that Judaism had found the source of its continuing vitality in the home rather than in the synagogue."

Shortly after the Scharpers' article appeared, however, Pope Paul VI produced a very different script. In his July 29, 1968, encyclical *Humanae vitae,* he repudiated the majority report of his own commission (who had not been notified) and reaffirmed the older teaching that each marital act must be open to procreation.[11]

The year 1968 was an explosive one in the United States, engaged as it was in an unpopular war in Vietnam, a passionate and bloody civil rights revolution, and a heated election campaign. A papal document responsive to its people in that critical year might have fostered a continuance of the passionate engagement of many married couples as vital agents in the Church in partnership with the clergy. Instead, the encyclical became a uniquely divisive event in American Catholic history; to Pope Paul's astonishment, it was widely rejected by the laity and remained unenforced by most clergy. From the mid-1960s on, the Catholic birth rate declined rapidly until it matched the national rate.

What We Became

In retrospect, an increase in moral decision making by Catholics exercising their own judgment on matters of sexuality after the encyclical might have helped the whole Church grow together as a community. Theologians like Charles Curran and activists like the Crowleys tried to keep communication channels open, but felt it their duty to express disagreement with the pope's decision in public; he had never claimed infallibility. The hierarchy did not seem to know how to handle such feedback and reacted defensively, instead of respecting the experience and moral courage of such witnesses. The Crowleys' own bishop stopped talking to them; CFM split on the issue and lost its momentum. Pope Paul and later John Paul II tightened their legal arguments; divisions widened but the topic was no longer discussed. There was a sharp drop in Sunday churchgoing

[11] In 1997 historian Charles Morris suggested a reason for Paul's action in *American Catholic: The Saints and Sinners Who Built America's Most Powerful Church* (New York: Times Books, 1997): "Consistency with past rhetoric . . . may . . . have been the decisive argument in the birth control decision. Better, presumably, to create painful moral dilemmas for millions of faithful Catholics than admit that the Church could have been wrong" (370).

in the United States from 1968 until 1975 as a result of anger and frustration over *Humanae vitae*. It then leveled off, but contributions to churches have remained significantly lower than they used to be.

As a result, according to moral theologian Lisa Cahill, the narrowness and internal inconsistency of Roman Catholic teaching on sexuality destroyed its ability to speak with authority to a culture which more and more minimized the moral significance of the body and placed almost no moral restraint on sexual acts.[12] Catholic families were left to fend for themselves; popular psychological advice on fostering self-esteem, fighting fair, and disciplining children with tough love replaced older marriage manuals on their bookshelves.

The economic and cultural pressures that marked the decades from the 1970s to the 1990s became far more significant than any Church pronouncements in shaping family life. The income gap between rich and poor widened. A sharp redistribution of earnings and government withdrawal of social supports raised the cost of rearing and educating children just as many more families felt it essential to send their children to college and even graduate school. Real wages declined precipitously as health and other costs rose, so that most families needed two incomes to maintain standards that took one in the 1950s and 1960s.

As high-powered advertising and marketing increasingly turned citizens into consumers, everybody's expectations were higher than they used to be. Even large families in the 1950s could lead a decent life because the constant pressure to buy cars, electronic toys, cell phones, stereo and home entertainment systems was not yet so overwhelming a factor. In 1960 over 70 percent of American households with children had two parents, with the father usually the sole breadwinner. By 1991 only 15 percent of American households met this description; more than two-thirds of all married women with children were working.

There were, of course, good aspects to these changes. Attitudes to the body and to sex were healthier; not much earlier the word "pregnant" could not be spoken over the radio. Greater tolerance developed not only to mixed marriages and the divorced but also to homosexuality.[13] Many middle-class husbands became more interested in raising their children than in their careers. Women gained more equality before the law and were welcome in many jobs closed to them before. Often they as well as

[12] See Lisa Sowle Cahill, *Women and Sexuality* (New York: Paulist Press, 1992) 4.

[13] By the 1980s, Catholics were more likely to accept homosexuals than Protestants and were not statistically different in their attitudes on abortion, though they still had a slightly lower divorce rate. See Andrew Greeley, *The Catholic Myth: The Behavior and Beliefs of American Catholics* (New York: Scribner, 1990) 97.

their children benefitted, and more cooperation was given to the mother's situation at home, especially since she often shared financial responsibilities and sometimes was the major breadwinner.

But by no means could all families find equal time for home and job, and some of the gains were at best ambivalent. With sexual tolerance—including the lack of shame that now accompanied childbirth outside of marriage—a dramatic increase in single-parent families came as well. The new permissiveness made it easier for husbands to walk out on wives. The pursuit of self-fulfilment was accompanied by a sharp rise in divorce and female-headed households, sometimes good outcomes—but agonizingly difficult in a culture which still places the burden of child-rearing largely on women. A rising tide of single mothers has taken on the heroic task of child-support and child-rearing with little sympathy or support from Church or society. Women and children form the majority of the genuinely poor people in the United States today.

Grandparents worry about the future of children. They believe men should help more and society should be supportive, but they see a whole generation of children who have no stable caretakers, who are shifted from babysitter to daycare center. An older nurse observes:

> It's ironic; some of the young women who work here feel they are selling out their stand as liberated women if they stay home for several years instead of just for six weeks. They are not selfish; their ideals, their solidarity with other women, and the drive for justice is part of their motivation. But the sad result is that too many children are not getting the consistent attention necessary for full human development.

Both the all-consuming nature of the work world and the woeful inadequacy of child care in the United States—unique among developed countries—are to blame. But despite his strong advocacy of higher family wages and the sexual union of "equals," John Paul II's words may well be contributing to the problem. He still manages to communicate a hidden sexism in his insistence that the highest role of women is motherhood. Many young Catholic women are so turned off by this attitude, which seems to undervalue any serious vocation they have, that they reject a moral authority that might have helped some make a different choice: either not to have children, or to guide their children in the crucial early years, planning early to make it possible to have a satisfying career as well. From another angle, Marvin Mich, an ethics professor and a father, sees the pope's emphasis on motherhood as troubling because he "distances the father from his parental role in conception, pregnancy, birthing and educating the child." Making the father an "outsider" like St. Joseph, he says, contributes to a man's not taking up the responsibility that is his. It impoverishes his own life, as well as the lives of his wife and children.[14]

Powerful forces in the American economy and government seem quite unwilling to think of a common responsibility to children despite the endless talk by politicians about them. The grandparents I consulted believe that the Church should concentrate its moral teaching on the needs of living children with respect and concern for their caretakers, whoever they may be. Being against abortion is not enough; it does not deal with the economic, social, or moral problems faced by men and women raising children today. At worst it compounds the number of neglected and alienated children who grow up to fill American jails with more prisoners than those of any other developed country.

As we begin a new millennium, American Catholic families face all the problems that other families do. For most, there is the constant scramble to survive and give their children a good education so they can get ahead. Rich and poor alike find it more and more difficult to pass on their beliefs and values when the media and their children's peers clearly have more influence than they do. In the last third of the twentieth century, when shopping malls replaced cathedrals as the great assembly halls of the people, the power of parents greatly diminished. They, too, are caught up in the maw of often malignant and omnipresent cultural forces.

"No one has time to sit down and eat, to be with each other as we were when I was young," sighs the pastor of a northeastern urban parish. "They're all doing different things, and there's such a push to luxury and lack of communication. Our culture doesn't help us talk about our feelings. But you can't have a healthy parish when the families aren't healthy," he says, "and a great many of them in my church are in trouble."

The good news is that he is able to do something about it in his largely Latino parish filled with recent immigrants negotiating a complex collision of cultures. Having learned Spanish so that his parishioners would feel at home in church, he is often asked to help with their marital troubles. Networking with other priests in similar situations, he uses a program to encourage couples to talk to each other honestly about their problems over a long period of time. The uninhibited emotional sharing in different families' homes keeps him awake at night, he says, but over three years of such work he has seen the lives of couples and their children transformed. Another key part of this work is that he and the other priests have been activists working with government at all levels to rehabilitate affordable homes for the people in his community.

[14] Marvin Mich, *Catholic Social Teaching and Movements* (Mystic, Conn.: Twenty-Third Publications, 1998) 335.

Such good relationships between pastor and people are perhaps more possible in urban parishes and with Latino families whose religion is centered in the home and the neighborhood. Among Mexican-Americans in the southwest, for example, the house is thought of as having a soul that is expressed by the altar, which often has a statue and a candle lit for particular occasions. Special foods are linked to religion in these homes, as they were earlier in Polish, Italian, and other immigrant families. In Texas, tamales are made only at Christmas; capitudara, a bread pudding, only during Lent. But as these immigrants, too, join the middle class, they are under great pressure to become assimilated into the Anglo culture around them.

In retrospect, the diversity of American Catholic families and their constant incorporation into mainstream culture has been a continuing thread until the present. Constantly influenced by the secular mainstream forces around them, Catholic families are still engaged in the struggle both to embrace American values and to preserve and pass on their core religious and cultural inheritance. Today, however, the pace is faster and the cultural environment is more hostile both to marital faithfulness and the healthy rearing of children.

Where We Are Now

"There is no such thing as the American Catholic family," snapped a well-known Catholic author in response to my question about its future. "I'm the only Catholic in my family today," said a psychologist mother of four whom I have long known to be a devoted churchgoer. Looking back on her life, an effective campus minister's recollection about the lack of communication and support she has received from the Church she continues to love and serve may help explain such answers:

> The church was the hub of my existence; now it is just a part. We have had to work things out for ourselves and grow up; it has been a wonderful and dangerous adventure, even more exciting now that we are grandparents. But the church seems to be in a state of arrested development. Sadly, none of our children go to church despite their education in all-Catholic schools. They never heard a sermon there that touched their lives. They are all seekers—especially the ones with children—and some have found a home in Protestant churches that are especially good with children.

Talking to older Catholic couples like these, middle-class and mainstream, to whom the sacraments, liturgy, and the Bible are the food of life, I hear two themes repeated in many voices. First, they love and admire their children who, they insist, are in many ways better than they were, more tolerant, more generous. Many live lives of dedicated service in their jobs as teachers, counselors, doctors, nurses, and lawyers.

Second, most of these children do not go to church. No longer possessing the largely unconscious anchors that religion and ethnicity gave their parents, they have separated their faith from the institution. The couples accept this situation, remaining close to their post-Catholic children, but are sad to think that their children will never receive the comforts they do from the liturgy and sacraments. They are equally close to their grandchildren and their values still form them, but they refuse to speculate on what connection the next generation will have with the Church.

Some indicators suggest that the culture is becoming more sympathetic to ideas of fidelity and care. Divorce has come down from the high of 50 percent in the 1970s and 1980s to roughly 40 percent in the 1990s. Having children seems to be back in vogue, and secular family historians argue strongly for a new communal emphasis on childrearing. If parents can communicate with their children despite real differences in belief and experience and both sides can learn, is it too late for people and the institutional Church to start talking honestly with one another? Before solving all their differences, could they perhaps work together on behalf of families in the wider community, as the Scharpers predicted they would before *Humanae vitae*?

The elements of necessary change in Church teaching already exist. We have long had solid reasoning that would permit artificial contraception with respect for tradition while affirming the primacy of conscience and mutual responsibility for one another. Both recent biblical scholarship and feminist theology have made sufficient corrections possible so that misogynist assumptions can be purged. Clergy and laity share a common commitment to social justice. Is it not possible to acknowledge that we are a Church of sinners and go on from there?

It might happen if, says Andrew Greeley, the institutional Church can rediscover the Spirit of God as she flourishes in the community and her people; if, say several married couples, the Church could become more inclusive, embrace its married priests, bring in women priests; if, says the retired pastor, "the Church can be seen as a friend of the family. No one expects the Church to be untrue to itself, but people do expect the Church to be patient, kind, prayer-promoting, encouraging, healing, forgiving. The Church can take the example of Jesus and its sacramental life and try to bring the family and family members in contact with God."

It is a recipe most American Catholic families would welcome.

Women and the Church: Rooting Out Stereotypes

Catherine Lupori and Mary Jo Richardson

Anyone having the temerity to write on women must recognize that generalizations about them will be not only suspect but almost certainly false. A writer or speaker discussing any group of women must note the diversities among them. American women in the Catholic Church in the twentieth century differ from each other in every decade—most visibly since Vatican II—and clear-sighted investigation of their history reveals they have always defied generalization. However marginalized in the mainstream, however invisible in written accounts until relatively recently, women have always differed from each other in multiple ways.

We proceed, then, acknowledging our inability to generalize, to do no more than simply record what we have observed or gained from our reading about women and the Church in the century just ended. It is significant to emphasize that we speak as women about women; we speak with our own voices, always having checked what we have read of others' observations against our own experience. It is important to emphasize as well that inevitably beliefs and ideas formed by our experiences—by our viewpoints—have influenced our observations and our interpretations of what we have read. Too often, even today, what has been said about women and the Church has been written by men, inevitably outside observers, who may well not realize how their unexamined assumptions about women affect what they see and interpret.

Two notable events of the twentieth century, the women's movement and the Vatican Council II, have affected American Catholic women in a special way. However they may differ about individual issues, all Catholic women have felt the impact of the two waves of the women's movement and the changes in the Catholic Church motivated by the documents of the council. Although there are some who would, it appears, like to return to the way things were before either movement, the turning point has occurred. There is no going back.

A female growing up in the first half of the century would have been unlikely to imagine how differently the world of Catholic women would appear in its last half. That imaginative lapse was largely due to the all too common lack of knowledge of any women's history and awareness of vigorous Catholic women of the past. In his history of American Catholic women James Kenneally observes that research on the history of Catholic women demonstrates that

> the legendary Catholic woman, acquiescent, parochial, uncultured, is more an image of the male mind than a historical reality. . . . The "new Catholic woman" of today often has as much in common with her contemporary coreligionists of yesterday as with her contemporary sisters. . . . Many Catholic women of the past, like their contemporaries today, have not been inhibited by the traditions of the male-dominated church.[1]

The story of American Catholic women, like any good story, is filled with contradiction, tension, and conflict. That has not always been recognized. Until they became aware of the contemporary research by women historians, especially of histories of women in the Church, present-day women uncomfortable with either the legendary view of ideal Catholic womanhood or their position in the Church might have thought that Catholic women active in the public arena or in conflict about the role of women in the Church are a new phenomena. But that is far from the reality. Indeed, as one churchwoman has observed, "In every century, including our own, history records women exercising leadership; in every century, including our own, that leadership has been contested."[2]

Accounts of American Catholic women in the first half of the twentieth century make it clear that Catholic women were not only workers in nearly all areas of the labor force but many were also valued leaders. In the labor union movement Catholic immigrant women were often in the forefront of organizing union members. Of women recorded in labor history one of the best known is the Irish immigrant Mary Harris Jones, referred to in the annals of the United Mine Workers as Mother Jones. Also prominent in histories of labor are Leonora Barry, a mill worker who became the first woman labor organizer in the United States, and Mary Kenny O'Sullivan.

At the turn of the century, O'Sullivan founded the National Women's Trade Union and later became the first woman organizer for the American Federation of Labor. She learned her skills as an organizer in Chicago where she lobbied for labor legislation and worked with Jane Addams of

---

[1] James J. Kenneally, *The History of American Catholic Women* (New York: Crossroads, 1990) ix–x.

[2] Sally Hill, Elder Learning Institute Lecture (Minnetonka, Minnesota, March 30, 1999).

Hull House to establish cooperative housing for working women. O'Sullivan linked her efforts in unionizing with support for the suffrage movement. Early on she pointed out that opponents of suffrage were most often women of leisure. She chastised them for obstructing the efforts of organized working women to achieve full citizenship.

The suffrage movement offers an example of the differences among Catholic women, who were found on both sides of the issue. One of the leading Catholic women opponents of suffrage was Katherine Conway, editor of three Catholic newspapers, including the *Boston Pilot*. Conway, who was a single professional woman all her life, took it upon herself to be the spokesperson for all women. In her opposition to suffrage she idealized the retiring wife and mother and took the view, apparently excepting herself, that women could have no vocation for public life. In this view, as well as in opposition to suffrage, she was joined by the majority of the Catholic clergy.

Several Catholic novelists, well known in the first half of the century, were strong proponents of suffrage, including Kathleen Thompson Norris, Margaret Culkin Banning, Katherine Kurtz Burton, and Elizabeth Jordan. Banning especially exhorted women to become active politically and to maintain their independence. Two Catholic women who worked for equal pay for teachers, Margaret Haley and Catherine Goggin, strongly supported suffrage; Haley campaigned for the measure in California and Ohio in 1911 and 1912. Another woman who connected work for equal pay and the right of married women to teach with work for suffrage, Grace Strachan Forsythe, founded the teachers' section of New York state's suffrage campaign committee.

One of the most militant of Catholic suffragists was Lucy Burns, who had left doctoral studies at Oxford to join the British suffragist movement. When she returned to the United States she brought the confrontational tactics she had learned in England to her work for the amendment here. She helped Alice Paul form the Congressional Committee of the National Women's Suffrage Association, organized parades, spoke at public rallies, lobbied for the cause, and was among suffragists arrested for picketing the White House. Burns spent more time in jail in either Britain or in this country than any other American suffragist.

When Catholic women from many backgrounds—union members, social activists, and well-recognized writers—joined the ranks of suffrage supporters, more women felt sufficiently empowered to challenge their clerical opponents. Changing their minds after the passage of the amendment, the United States bishops in a pastoral letter acknowledged that the women's sphere was no longer confined to the family and urged women to vote, although they continued to reaffirm the superiority of traditional roles for women. Churchmen combined the two positions by urging women to vote "to purify and elevate our political life."[3]

The concept of ideal Catholic womanhood—that a woman's activity should rightly be confined to the private realm of the home—was still widely preached in the early part of the century. This concept ignored and marginalized wage-earning women, whether or not they were faithful daughters of the Church in their religious life.

Still as more Catholic women became active outside the home, the attitude of the hierarchy slowly modified, especially about activity related to institutional organizations. In areas important to the vitality of the Church, such as education and social welfare, women's contributions were more often appreciated.

No observer of the Church in the twentieth century could fail to recognize that it was strong women in religious orders who grounded the development of Catholic education from kindergarten through graduate school. The story of these women is largely unsung; what is slowly emerging in oral and written histories is how frequently Church leaders challenged the orders' initiative and independence in the dioceses in which they were located.[4] Because many of the religious communities staffing Catholic schools had to adapt to a different culture when they came from Europe to America, nuns had learned how to use their initiative to adapt creatively to new ways. It has often seemed to us that American nuns acted for women's independence many years before the women's movement, one generalization about women that is clear in the historical records.

Especially significant for the development of Catholic women in the twentieth century (and later for their response to both the women's movement and Vatican II) was the founding and growth of Catholic women's colleges. Through them higher education became available not only to young women of privilege but also to young Catholic women who were the first of their families to have access to it. At their zenith, about 1955, there were 140 Catholic colleges for women, of which 116 were baccalaureate and 24 were two-year junior colleges.[5] The educational experience they offered at its best

---

[3] James J. Kenneally, "A Question of Equality," *American Catholic Women: A Historical Exploration*, ed. Karen Kennelly (New York: Macmillan, 1989) 140.

[4] Two examples of written histories recording struggles of this kind are *Building Sisterhood: A Feminist History of the Sisters, Servants of the Immaculate Heart of Mary*, comp. Sisters, Servants of the IHM (Syracuse, N.Y.: Syracuse University Press, 1997); and Mary Richard Boo, *House of Stone: The Duluth Benedictines* (Duluth, Minn.: St. Scholastica Priory Press, 1991).

[5] Abigail McCarthy, "A Luminous Minority," *Educating the Majority: Women Challenge Tradition in Higher Education*, ed. Carol Pearson, Donna Shavlik, and Judith G. Touchton (New York: American Council of Education and Macmillan, 1989) 178.

gave young Catholic women the tools to think for themselves, to value their own experience, and to find their own voices. Equally important for the development of young women's self-sufficiency was the presence of women in leadership positions throughout these colleges. Their example made clear women's capabilities to envision, to organize, and to administer.

The relevance of the strong Catholic women's colleges to the history of Catholic women in the twentieth century cannot, we think, be overstated. And in some quarters it was recognized early: in 1902, Archbishop John Ireland of St. Paul spoke of his belief in the higher education of women and said of the Sisters of St. Joseph of Carondelet, who were then founding the College of St. Catherine, that the college would be "the chief contribution of their community to religion during the half century to come."[6]

Before mid-century, Sr. Madeleva Wolff, president of another Catholic women's college, appalled that women could not be admitted to theology programs in seminaries or Catholic universities, established a graduate program in theology at her institution, St. Mary's College in Indiana. The School of Sacred Theology began in 1944, with formal approval of Pius XII. By 1970 St. Mary's had awarded 76 doctoral and 354 master's degrees. It was phased out then because graduate work in theology had become available to women and laymen at several large Catholic institutions and many seminaries. Indeed, ten years after the founding of the St. Mary's program, the Vatican set up its own school of theology for women, Regina Mundi in Rome, after much consultation with the program in Indiana.[7] Sister Madeleva's foresight launched what was to become one of the major contributions of Catholic women post–Vatican II.

In the other area in which women's activity was often appreciated, work for social welfare, nuns had led the way with work for the poor, but other women within the Church often found themselves confined to being auxiliaries in organizations led by men. In 1920 when the National Council of Catholic Women (NCCW) was founded, its leaders thought that incorporation of several women's organizations would make more autonomy possible. However, because they were part of the National Catholic Welfare Council, NCCW leaders found it necessary to move more slowly than they might have liked on issues important to women.

Three organizations led by women—the Catholic Worker, Friendship House, and the Grail—represented, as one commentator noted, "an alternative vision based upon the conviction that the spiritual solidarity that bound

---

[6] Kenneally, *The History of American Catholic Women,* 94.

[7] Gail Porter Mendell, *Madeleva: A Biography* (Albany: State University of New York Press, 1997) 184–8.

together the Mystical Body of Christ had radical social implications that could only be realized in small communities."[8] Of the many individual women who worked, often as volunteers, for the betterment of society, no woman is better known than the Catholic Worker's Dorothy Day, whose activities spanned the century from the time of the great Depression until her death in 1980.

In his biography *Dorothy Day: A Radical Devotion,* Robert Coles noted that Day was acutely aware of the signs of her times. She had heard well Pius XI's lament that the workers of the world were lost to the Church. Coles argues that she never forgot that statement. "It can be said," he wrote, "that her entire life from 1932 until her death was dedicated to working against its assumptions."[9] In her commitment and dedication to the movement she founded with her colleague Peter Maurin, she followed the spirit within her and did not wait for direction from the Church.

While she loved the Catholic Church, Day lived in a state of permanent dissatisfaction with much of its practice. In fact, the Church of her time was often a scandal to her, especially in what she saw as its lack of responsibility for the poor, the worker, and the oppressed throughout the world. In the Church's practice, she said, "There is plenty of charity but too little justice."[10]

All her life, she was willing to challenge members of the hierarchy when she thought their decisions were unjust. Her relationship with Francis Cardinal Spellman of New York was legendary. Once, in response to his treatment of striking cemetery workers, she wrote of him in *The Catholic Worker* as one "ill advised, [who] exercised so overwhelming a show of force against a handful of poor working men, he [became an example] of that most awful of all wars, the war between the clergy and the laity."[11]

Yet Dorothy Day appreciated keenly the support the Catholic Worker Movement received from members of the clergy, including many bishops. As she noted in her autobiography *The Long Loneliness,* "The stories in *The Catholic Worker* of poverty and exploitation aroused priests to start labor schools, go out on picket lines, take sides in strikes with the workers, and brought an emphasis on the need to study sociology in seminaries."[12]

[8] Debra Campbell, "Reformers and Activists," *American Catholic Women,* ed. Kennelly, 175.

[9] Robert Coles, *Dorothy Day: A Radical Devotion* (Reading, Mass.: Addison/Wesley, 1987) 11.

[10] Ibid., 87.

[11] Ibid., 81.

[12] Dorothy Day, *The Long Loneliness* (San Francisco: Harper/Collins, 1952) 221.

Not as well known as the movement for workers which she founded, nor as widely accepted, were Dorothy Day's pacifism and her work for nuclear disarmament. In the 1940s, one of us remembers, she was not welcomed as a speaker on many Catholic college campuses.

As the century progressed, many Catholic women, responding with other American women to the second wave of the women's movement, were beginning to find new understandings of themselves and to question their roles in the Church as well as in other parts of society. Other women perceived the new understandings and questions as threats to values and structures important to them. An issue about which there was disagreement, as strong as divisions among Catholic women about suffrage, was the proposal for a federal guarantee of women's legal rights, the Equal Rights Amendment.

Over the several decades during which the ERA was debated, there were both challenge and support among Catholic women as well as among members of the clergy. Soon after its formation, the NCCW publicly opposed the ERA and lobbied against it on the grounds that it would endanger the family and remove legislative protection from working women. The latter argument was precisely why other Catholic working women supported the amendment. Two, Mary A. Murphy and Maggie Hinchey, argued that so-called protective legislation instead denied women opportunities for work. When New York legislated against night work for women, Murphy had lost the work she had chosen so she could be with her five children during the day. Hinchey was among fifteen hundred females dismissed when regulatory legislation forbade transit work for women. Both Murphy and Hinchey joined organizations lobbying for the ERA; both went to the White House with petitions for its passage.

In the 1940s both Catholic support for and denouncement of the ERA grew. Winifred Stanley, a Catholic congresswoman from New York, endorsed it; novelists Margaret Culkin Banning and Kathleen Norris, who had worked for suffrage earlier, were advocates of equal rights as well. On the other side, the NCCW, several diocesan and archdiocesan councils for women, and Catholic lobbyists increased their campaign against the amendment. Clergy and the hierarchy were also divided: Bishop Edmond J. FitzMaurice delivered the invocation at a regional meeting of the National Women's Party (NWP) in which he "besought all 'noble souls' to join in the war against discrimination and injustice and concluded by begging God to hasten the day when women would enjoy equality with men."[13] After behind-the-scenes support for the amendment for more than

---

[13] Kenneally, "A Question of Equality," 143.

ten years, in 1945 Cardinal Dennis Dougherty made his endorsement public with a letter to the NWP of strong support for the ERA, an action which, it was said, influenced senate hearings on the measure.[14]

In the 1950s, both attention and vocal support of the ERA lessened, but in the 1960s religious women joined public endorsement. Both the National Assembly of Women Religious and the Leadership Conference of Women Religious became active supporters. In the 1970s the NCCW renewed its opposition and the American bishops warned that the amendment might "destroy family relationships."[15] In the mid-1970s some Church groups increased opposition by linking abortion to the measure. Efforts to make clear that the two were separate issues were mostly unsuccessful.

A final shift of clergy position came in 1982 when twenty-three bishops issued a joint statement calling upon legislators to approve the ERA. But by that time, a conservative Catholic, Phyllis Schafly, had launched what became a successful campaign against the amendment. Her group claimed that passage would lead to such results as the weakening of the family, lesbianism, the forced abandonment of Catholic single-sex schools, and the ordination of women. The ratification of the amendment came three states short by the end of the deadline, but the struggle for women's equal rights—and the opposition from many Catholic groups—continued.

At the same time, Catholic women who had begun to question their roles in society and in the Church were encouraged by pronouncements from the Church which appeared to be acknowledging the changing status of women as a sign of the times.

In the 1963 encyclical *Pacem in terris,* John XXIII noted, "Since women are becoming ever more conscious of their human dignity, they will not tolerate being treated as mere material objects, but demand rights befitting a human person in domestic and public life."[16] In 1964, when Vatican II entered the third of its four sessions, twelve women were admitted as auditors; there were women among the periti, experts who were in Rome during the sessions and gave lectures attended by many delegates to the council. *Gaudium et spes,* the Pastoral Constitution on the Church in the Modern World, included statements declaring that

> every type of discrimination, whether social or cultural, whether based on sex, race, color, social conditions, language, or religion, is to be overcome and eradicated as contrary to God's intent . . . it must still be regretted that fundamental personal rights are still not being universally honored. Such is

[14] Ibid., 145.
[15] Ibid., 146.
[16] John XXIII, *Pacem in terris* (New York: America Press) 114:14.

the case of a woman who is denied the right to choose a husband freely, to embrace a state of life, or to acquire an education or cultural benefits equal to those recognized for men.[17]

In 1970, the Church declared as Doctors of the Church two women who were known in their time as reformers, St. Catherine of Siena and St. Teresa of Avila. The significance of this recognition to Catherine of Siena, known to have remonstrated with popes, was not lost on the women who rejoiced in the Church's action. Indeed, Catherine expressed in her time a recognition of discrimination against women: "My very sex, as I need not tell you, puts many obstacles in the way. The world has no use for women in work such as that, and propriety forbids a woman to mix so freely in the company of men."[18] As Mary Jo Weaver comments in *New Catholic Women,* "Catherine and Teresa sustained an independent position in a church that even more than today discouraged and often punished female initiative."[19]

Because of all of these statements and actions, to many women, including both of us, the possibilities—even probabilities—for women's full participation in the life of the Church seemed imminent.

In the late 1960s and the 1970s, women were to be found in many areas of Church life where they had not been seen before. They were appearing as lectors, eucharistic ministers, parish council members and directors of liturgical planning. They were invited to membership in archdiocesan councils and were appointed to national Church-related offices. Commissions on the status of women were created in many archdioceses. Women who had been admitted to graduate work in seminaries and earned degrees in theology and pastoral ministry became hospital or prison chaplains, campus ministers, associates in parish administration. It is now estimated that over half of the students in seminaries other than Catholic are women. Many of these include women on their faculties.

What women in the first part of the century had been unable to imagine about women and the Church was occurring. Nuns, always before identifiable by their habits, and usually to be found living together in convents, became hard to distinguish from other Catholic women, and might be the new neighbors in the next house or apartment. Some of the new neighbors were still members of their religious communities but living outside the convent. Others were among the hundreds of nuns, who, for a

---

[17] *Gaudium et spes,* 29 (Boston: St. Paul Books & Media, n.d.) 28.

[18] "Catherine of Siena," *Mystics, Visionaries, and Prophets: A Historical Anthology of Women's Spiritual Writings,* ed. Shawn Madigan (Minneapolis: Fortress Press, 1998) 211.

[19] Mary Jo Weaver, *New Catholic Women: A Contemporary Challenge to Traditional Religious Authority* (New York: Harper & Row, 1985) 196–7.

wide variety of reasons, had, especially in the 1960s and 1970s, left their religious communities to take up professional positions elsewhere.

By the late 1980s there were more women, religious, married, or single, working as full-time parish administrators, especially in rural areas. They often functioned as the sole ministry staff of the parish, carrying out almost every pastoral task except presiding at Mass. A National Pastoral Life Center study in 1997 recorded that of an estimated 26,000 people employed as parish ministers, 82 percent were women. However, another study by the National Association of Church Personnel Administration found that women held only 25 percent of top administrative positions.[20]

From the early 1940s women had begun to organize in groups to work on issues they wanted to advance. Women religious concerned about the preparation of young nuns for teaching and other forms of ministry organized the Sisters Formation Conference in 1954, followed by the Conference of Major Superiors of Women (now known as the Leadership Conference of Women Religious—LCWR). An offshoot, the National Assembly of Women Religious, founded in 1968 as a grassroots group, later became the National Assembly of Religious Women to indicate that both sisters and laywomen were working together on the mission they defined as "public action for the achievement of justice."[21] In many urban areas Leagues of Catholic Women sponsored programs to assist under-served people through neighborhood nurseries, homes for adolescent girls in trouble, and shelters for abused women.

The majority of these organizations worked for social justice and the empowerment of women. Some, like the LCWR, did not hesitate to call themselves feminists, following an understanding of Catholic feminism as "that movement among U.S. Catholics which regards sexism (the exploitation and domination of one sex by the other) as an injustice to be eliminated if the 'good news' of true equality in Christ is to become a reality."[22]

Two organizations which focused fully on a specific feminist agenda in the Church were a division of the British Catholic St. Joan's Alliance, established in the United States in 1965, and the Women's Ordination Conference (WOC, 1976), both of which worked toward what they saw as essential for women's full participation in the Church. WOC continues to hold national conferences. Still another group held a regional conference, "Women-Church

---

[20] "Women Ministers in the Catholic Church," *A Call for National Dialogue on Women in Church Leadership* (brochure published by FutureChurch, Cleveland, and Call to Action, Chicago, n.d.) 1.

[21] Rosemary Rader, "Catholic Feminism: Its Impact on U.S. Catholic Women," *American Catholic Women,* ed. Karen Kennelly, 188.

[22] Ibid., 183.

Speaks." Following the conference, Women-Church groups formed throughout the country: there is currently a coalition of groups including the Women's Alliance for Theology, Ethics and Ritual (WATER) of Silver Spring, Maryland, the Quixote Center, and the Center of Concern, Washington, D.C., whose programs principally or frequently focus on women's experience and the Church.

Of all the Church conferences bringing women together during the last decade of the century, probably the most discussed pro and con was the Re-imagining Conference held in Minneapolis in 1993. Described as a "global theological colloquium," it was initiated as part of the World Council of Churches' Ecumenical Decade: Churches in Solidarity with Women (1988–98). Among the two thousand women and men who attended the five-day ecumenical conference were hundreds of American Catholic women.

The first of three theologians speaking at the opening session of the conference was a Catholic, Mary Farrell Bednarowski, professor of religious studies at the United Theological Seminary of the Twin Cities. In her address, "The Spirit of Re-imagining: Setting the Stage," Bednarowski said:

> My commitment to the equality and full participation of women in our religious traditions had its beginning in my own history, but also in the reading of history, primarily because of what I didn't find there. My understanding of what this conference means and where it came from has its roots in my study of women in American religious history. The conference does not come out of nowhere. It is part of the long history of women's involvement in religion in America and all over the world. It is the result of some of the questions and issues concerning gender roles and religion that we are learning to ask as part of our particular time in history.[23]

From many of the denominations whose members attended the conference there was strong criticism and, in some, churchwomen lost positions. Somewhat smaller conferences were held each year from 1993 to 1998. A second international conference is to be held in 2000 in Minneapolis.

Not all Catholic women welcomed the changes promulgated by Vatican II. Furthermore, many thought the phrase "Catholic feminism" was oxymoronic and were particularly appalled at calls for ordination of women, seeing this as a threat to the orthodoxy of the Church or the stability of the family. The Catholic Charismatic Movement was developing at the same time as the establishment in the United States of St. Joan's Alliance, and in 1984 the United Catholic Women of America, with a mission to "restore

---

[23] Mary Farrell Bednarowski, "The Spirit of Re-imagining: Setting the Stage," *Church & Society* (May/June, 1994) 14.

Marian values," was organized.[24] Groups and individuals deploring feminism and feminists in the Church continued into the 1990s. A 1991 book, *Ungodly Rage: The Hidden Face of Catholic Feminism,* speaks of Catholic feminists as "witches engaged in a diabolic conspiracy to subvert the Church."[25]

The response of the institutional Church to women's expanded activity as well as to those who were ambivalent about it was an effort to articulate an official position on women and the Church. In 1975, the bishops of our own diocese, Minneapolis/St. Paul, appointed a committee to draft a paper on the topic "Contemporary Woman from the Perspective of Social Justice." The Social Action/Social Welfare Department of the Minnesota Catholic Conference was called upon to work with a committee of seven women approved for the task. After five drafts in four years, "Woman: Pastoral Reflections" was published. It contained two papers: the one written and rewritten by the committee, which focused on social justice and women, and an accompanying one from the bishops themselves focusing on what they defined as a complementarity of women's and men's roles, especially in the family, which they felt had not been addressed adequately in the committee's paper.

The challenges in Minnesota presented by the preparation of statements that both the bishops and the women on the drafting committee could approve were a kind of preview of the experience of the drafting of a national pastoral on women and the Church. The differences among women in the Church and among women and the hierarchy became very apparent during the ten years (1982–92) that the pastoral was in process. At the start, forums, called listening sessions, were held in one hundred dioceses, sixty colleges, and forty-five military bases. The sessions provided opportunities for bishops to hear from women in each locale. Forums revealed, as one commentary noted, "the contrast between those who advocate change and those who are wedded to preservation."[26] Ultimately, after pleas from women's groups to defer publication on the one hand, and objections from the Vatican on the other, the last draft of the pastoral, having failed to get the two-thirds vote required or release, was tabled by the bishops.[27]

By the early 1980s, when the national pastoral was begun, Catholic women like us were becoming more and more aware of the growing amount of writing about women and the Church. Concurrent with the

[24] Kenneally, *The History of American Catholic Women,* 199.

[25] Quoted by Rosemary Skinner Keller and Rosemary Radford Ruether, eds., *In Our Own Voices: Four Centuries of American Women's Religious Writing* (San Francisco: HarperSanFrancisco, 1996) 429 and 504.

[26] Kenneally, *The History of American Catholic Women,* 200.

[27] Keller and Ruether, eds., *In Our Own Voices,* 57.

movement of women into other areas of scholarship formerly totally dominated by men was the movement of women into the study of theology, biblical research, and the history of religion. Research on women in early Christianity helped Catholic women reclaim their own history, similarly reclaiming women leaders and activists in secular American history. In 1968 Mary Daly, one of the graduates of the School of Sacred Theology of St. Mary's College in Indiana, brought out her first book, *The Church and the Second Sex.* Although some years later Daly separated herself from the Church, American Catholic theologians recognize how influential that book was.

A few years later, in 1972, there was a gathering of women doing theology in Grailville, Ohio. A participant at that time, theologian and biblical scholar Elisabeth Schüssler Fiorenza, refers to it as "one of the birthplaces of feminist theology—a movement that has since profoundly changed both theology and Church."[28] Whatever their response to the issues raised by the increasing number of Catholic feminist theologians, Catholic women involved in consideration of the Church and its future have at least heard names such as Schüssler Fiorenza, Rosemary Radford Ruether, Anne Carr, or Elizabeth A. Johnson, to cite a very few of the many scholars and researchers working today.[29] In her introduction to a new edition of *Transforming Grace: Christian Tradition and Women's Experience,* Anne Carr lists, in addition to the names above, nineteen women as among "many more" who have "forged a real sub-discipline, a theological specialty, a new area that is now recognized as feminist theology." And she notes:

> feminist theology has grown more complex. The sub-title, about 'the experience' of women, suggests that a single category can easily encompass all women, everywhere. . . . The last decade has given the lie to that initial assumption. . . . The emergence of womanist and mujerista theology in the United States . . . indicates that 'woman's' experience is not simply one reality but is rather a pluralistic and diverse set of experiences, and it is difficult, if not impossible, for one voice to speak for all.[30]

The contribution of womanist and mujerista theologians is not only bringing new voices but also authenticating the importance of hearing the stories of people in the Church. For womanist theologians like Shawn Copeland,

---

[28] Elisabeth Schüssler Fiorenza, *Sharing Her Word: Feminist Biblical Interpretation in Context* (Boston: Beacon Press, 1998) 1.

[29] A compilation, "100 Books by Women on Theology, Scripture, and Spirituality," is available for $2.00 from Women at the Well, 1884 Randolph, St. Paul, MN 55105.

[30] Anne E. Carr, *Transforming Grace: Christian Tradition and Women's Experience* (New York: Continuum, 1996) xi–xii.

Jamie Phelps, and Diana Hayes, and mujerista theologian Ada Maria Isasi-Diaz, collecting women's stories is part of doing theology.[31]

The inclusion of story in theological study brings the name of a distinguished writer into the story of American Catholic women of the twentieth century. It is not surprising to us to learn that writings by Flannery O'Connor are apt to be part of course work in seminaries. *The Habit of Being,* collected letters of O'Connor, contains many passages relevant to theological study. In a letter to a reader who was "someone who recognizes my work for what I try to make it," O'Connor speaks of herself as a "God-conscious writer," and says "I write the way I do because (not though) I am a Catholic." About her stories she comments, "The stories are hard but they are hard because there is nothing harder or less sentimental than Christian realism."[32]

Another aspect of American Catholic women's experience in the last decades of the century, no doubt influenced by the wealth of writing about women and the Church, but growing out of a felt need for growth, has been the development of women's spirituality groups. These have taken many forms—workshops, retreats, lectures, creative rituals—and a multitude of other explorations of ways of finding meaning related to women's (diverse) experience. One example from our locale is a program called Theological Insights, which for more than ten years has offered two series annually in programs originally patterned after one coordinated by Elizabeth Dodson Gray of Harvard Divinity School. As at Harvard, each session has two speakers, one using her experience, the other offering a more academic focus.[33] Many participants say the programs have become their spiritual community.

Often ecumenical, the spirituality groups frequently may focus on women's connection to peacemaking, protecting the environment, and building community. As spiritual writer Joan Chittister says in a recent book:

> Spirituality plunges us into life with an eye to meaning and purpose. When it is authentic, it is never an invitation to withdraw from life. Real spirituality, like Jacob wrestling with the angel, takes life in both hands and grapples with it. The greatest contemplatives . . . Bernard of Clairvaux, Teresa of Avila, Catherine of Siena, Thomas Merton . . . were often our most active people. The greatest activists . . . Dorothy Day, Martin Luther King,

[31] Interview with theologian Joan Mitchell, St. Paul, MN (May 1999).

[32] Flannery O'Connor, *The Habit of Being,* ed. Sally Fitzgerald (New York: Farrar, Straus, Giroux, 1979) 90.

[33] Co-sponsored by the College of St. Catherine and Wisdom Ways, an Ecumenical Center for Spirituality, St. Paul, MN.

Jr., Mahatma Ghandi—were intensely contemplative, deeply visionary, intrinsically spiritual people.[34]

One of the hallmarks of women's spirituality groups, whatever their form, is the conscious and emphatic use of inclusive language and of images of God that are not solely patriarchal. The importance of language which includes both genders, inclusive images of God, and acknowledgment of the presence of a variety of races cannot be overemphasized as an issue for women. Only the experience of feeling excluded, as has been the common experience of women, can make anyone understand why inclusive language is a critical issue. As students of language know, the words we use and hear shape our attitudes and define our reality. Yet recognition of this has been slow in coming to implementation in the Church. Twenty years ago, at a conference on women and the Church, we were among women who recommended the implementation of inclusive language throughout our archdiocese, a recommendation which met with a positive response. Today, both of us belong to parishes that are very sensitive to this issue. We were surprised to learn as we were preparing these observations that, according to a recent archdiocesan survey, fewer than half of the parishes have attended to the use of inclusive language in hymns, homilies, and parish communications, and a very small number to inclusive language for images of God. It makes us wonder whether this is typical of other parts of the country. If so, it is not surprising that women's spirituality groups make language an issue.

As the twentieth century ended, the institutional Church was still struggling with aspects of the role of women in the Church. In October 1998 the National Council of Catholic Bishops issued two statements they approved to augment the 1994 pastoral reflection "Strengthening the Bonds of Peace." The first text, written by the NCCB's Committee on Doctrine, is titled "Ten Frequently Asked Questions About the Reservation of Priestly Ordination to Men." The second, by the NCCB's Committee on Women in Society and in the Church, is titled "From Words to Deeds: Continuing Reflections on the Role of Women in the Church." This statement is organized around three goals: "To appreciate and incorporate the gifts of women in the Church; to appoint women to Church leadership positions; to promote collaboration between women and men in the Church."[35] The discussion of each of the goals includes suggestions for

---

[34] Joan Chittister, *Heart of Flesh: A Feminist Spirituality for Women and Men* (Grand Rapids, Mich.: Eerdmans, 1998) 2.

[35] NCCB's Committee on Women in Society and in the Church, "From Words to Deeds: Continuing Reflections on the Role of Women in the Church," *Origins* (October 28, 1998) 334.

implementation. In the discussion of the second goal, the bishops say, "In the past, we have encouraged Church leaders to identify the Church roles, especially leadership roles, that are open to women. We now need to shift our thinking. We assume that all roles in the Church are open to women, unless stated otherwise by canon law."[36]

We especially noted that while the statement acknowledges the many contributions of women to the Church, there is also acknowledgment that the very language of the Church excludes women. A pastoral suggestion to use inclusive language "as permitted" asserts, "Sensitive use of language helps to build a foundation by acknowledging the presence and participation of women."[37]

At the end of the twentieth century, as at its beginning, American Catholic women continued to differ from each other, according to our observations of them and our reading by and about them. Some are not only content to maintain a traditional role, but also want others to maintain the same. Others, content to live with whatever the status is, do not object if other women want to change it to participate more fully. Still others strongly oppose the inequality they see as a result of a patriarchal system and work toward a transformative change. And there are, sadly, many now former Catholic women who have left to join other communities—different churches or other sources for their spiritual needs. What one commentator observed in the 1980s seems to us still true:

> The American experience indicates that diversity has always been a characteristic of American women. The diversity itself has always been a sign of vitality and growth; without prophets raising issues, challenging shibboleths, and living lives of sacrifice, the Church itself becomes moribund. The history of American Catholic women . . . indicates there is little chance of such stultifying tranquillity in the future.[38]

If that is so, we may hope that in accounts of the twenty-first–century Church, women will be so fully integrated into its life that a separate chapter on women will seem as unnecessary as a separate chapter on men in the Church. As St. Paul reminds us: "All baptized in Christ, you have all clothed yourselves in Christ, and there are no distinctions between Jew and slave and free, male or female, but all of you are one in Christ Jesus" (Gal 3:27-28).

---

[36] Ibid., 357.
[37] James Kenneally, *History of Women in the Church,* 200.
[38] Quoted in James Kenneally, *History of Women in the Church,* 200.

Catholic Youth: The Presumed Become the Pursued

David J. O'Brien

When it comes to young people, confusion reigns, perhaps everywhere, certainly in the Catholic Church, nowhere more than in the United States. As always, parents complain that the young are less respectful of their elders than they once were, while religious leaders decry the multiple dangers that surround them. Few conversations about generations, at least among Catholics, escape themes of "decline and fall." And there is plenty of evidence to back them up. Church attendance is down among young adults, attendance at religious education programs all but ends with confirmation in the mid-teens, and vocations to the priesthood and religious life, once a dramatic marker of U.S. Catholic prosperity, have fallen far below replacement levels. One need not add that their theory and practice regarding sexuality are at odds with the teachings of Catholic authorities.

Still, young Americans remain very religious. Studies show that vast numbers of them affirm the basic Christian doctrines of incarnation and redemption. They pray and large numbers claim a personal relationship with Jesus. Their moral views on questions of racial equality, war, and social justice correspond closely to those of moderate Christian religious leaders, including the U.S. bishops. Evangelical Christian movements make a strong appeal and young Americans flocked to see Pope John Paul II, a hero in their eyes, even while they have doubts about many of his teachings regarding sexuality or the role of women within the Church. Even those most disturbed by "religious illiteracy" acknowledge that young people are interested in religion, like to pray, and regularly volunteer to help poor people. As sociologist Andrew Greeley has been saying for thirty years, young people love religion; it's churches they have trouble with.

At the close of an old and start of a new century and millennium, as the pope appeals especially to the young to renew their acquaintance with Christ and the Church, it may be worthwhile to undertake a brief review of Catholic projects related to young people. Our review will have three parts. First, we will look at the long Catholic culture war against modernity, when youth was an important battleground. Second, we will look at the mixed results of a more positive approach to the young following Vatican II. Finally, we will try to locate the issue of youth in the context of the American Church at the end of the century.

Catholicism and Culture Wars

Between Martin Luther's unleashing of rebellion against Christendom in 1517 and the conclusion of the bloody Thirty Years War in 1648, everything changed. The Reformation, among other things a young people's movement, shattered the hegemony of Catholicism and the unity of Europe. In its wake came modern states, with governments in control of religion, with religious establishment the universally accepted norm, and with an international system based on non-interference by states in one another's internal affairs. Few political or ecclesiastical leaders tolerated religious dissent, so in most places the transmission of specific religious viewpoints was not a self-conscious problem or a popularly acknowledged responsibility. Counter-Reformation Catholics worried about the religious literacy of Catholics generally, and they produced catechisms and a variety of pastoral initiatives to educate Catholics and insulate them against proselytizing, but rarely did they look upon children or young people as a distinct endangered group. Even the Jesuits and others who took steps to educate old and new elites, including the new middle classes, did not regard young people as a group in need of special attention. If there was an exception among Catholics it was in Maryland, where parents, economically prosperous but politically vulnerable, took deliberate steps to ensure that their heirs understood their responsibilities as a persecuted religious minority and developed the skills needed to negotiate their place on the margins of civil society. "Deliberate" was, and would remain, the key word.

What triggered more widespread attention to the young was the French Revolution, which attacked the Church along with the other institutions of the *ancien régime.* By depriving the Catholic Church of the financial support of the state, seizing its treasures and endowments, and breaking its hold on education and civil registers, revolutionary liberalism forced a new sense of strategic deliberation upon Catholic leaders. From that point on children and youth became objects of political struggle as contending groups sought to win the allegiance of young men, and to a lesser degree young women, who now had real choices available to them.

Alexis de Tocqueville, in one of those brilliant insights that mark his work, suggested that when Catholic authorities lost the capacity to control society and shape culture by means of their influence on the state and its legal, educational, and civic institutions, they adopted a domestic strategy. Once the Church controlled personal and family life through its alliance with the state; now it would influence state and society by its formative role in personal and family life. Years later sociologist Gene Burns developed a similar argument to explain the preoccupation of the twentieth-century Church with sexual ethics.

This is a special Catholic argument, because Catholic leaders were never satisfied to see Catholicism become simply a denomination like others. Instead, as leaders of once established churches, they thought of themselves as an establishment in exile, ready and able to once again take responsibility for the spiritual and moral life of the entire community.

If there is truth in this argument, it explains the vigorous effort of the European Church in the nineteenth century to sharpen its conflict with the emerging culture of modernity. Catechisms, parish missions, reform of the diocesan clergy, and reinvigoration of pastoral ministry all aimed at turning baptized Church members into "practicing Catholics," dependent on the clergy for the sacraments, which were increasingly defined as the primary if not sole channels of divine grace. Loyalty and solidarity were taught, and practiced, and in the process competing associations were kept at bay. Where the Church faced overt competition from Protestants or socialists, parish mobilization was supplemented by a variety of movements and organizations, some of them aimed directly at youth. These included Catholic trade unions, farmers associations, student groups, confraternities, and in some cases political parties.

Mobilization of this sort was politically loaded. Not only were other ideological groups anxious to attract the young, but modern states very much desired to break down internal divisions in order to unify the nation and strengthen the government. Bismarck's Germany, the French Third Republic, and liberal regimes in Italy, the Low Countries, and later eastern European regimes all took steps to limit Catholic organization among the young. Later fascist regimes, at one level sympathetic to the Church, as in Austria, Portugal, or Italy, ran into the Church when they tried to develop new forms of youth mobilization. In Italy and Germany it was clashes of this sort, rather than problems of racism or militarism, that led to clashes between Church and state in the 1930s.

Much Catholic youth work was defensive then, as the Church sought to strengthen its subcultural resistance against secularism and anti-clericalism. But there were more positive efforts to tap youthful idealism for apostolic purposes. Youth groups joined other lay organizations in national Catholic congresses in Germany, France, and Belgium in the 1870s and

1880s. Here plans were made to promote Catholic education, support the growing Catholic press and new publishing ventures, develop programs to assist the new working class, and mobilize intellectual and organizational resources to make the case for Catholic positions in public life. When Pope Leo XIII loosened the Catholic alliance with monarchy, Christian democratic groups sprang up to promote a positive Catholic response to social questions. *Le Sillon,* in France, for example, inspired young Catholics to work for social justice and authentic political democracy until its energetic lay leaders ran afoul of anxious ecclesiastics worried about power. Similar movements appeared, and met a similar fate, in Italy. In time the Church would identify such organizations as "Catholic Action" made official when and only when it took place with episcopal authorization and clerical control.

Between the wars, as liberalism declined as a result of war and depression, the culture wars between the socialist left and the fascist right intensified, and Catholics developed their own movements to reform society and construct a more Christian social order. Most notable were the so-called JOCists, specialized Catholic-Action groups associated with Canon Joseph Cardijn of Belgium, Young Catholic Workers, and Farmer and Students. They came together in networks of small units, sometimes called cells, for prayer, self-education, and mutual support as they attempted to combat the influence of secular ideologies while backing the legitimate work of unions and trade associations. These groups developed a methodology of social action that proved remarkably resilient. JOCist groups flourished in the post-war period, extending throughout much of the Catholic world, including the United States. But American organizations remained modest in size, religious rather than political in emphasis, and safely under Church control.

The School Question

Obviously the school question was at the center of these culture wars. In Germany, France, and Italy nationalist governments sought a monopoly of education, and Church leaders battled back to ensure clerical influence over the education of the young. Fights over control of education persisted and spread to eastern European countries whenever governments embarked on modernization schemes. School fights were almost always three sided. One party was the Church, another was competing churches and social groups, the third was the state. The goal of the Church was to ensure the continued faith and loyalty of its people. The goal of alternative groups was to win support of the young for their vision of religious and political truth. The goal of the state almost always was the integration of society, so that populations could be mobilized for public purposes, especially war.

In continental Europe the battle was fought with considerable bitterness in France, Germany, and the Low Countries. Church leaders sought to control elementary and later secondary schools, with public financial support provided for schools under ecclesiastical supervision and often with teaching provided by religious orders of men and women. Competing groups battled to break the Church monopoly and were usually ready to ally themselves with the state in order to do so. Political leaders feared the divisiveness of Church power, while state supported teachers feared the backwardness and obscurantism they identified with Church control. Once again the subcultural preoccupations of the pre–Vatican II Church were evident: the school question was framed and answered in terms of the Church. Keeping Catholics Catholic was the first priority and the clearest principle governing Catholic youth work.

The American Exception

The United States was different, but not all that different. Here there was almost none of that tone of restorationism: Catholics never dreamed of running the state or controlling society as a whole. Battles over education were chronic, from early battles to purge public schools of Protestant practices through the Grant Administration's effort to nationalize education to the climactic battle in the 1920s over an Oregon law requiring attendance at public schools. That case established the principle of parental control and the freedom of churches to run schools. School fights after that were often bitter, but they were usually about money, with Catholics complaining of double taxation and public school advocates worrying about Catholic assaults on the public treasury.

Despite the commitment of the Church to its own schools, Catholics attended public schools in large numbers, and in many heavily Catholic industrial cities Catholics provided the largest numbers of teachers, principals, and school board members. In Catholic schools textbooks were often indistinguishable from those used in public schools, educational officials easily accepted state and local guidelines and even tests on "secular subjects," and everyone proclaimed loyalty to God and country. The American school question for Catholics at least had the flavor more of contentious interest groups than impassioned culture wars.

More broadly, in the United States battles over youth were far less fierce than in Europe. Catholic leaders worried constantly about inroads into the ranks of Catholic young people by Protestant sponsored scouts or the YMCA. In the nineteenth century, official discrimination had forced real battles in courtrooms about access to Catholics accused of crimes, to orphans of Catholic parents, and to public institutions. But the war for equal treatment was usually won, priests gained access to institutions, and Catholic social agencies ended up cooperating with non-Catholic agencies in community fund raising and, as a result, community services. In that complicated mix of private and public partnerships, so different from the sectarian divisions over the school question, Catholic institutions played their part. If there were Protestant Scouts there would be Catholic Scouts; if the YMCA, then the CYO (Catholic Youth Organization). As parishes often failed to reach thousands of urban children from Catholic families, outreach efforts became something of a crusade, especially in the decades on either side of the Second World War. In the 1930s it was the CYO, with its athletic leagues and social events. In the 1950s it was more often parish-based diocesan youth councils adding to the leagues and dances, parades, concerts, and demonstrations of mass support.

Apostolic movements made their mark as well. From the 1880s on, the parish-based St. Vincent de Paul Society was a major vehicle for youthful idealism. The Catholic Worker movement, founded in 1933 by Peter Maurin and Dorothy Day, appealed to cadres of young Catholics worried about the social question, later about war and weapons. The Grail, aimed at idealistic young lay women, also enjoyed a period of popularity after World War II. JOCist groups were less successful. Fr. Louis Putz, c.s.c., launched Young Christian Students (YCS) and Young Christian Workers (YCW), and from 1945 through the 1950s they were prominently represented at Catholic youth gatherings. All of these groups supplemented the work of religious orders, some of which had their own youth arms, like the Jesuit Sodality of Our Lady. But together they were limited in number and impact.

In the United States, without Catholic trade unions or political parties, and with the parish the basic focal point of Catholic life, lay organizations generally, and independent youth movements in particular, had a hard time getting solid footing. One reason was clearly the fact that parishes, and the vast project of Catholic parochial school education, required enormous resources, so that all proposals for innovation had to be tested against the ever pressing needs of Catholic parishes. That which strengthened parishes won approval, that which did not (or which was so perceived), like the most successful lay organization of the post-war years, the Christian Family Movement, did not. Add to that the continuing demands of ethnic solidarity, the preoccupation of religious orders with their own pressing apostolic commitments, and the general perception that religion was a matter of family and private life, not public life, and it becomes clear that vigorous youth movements would have little room to breathe in the American Catholic Church. What did flourish especially in the post–World War II years were secondary schools and parish-based youth groups which shaped barriers against intermarriage, strengthened morale, and sustained beyond the immigrant generation the thick social networks which formed Catholic identity.

In 1972 Archbishop Jean Jadot, the Belgian-born Apostolic Delegate to the United States, told a student group that his biggest surprise since coming to the United States was the near total absence of lay organization in this country. In Belgium he had served as a student chaplain. Students and their chaplains were well organized apart from parishes. They even had their own access to the hierarchy. In the United States the Newman movement struggled for support with only grudging support from Church leaders. Jadot attributed this to the clergy's preoccupation with the parish, the dominant institutional fact of American Catholic life.

Vatican II and Beyond

The Second Vatican Council came at a time when the Catholic subcultures of Europe and North America were undergoing dramatic change. In Europe Christian Democratic parties, independent at last of clerical control, played a major role in post-war reconstruction. Anti-communist enthusiasms sustained new forms of culture-war mobilization, but political success and economic resurgence ate away at the hard edges that had long separated ideological groups. At the same time, after a brief period of revival, religious practice began a long decline. Below the surface hard questions about the mission and purpose of the Church provided the backdrop for the call to renewal issued by Pope John XIII and the council he convoked.

In the United States the immigrant church gradually gave way to a Church dominated by a new middle class, educated under the G.I. Bill of Rights and relocated in the automobile suburbs rather than urban neighborhoods. Between 1945 and 1965 church attendance reached spectacular heights, parochial school enrollments doubled, and vocations to the priesthood and religious life almost kept pace with the burgeoning Catholic population. On the other hand, middle-class arrival, shared patriotic enthusiasms, and mass popular culture shattered old boundaries, eroding ethnic and religious differences. Even if there had never been a Vatican Council the American Church would have experienced enormous strains in the 1960s.

But the council did happen, and it happened just as the country itself shook with the civil-rights movement, urban riots, political assassinations, and a cruel and unpopular war. The solidarity of pre-conciliar Catholicism was shattered, school attendance and vocations dropped dramatically, ecclesiastical reassertion of traditional sexual morality clashed with popular practice, and the once solid Church gave way to what Andrew Greeley called "do it yourself Catholicism."

Once the Church was built around the need to instruct the young in the culture of their immigrant parents. Remarkably the American Catholic hierarchy succeeded in sustaining this family-centered subculture through the process of Americanization. But by the end of the 1960s it no longer seemed enough, at least in those sectors of the Church associated with the Americanized descendants of the European immigrants.

In the first place, "keeping the kids Catholic" remained an important motivation for Church membership. Vast resources poured into parish-based CCD (Confraternity of Christian Doctrine) programs of religious education. After confirmation, education gave way to new forms of "youth ministry," often directed by professionally trained lay people. Results were ambiguous. On the one hand large numbers continued to self-identify as Catholics, and religious practice remained fairly high, at least until the mid-1990s. Most important, survey data and pastoral reports showed that people prayed often and testified to personal experiences of the presence of God. On the other hand liturgical practice among the young dropped off sharply, with many resuming practice when they had their own children. Complaints multiplied that CCD-educated Catholics were illiterate in Catholic history and doctrine. And youth ministry and the less widespread young adult ministry aimed at post–high school non-college young people were often inadequately funded and lacked strategic coherence.

Second, almost no efforts have been made since Vatican II to mobilize youth or young adults for apostolic purposes. Young Catholics surely participate in such peace and social justice movements as the Catholic Worker, or in evangelizing efforts associated with charismatic renewal. Campus ministry programs on Catholic campuses provide well-attended liturgical services, large social service programs, and intense experiences of social ministry at home and overseas. These result in numerous volunteers for post-graduate service programs, but so far seem to have had little impact on Catholic parishes or dioceses, or even on the Church's own impressive array of social ministries. Almost no efforts are made to mobilize committed students across campuses, or to develop pastoral strategies for their later participation in the American Church. The social activities of the Church generally are fragmented and local.

In addition, ecclesiastical support for campus ministry on non-Catholic campuses is restricted to provision of pastoral services, and there are signs of erosion of even that support. Surprisingly European-based conservative youth mobilizations have had little success in the United States, at least so far. One reflection on this lack of interest in organizing on the basis of youthful idealism, on left and right, may be the declining resources of religious orders of men and women who so often in the past provided leadership and ecclesiastical access for energetic young Catholics.

Finally, it may well be that these trends point to larger issues. Many have characterized the recent experience of the Church in the United States as Americanization, the adaptation of the immigrant Catholic enclave to the demands of American culture. Older Americanists once championed that adaptation. Some even looked forward to the day when Catholics would find all the outlets they needed for apostolic service in non-denominational political and social movements. Americanists generally did not lament the decline of specifically Catholic organizations for young people. Radical Catholics and later conservatives saw that overall Americanist strategy as disastrous and advocated a recovery of Catholic integrity by countercultural resistance to American consumerism and violence, even adopting Pope John Paul II's language of "the culture of death" to describe their country.

This dialectic of pro- and anti-Americanism is rooted in a long history, but it has reached levels of intensity reminiscent of the internal Church battles of a century ago, which led to a papal condemnation of that generation's brand of Americanism. Rarely noticed in this recent debate is the religious culture to which Americans have adapted, perhaps over-adapted. It is marked (1) by individualism, and thus by an emphasis on religious experience; (2) by pluralism and thus by an emphasis on evangelization, "selling God" and personal decisions, consumer choice, and (3) by voluntary communities, congregations, and thus by fragile structures of ecclesiastical authority and theological orthodoxy. This is the religious culture that was kept partially (and only partially) at bay by Catholic subcultural strategies grounded in the immigration experience. Now American Catholics are beyond recall Americans, part of a culture they have helped transform as they made it their own.

This explains why we have seen the growth of evangelical forms of piety among Catholics in recent years. For in this environment religion must be a matter of personal conviction and free choice. Piety based on Scripture and the person of Jesus, revivalist appeals for decisions for Christ, and formation and reformation of congregations are part of every Christian group's American destiny.

It is no surprise, then, that young Catholics pray, read Scripture, and respond to Jesus, and that they are puzzled by more collective symbols of Eucharist and body of Christ. The evangelical thesis also helps explain the appeal of personal social responsibility and the weakness of appeals to the common good. Catholic wisdom about sacrament and liturgy, solidarity and organic social obligation that precedes and grounds personal choice is hard to grasp.

This is not just a youth problem, for questions of literacy and theological coherence can be raised at every level of the Church. Can Catholic wisdom be retrieved? Can Catholic ideals of solidarity be renewed in such a way as to enrich American culture? Probably not by the simplicities of Americanism or counter-cultural restorationism. The one risks losing the ground for religious commitment, the other risks confusing alienation with integrity. Catholicism cannot and should not lead its young away from American culture, because it is our culture and we share responsibility for it. But neither should Catholicism submit to the impulse toward cultural surrender, because there is much in our culture which betrays not only Christian principles of human dignity but America's own foundational promise of liberty and justice for all.

Another road is needed. Perhaps it can be relocated through a retelling of American Catholic history. Rather than a story of questionable Americanization, perhaps it can be told as a story of liberation. Families once poor and on the margins, exploited workers in mines and factories, insulted immigrants in squalid tenements, over three or four generations moved up and moved in. If liberation has to do with overcoming economic insecurity and dependence, lack of education, cultural marginalization, and political powerlessness, then this is a liberation story. Of course it was messy and ambiguous, like all historical journeys since Exodus. Like that story this one will find its meaning in what each generation does with the freedom and the resources it is given. The question now is: "liberation for what?" Perhaps it always was.

In this perspective the youth question changes. Once that question was one of defensive protection against dangerous outside enemies. In the United States it had to do with generational continuity amidst rapid social change. Since the Reformation and the French Revolution youth were pawns in culture wars, recruits in a struggle for souls and for history. Now external enemies are less visible, so boundaries are blurred. Generational transmission of faith is complicated by the individualism of the culture that engulfs old and young alike. Church insiders fight about who will control ecclesiastical policy, basing their claims on conflicting ecclesiologies, differing answers to the question "what is the Church?"

But the better question is why. If the story is one of liberation, then the meaning of the historic journey will be found in the choices Catholics and their Church make. Youth has to do with the future, and the future is about mission. What is the Church to do? How is the work of God's kingdom to be forwarded? How are we to use the freedom which our forebears gained for us? Answering that challenge is the work of social theology and ministry which deals with the relationship between faith and the human project. The road to revitalizing youth ministry lies through the renewal of the Church's sense of mission and purpose. Those who would renew the Church's youth programs might begin with a deeper exploration of the social meanings of faith and the people's own stories of liberation.

Catholic Education: Helping Shape Intellectual, Cultural, and Civic Life

Jeanne Knoerle, S.P.

As we look at the history of American Catholicism in the twentieth century, it is hard not to be impressed with the growth of the Catholic Church and the expansion of its influence in almost all areas of civic life and American culture. A slow awakening to and then conscious recognition of its power to make a difference, a hesitant flexing of its muscles to see just how strong it is, a careful looking around to assess the best way to take its place in an unfolding democracy—all these are part of the greater self-consciousness American Catholics experienced as the century progressed.

The twentieth century was a time of growth in almost every area of the Church's life. It was a time of moving from a perception of itself as a transplanted European church reconstituting itself as an American church with no intention of disturbing any of its original characteristics, to a perception toward the end of the century that, while it retained the fundamental marks and universality of its parent, its own characteristics are uniquely and self-consciously American. American Catholicism truly came of age, of "American age," as it moved across the twentieth century—with all the positives and negatives that separation from parents and maturation always imply.

From the earliest colonial times, when a mere handful of Catholics was present in an overwhelmingly Protestant population, up to the end of the twentieth century, by which time Catholics had become the largest single denominational group in a constantly diversifying population, Catholics have played a significant role in shaping American culture. At the same time, the impact of the culture of this constantly growing and changing nation has also significantly formed contemporary American Catholicism. And one of the strongest, if not the strongest, influence in that mutual process has been education.

From their very earliest days on these shores, Catholic parents and Catholic ecclesiastical leaders were concerned about how to educate children in the faith they felt had served them so well. And this concern, while it frequently (in fact, fairly constantly) placed them at the center of controversy, resulted in several positive outcomes. One result of that concern is that the constant questioning and prodding by American Catholics about the education of children, and their fear that they were being oppressed by the methods prevailing in America, continued to raise the question in the public arena: who is responsible for providing education for children and how is that education best organized, delivered, and paid for so that all citizens are served well? That debate has been, and still remains, a powerful, if irritating, incentive to clarify what fundamental American values are and to trace how they have been shaped over the last several centuries.

A second impact of this continuing conflict was that the issue of education was consistently brought to the forefront of discussion and the center of decision-making among Catholics, most especially in the twentieth century as they moved up the economic ladder and began to take a more prominent place in American society.

This concern eventually led to a third result which impacted the role of women in the American church. It provided a greatly expanded role for those religious communities dedicated to providing education, encouraging them to professionalize their preparation for teaching in order to meet and exceed many of the standards required for public education. And because many of these were women's communities, it consequently expanded the education of these women in a way that might not have been possible otherwise. As a result, in a Church without the leadership of female clergy, this education eventually gave women positions of some power and, perhaps more important, a place from which to exercise influence in a variety of arenas. It also provided, after the mid-century move to educate sisters to a high professional level, a cadre of contemporary religious and former religious women who are now exercising a good deal of leadership in the present-day Church.

Some of the Basic Conflicts

The belief that public authority should control education seemed self-evident in colonial times. Schools were primarily perceived as a way to form a child's nature, which was thought of by the religious leaders of the time as inherently evil. "Since the child was prone to sin, the best way to keep him under control, was to instill in him a fear of breaking God's laws and a fear of the awful and dreadful consequences of sin."[1] Authority at

---

[1] R. Freeman Butts and Lawrence A. Cremin, *A History of Education in American Culture* (New York: Henry Holt and Company, 1953) 66.

that time was in the hands of Protestant-Calvinist leaders who fully accepted this view of religious orthodoxy.

It soon became evident, however, that, if education were to include the inculcation of religious beliefs, government control of public schools could not be sustained in a society where mixed religious beliefs inevitably developed into hostile sectarian rivalries. By the eighteenth century, education had begun to splinter along religious lines as Protestantism began to break into more identifiable sects. A new public doctrine of education began to develop based on the presupposition that, by reading the Bible in public schools without comment, these schools could teach moral principles that were common to all the sects. By this time, Catholics had become more numerous and they expressed clear and vocal opposition to this possibility, which they felt was essentially an imposition of the doctrine of personal interpretation of the Bible. This, they felt, was contrary to Catholic practice, and would seriously harm the faith of their children.

By mid-nineteenth century, the practice of Bible reading without comment provided an invitation to an increasing number of American Catholics to make a bold move. Under the leadership first of Orestes Brownson and then of Isaac Hecker (both Protestants who had converted to Catholicism), they attempted to illustrate the merits of having an authoritative doctrine of interpretation rather than personal interpretation, in order to give children, who were surrounded by a rash of sectarian creeds, more security about reading the Bible.

According to Brownson:

> If democracy commits the government to the people to be taken care of, religion is to take care that they take proper care of the government, rightly direct and wisely administer it. But what religion? It must be a religion which is above the people and controls them, or it will not answer the purposes. If it depends on the people, if the people are to take care of it, to say what it shall be, what it shall teach, what it shall command, what worship or discipline it shall insist on being observed, we are back in our old difficulty. The people take care of religion; but who or what is to take care of the people? We repeat, then, what religion? It cannot be Protestantism, in all or any of its forms; for Protestantism assumes as its point of departure that Almighty God has indeed given us a religion, but *has given it to us not to take care of us, but to be taken care of by us.* . . . The Roman Catholic religion, then, is necessary to sustain popular liberty, because popular liberty can be sustained only by a religion free from popular control, above the people, speaking from above and able to command them—and such a religion is the Roman Catholic.[2]

[2] Ibid., 174.

This move and the later decision of the Third Plenary Council of 1884 to mandate the building and attendance at Catholic schools by all Catholic children (with some government support, they hoped) only served to solidify Protestant opposition and draw many disparate Protestant groups together in an effort to establish a common nonsectarian public school system and oppose any diversion of public funds to a separate Catholic system.

And there the complex controversy lay at the dawn of the twentieth century, with Catholics, for different (though not necessarily inconsistent) reasons at different periods of American history, almost always standing in opposition to the prevailing educational beliefs reigning on the national scene. Given the growing number of immigrant Catholics in the United States and increasing pressure to find economically feasible ways to educate their children, Catholics were faced with an urgent need to articulate reasons why education was a joint responsibility of the parents and of the state. They believed and argued that—since America is a Christian nation and morality rests upon religion—education, even public education, must include religion if Americans are to be and remain a moral people. Therefore, they argued, the government should promote Christianity by a free "cooperation" between the state and the churches. While many Protestants agreed with the fundamental presuppositions of this statement, heated controversies erupted and flamed intensely when the issue came down to choosing among the practices and doctrines of a particular form of Christian religion.

From the 1910s through the 1920s, the religious issue was less central to the discussion, with controversy focused primarily on whether America should continue its experiment to maintain public and private systems of schools side by side, whether it should give still greater emphasis to public education, or whether the government should encourage private institutions to become the major deliverers of American education.

Two important Supreme Court decisions in the 1920s illustrate the issues and emotions generated in those questions. Between 1917 and 1921, thirty-one states passed laws requiring all instruction in public schools to be given in English. Nebraska, however, included private schools in its law, which led to a ruling by the Supreme Court declaring the law unconstitutional. The Supreme Court argued, in part, (*Meyer v. Nebraska,* 1923) that the state can compel children to attend some school, that it can establish reasonable regulations for all schools, including the giving of instruction in English, and that it can prescribe a curriculum for public schools which it supports, but it cannot prohibit instruction that interferes with the religious and private rights of parents to seek the kind of instruction they wish.

In 1922, Oregon adopted a compulsory education act that required all children to attend a public school and required any who attended a private

school to obtain permission of and be examined by the county superinten-
dent of schools. That act led Catholics into legal action, resulting in another Supreme Court decision (*Pierce v. Society of Sisters*, 1925) a part of
which read:

> Under the doctrine of *Meyer v. Nebraska*, we think it entirely plain that the
> Act of 1922 unreasonably interferes with the liberty of parents and
> guardians to direct the upbringing and education of children under their
> control. . . . The fundamental theory of liberty upon which all govern-
> ments in this Union repose excludes any general power of the State to stan-
> dardize its children by forcing them to accept instruction from public
> teachers only.[3]

This decision was widely taken as a charter of privileges for private and
religious schools, leading Catholics to argue more forcibly for public
funds to support their schools. Some Protestant educators began to argue,
as a new counter to this emerging set of educational realities, that, if children were to learn to cooperate with other religious and cultural groups,
they could do it best only if they all learned to live, work, study, and play
together in a common school, and that a great expansion of private education would simply create a dual system that would have the effect of creating sharp cleavages in American society along religious lines.

As a result, in the 1930s and 1940s the pace of controversy increased
and the question became: Shall public funds be used for the support of religious schools and, if so, for what purposes? Many Americans, by the time
this question had become dominant, had moved from approving direct support for religious schools and seemed to be in general agreement that the
best interests of the nation and of religion would be served if public funds
were not granted to religious schools. As a result, the delicate balance in
which the phrase "the separation of Church and state" always hung col-
lapsed again and three positions came into conflict in the public square:

> (1) Public funds should be granted to religious schools as a recognition of their
> role in serving the public welfare and in meeting the requirements of compul-
> sory attendance laws—there was strong Catholic support for this position;
> (2) Even though direct aid for religious schools was contrary to good pol-
> icy and the doctrine of separation, it was nevertheless justifiable for the state
> to use public funds for indirect aid to parochial schools—many Protestants
> joined many Catholics in support of this position;
> (3) Direct aid from public funds is unconstitutional and indirect aid in the
> form of "auxiliary services" is also unconstitutional—this position was
> based on the slippery slope argument and many Protestant, most Jewish, and

---

[3] Ibid., 527.

many non-religious groups held it, while the National Catholic Welfare Conference took a strong stand against it.

It was in such an environment of controversy, excitement, fine-pointed arguments, attempted compromises, religious and political disagreements, battles won and battles lost, that Catholicism lived throughout most of the twentieth century.

The Education Lens

It is interesting and instructive to view American Catholics in this century solely through the lens of their views on education. They had often been perceived by many of their fellow citizens as one of the following: ignorant immigrant laborers, unschooled and possibly unable or uninterested in advancing far in their schooling; a people never encouraged, or even allowed, to think independently because of the strong authoritarianism of their Church; persons uninterested in philosophy and higher studies because of their continuing (and possibly permanent) position on the lower rungs of the economic ladder; a people unwilling to enter fully into American society because their religious beliefs—to which they clung tenaciously—were clearly at odds with the predominant views around them and their allegiance to the pope was incompatible with full-fledged American citizenship. As a result, Catholics were clearly outsiders—often angry because they felt oppressed by the dominant culture around them—yet, at the same time, fundamentally proud to be different because it gave them a sense of identity and an unchanging moral ground on which to stand.

Despite all these characteristics, and in some instances because of them, and despite having to deal with the continuing conflicts outlined previously, these are the people who nonetheless built and maintained the largest non-public school system in the history of the world. Between 1912 and 1963, the country's Catholic population nearly tripled, from 15,015,569 to 43,851,538, comprising almost 22 percent of the total population.[4] During these years the number of educational institutions and of students educated in those institutions expanded at an unbelievable rate—by 1965 there were 5.6 million children enrolled in Catholic elementary and secondary schools, organized and supported by untold numbers of teaching and administrative staff.

And Catholics had funded this educational system essentially from their own resources. Says Timothy Walch:

---

[4] James Hennessey, *American Catholics* (New York: Oxford University Press, 1981) 286 and 329.

The rapid growth in Catholic school enrollment quickly became a preoccupation of a new generation of bishops. In virtually every diocese across the nation, bishops and other Catholic leaders built dozens of new schools in the 1950s. In each of the major archdioceses of New York, Boston, Philadelphia, Chicago, and St. Louis, the number of new schools built during the decade climbed into the hundreds. Yet, for all their efforts, these bishops could not build and staff enough schools to meet the demand.[5]

The twentieth century was also a time when Catholic institutions of higher education were exploding across the country, fueled by the improving economic position of Catholics who wanted to give their children the advantage of a college education as well. Those religious communities that had educated their sisters, brothers, and priests to teach in the elementary and high schools they had established were enthusiastic in their willingness to establish colleges where their graduates' faith would be safeguarded and where it could be developed and expanded to meet the more mature challenges their lives would place before them.

After World War II, the G.I. Bill provided educational funds for returning veterans (at the time by and large male, of course), and this entitlement gave Catholic colleges and universities a powerful boost in enrollment. That enrollment was further expanded when parents found they could now send their daughters to a Catholic college, since their sons' education was being provided by the government. Many of these women would not have been able to attend college, even a nearby, less expensive state institution, much less a Catholic college, had that bill not provided their parents the discretionary money that earlier would have gone to educate their brothers. The number of these colleges and universities peaked in 1965 at 309 institutions. They comprised then, and still do—though the number is now 220—the largest single group of church-related colleges in the country.

It is not possible to exaggerate the role of the religious communities of women and men who provided not only the raw material but the core support for the feat of establishing, organizing, and overseeing all of these educational institutions. Both before the rise in the numbers of religious who staffed these schools, and since the late 1960s when their numbers have significantly decreased, the Church, through its ordinary parish financing, found it almost impossible to maintain such institutions. The history of the American Catholic Church is rife with examples of schools opened with enthusiasm and then closed for lack of funds.

---

[5] Timothy Walch, *Catholicism in America: A Social History* (Malabar, Fla.: Robert E. Krieger Publishing Company, 1989) 79.

Establishing schools was not considered a central religious activity in the European church from which these American Catholics had come. Therefore, they had little understanding or agreement about how to fund them. Money was always a major issue in Catholic parishes. And in a parish with a school it was even more difficult to adjudicate how available money would be allocated. There were many causes to which Catholics were asked to contribute, particularly in the earlier part of the century— hospitals to take care of the sick, orphanages, the destitute poor who could depend only upon their fellow Catholics for assistance, those who were temporarily "down and out" and needed a helping hand. Further, there was little history of philanthropy among a laboring people who had always had very little discretionary money to share, and the Protestant concept of "stewardship" had not penetrated the Catholic psyche.

Therefore, the role of religious communities took on great importance relative to the maintenance of schools. The financing was done in many ways. There are many examples of funding for "poor schools" being made possible, for instance, by these communities from their own funds, even though they depended entirely for their livelihood on the stipends contributed by their members.

> A practice, common in many dioceses by the 1860s, whereby sisterhoods were expected to borrow money to purchase land and construct parochial schools, demonstrates the extent of their subsidization. Once the schools opened, their debts and sister-teachers' stipends alike were supposed to be covered by tuition charges. But since most children in these schools were too poor to pay even minimal tuition fees, the sisters had little choice but to open "select schools" to support themselves as well as the schools.[6]

These practices and many others initiated by religious communities over these years allowed such schools not only to exist but often to flourish. Clearly, the recent decrease in the number of Catholic schools, which has resulted from the rapid decline in the numbers of sisters, brothers, and priests, is further illustration of the powerful financial impact of these religious on the Catholic schools and within American Catholicism—and the challenging changes in education which lie ahead as we enter the twenty-first century.

A "New" Century

As we look at the full breadth and length of the twentieth century, it becomes more and more clear that American culture begins to splinter and

---

[6] Mary J. Oates, *The Catholic Philanthropic Tradition in America* (Bloomington: Indiana University Press, 1995) 151.

become much less cohesive toward the end of the 1960s, and that many of the coherent characteristics we think of as "American" are no longer patently that. And as American culture began to split into a number of disparate forms and colors, American Catholicism did the same. Education had produced a critical mass of Catholics who were no longer perceived by their fellow non-Catholic citizens to be uneducated laborers, uncreative persons programmed to accept authority rather than think for themselves, persons who stood on the margins of society as lookers-on. However, that very educational phenomenon that had solidified Catholics' sense of cohesion and pride in one period of history began slowly to destroy that cohesion in another. The very same education that so many Catholics had labored so hard to make as widely available as possible began to change its recipients considerably, opening them to new ideas and to the possibility of taking new and unheard of roles both in their society—and in their Church.

Further, the demographics of the Catholic population during these last forty years began to change dramatically. Just as more and more Catholics who had taken advantage of the education offered to them were forming a critical mass of educated Catholics, a new wave of immigrants, some educated, some not, began to dilute that mass, creating new demands for ways they could be helped to climb that same ladder their brother and sister Catholics had climbed early in the century. Yet the instruments to provide that education were not so readily at hand as they had been earlier, and the issue of where religion fit in the educational scene was much less urgent than in the past. And so the questions were different—not how do we find religious communities to build new schools and provide new teachers and how do we finance such a system, but how do we sustain and nurture the faith of our children when most of them will be educated within the public system and is it possible or wise (or even desirable) to push for voucher laws to support and strengthen the Catholic educational system?

Or is the more practical solution, rather than supporting the continuation of a school-based program which is beginning to weaken under the weight of the late twentieth-century American cultural forces, to more fully and intensively support a comprehensive parish-based religious education program (the CCD model)? Such a program would depend not on developing a full-blown school, with all that implies of professional training and certification in all areas of teaching, plus long-term personnel and a financial commitment, but would depend instead on the less-expensive alternative of asking an educated Catholic laity, under the direction of a professionally trained director of religious education, to share their knowledge of their faith with children in the parish in the evenings or on weekends.

Weighing the outcomes versus the costs of parish-based in contrast to school-based religious education has been an ongoing argument among American Catholics for over a century. Innumerable studies have been conducted to finally "settle" the issue and "prove" the advantages of one way over the other. Yet the criteria for validating the value of one over the other have never been widely agreed upon, and none of these studies has proven sturdy enough to answer the question with sufficient clarity and authority to settle the argument. Therefore, a continuing dual system of Catholic education seems likely to be an ongoing scenario, at least during the early twenty-first century, with the pros and cons still hotly debated, and parishes and individual Catholics lining up on both sides of the argument.

In the light of all these changes, to look at American Catholics in the last third of the twentieth century through the lens of education provides a very different view of them than in the earlier portion of the century. Their characteristics make it almost a "new" century. It is a time when Catholics are beginning to see themselves as integral to the American scene rather than outsiders. It is a time of much more prominent leadership among Catholics on the civic scene, solidified initially by the election of President Kennedy. It is a time when Catholics no longer feel they must differentiate themselves from their fellow citizens by a set of Catholic propositions to counter a set of Protestant propositions or a set of Catholic associations which mirror a set of secular associations, e.g., the Catholic History Association side by side with the National History Association.

Most especially it is a time when acceptance of ecclesiastical authority is tempered significantly by dependence on the internal authority that comes from education. Catholics have indeed come of age and their strong American strain of independent thinking brings them often into conflict with the rigidities of a European church. Somewhat like their earlier experience of needing to establish their position vis-à-vis prevailing American educational policy which neither understands nor values Catholic doctrines and ecclesiology, they now find themselves needing to clarify their position vis-à-vis a European church that neither understands nor values American principles of freedom and individual rights.

The results of such quasi-adversarial situations are frequently more strengthening than weakening. Since such situations require that each party clarify and synthesize their values, they can sometimes result in useful—if not perfect—compromises. American Catholics, at the start of the twenty-first century, seem positioned in just such a relationship, both with their Church and with their government.

One illustration of such a troubling relationship with their Church is the present conversation around the apostolic constitution *Ex corde eccle-*

siae, addressed to all Catholic colleges and universities throughout the world. The document is, first of all, a clear affirmation by the Vatican of the values of higher education, both to the Church and to society. However, accompanying strong positive statements of support for such indispensable marks as institutional autonomy and academic freedom as essential components of a Catholic university are what many college and university administrators perceive as statements contradicting those marks.

Especially troubling to these administrators is the return in the document to the demand of Canon 812 from the 1983 Code of Canon Law, requiring that "teachers of theological disciplines in any institution of higher studies must have a mandate from the competent ecclesiastical authority." A further concern is the statement that diocesan bishops should "reserve to themselves, insofar as possible, such powers as to enable them to preserve and strengthen the Catholic identity of the university." Such requirements, and several other statements in the document as well, fly in the face of institutional governance patterns and structures common to American law, especially law governing higher educational institutions. Presidents of American colleges and universities see these requirements as juridical norms imposed to assure that an institution is Catholic, effectively removing responsibility for the Catholicity of an institution from its board and placing it instead in the hands of a Church official external to the institution.

Interestingly, however, beneath this uneasy layer of confrontation and/or potential confrontation, lies also a strong layer of loyalty to a Church which still exercises a strong power over and influence on them. These are Catholics who proudly believe they are part of a worldwide religion with a tradition that stretches back to the first centuries of Christianity and stretches ahead to an unknown future. But these are also Catholics who are proud of their American culture and its ability to create new jobs and new ideas and new technology to shape a new century. There is little evidence that American Catholics desire to jettison either of these anchors.

And so this "new" twentieth century segues into the twenty-first, with American Catholics strongly positioned to exercise a leading role in the American scene and in the international Church. It will be instructive to see what roads are taken and what compromises are struck.

Biblical Scholarship:
When Tradition Met Method

Patricia M. McDonald, S.H.C.J.

Although family photographs may interest another family member, we tend to hold back from showing them (at least in quantity) to those who do not know well most of the people depicted in them. Similarly, someone trained in biblical studies may hesitate to write a whole chapter about the progress of that discipline in the twentieth century. It is, after all, a rather specialized field. Nevertheless, the risk should be taken. Many who would like to integrate the Scriptures into their lives find the task daunting because it seems that biblical studies have become just another narrow area of expertise to which they, as specialists in other fields, have no easy access. They may even feel as though other people's academic study of the Bible has spoiled their innocent understanding of it without supplying a substitute. A sense of how the discipline has developed during the century may help them to understand the situation better.

Despite the Catholic rejection of the Reformers' claim that Scripture, without the Church's tradition, is sufficient for salvation (*solā scripturā*, "by Scripture alone"), Catholics have never regarded the Bible as "just another book." So biblical scholarship in the Church of the twentieth century can be understood as the narrative by which, in a particular set of historical circumstances, two dynamics were at work. One is that biblical scholars worked diligently and with great seriousness to understand the Bible and to interpret it for their contemporaries. At the same time, those with a particular responsibility for the well being of the Church took equal care to preclude the possibility that the results of such scholarship might imperil either ordinary Christians or the whole body.

Because understanding the Bible aright is central to Christian living, both sides expended much energy. At times, one element predominated over the other: hierarchical control in the 1920s and 1930s, and the historical critical method from the 1960s to the 1980s. At other stages, particularly at mid-century and toward its close, this imbalance was, in significant measure, countered by an awareness that for the Bible to animate the Church's life, the best possible intellectual insights must somehow be combined with an uncompromising fidelity to the tradition. This dialectic continues today, which is another reason why a consideration of twentieth-century biblical studies might throw some light on contemporary experiences.

Setting the Scene

During the nineteenth century, there was a great expansion of what was initially called "higher criticism."[1] Now usually referred to as the historical critical method, higher criticism was developed and initially practiced mostly by German Protestant scholars. Newly aware of the Bible's affinities with other literature, artifacts, and cultural practices of the ancient world, they tried to establish how Scripture came to reach its present form. For example, they found parallels to various Old Testament stories in other ancient Near Eastern traditions, and suggested "sources" for the Pentateuch and for the Synoptic Gospels. People came to realize that the Bible, in addition to containing much ancient history, also had a history of its own, because of the cultural contexts in which it was produced.

Although within liberal Protestantism these developments could lead to the Bible's being considered as merely a human book, that was certainly not the case for most Christians. For them it never ceased to be also the Word of God, the witness to the community's experience of Jesus. They needed to develop ways of talking about what made this book special and how that related to what scholars were discovering, or claiming to discover, about the stages and conditions in which it came into existence. In 1870 the Vatican Council I had referred to God as the author of Scripture (*Dei Filius,* chapter 2, "On Revelation"). However, the meaning and implications of that phrase still remained to be decided, since the books already had human authors. So, even as some Catholics took up the challenge of Leo XIII's 1893 encyclical *Providentissimus Deus* by setting themselves to learn ancient languages, to study the literature and other cultural artifacts of the societies that produced them, and to use historical methods to further the Church's theological understanding, others continued to ponder and argue about what it meant to say that God is the author of Scripture. Even people who were not theologians, but were familiar

---

[1] It was thus distinguished from "lower criticism," now known as textual criticism. The latter is the art and science by which scholars construct as best they can the original Hebrew, Greek, or, occasionally, Aramaic texts of a biblical book. For this they use all the available manuscripts, none of them the document actually penned by the sacred writer.

with current developments in history and the secular sciences, became interested in "the biblical question."

As the twentieth century opened, then, biblical studies were a vibrant center of attention. In 1890 the Dominican Marie-Joseph Lagrange had founded in Jerusalem the Ecole Biblique for the study of archaeology and the Bible. Two years later, he established the *Revue Biblique* (1892), the first scholarly journal devoted to biblical studies (excluding a very short-lived one edited by Alfred Loisy). Biblical topics were prominent at the Fourth International Catholic Scientific Congress that took place in Fribourg, Switzerland, in 1897.

Pope Leo XIII followed up on his encyclical of 1893 by founding the Pontifical Biblical Commission in 1902. Like the encyclical, the commission had a twofold purpose: to foster the understanding of Scripture and to defend it from "every breath of error . . . [and] . . . temerarious opinion," in the words of the apostolic letter establishing the commission. From 1904 its functions included granting advanced academic degrees in Scripture, a new departure. The Biblical Commission consisted of a small group of cardinals, two secretaries, and a number of "consultors" (initially twelve but soon about forty). The latter were biblical scholars from different countries who were appointed for indefinite terms to provide expertise as required. Among the original consultors was Charles Grannan (1846–1924), an American priest of the Archdiocese of New York.[2] Leo had also intended to establish a biblical institute but died before he could do so. In 1909 his successor, Pius X, founded the Pontifical Biblical Institute and entrusted it to the Society of Jesus.

The United States: Seminaries and "The New York Review"

Although Americans had a representative among the consultors to the Biblical Commission, the Catholic biblical scene in the United States at the start of this century was very small and restricted. It consisted of a mere handful of priests who taught in the Sulpician-run seminaries on the east coast (in Baltimore, Maryland; Brighton, Massachusetts; and Yonkers, New York), at the Jesuit Woodstock College near Baltimore, and at the Catholic University of America, founded at Washington, D.C., in 1887. These priests had strong links with Europe: nearly all of them were born and educated there, and most had an institutional connection with Paris or Rome, through the Sulpicians or Jesuits. So they were very much involved in the revival of

---

[2] Since its reorganization by Pope Paul VI in 1971, the Pontifical Biblical Commission is an advisory body to the Congregation for the Doctrine of the Faith. Its members are not cardinals, but twenty biblical scholars appointed by the pope for five-year terms.

interest in biblical studies that was taking place in Europe. They were soon joined by others (also mostly from Europe), as the Catholic University of America recruited the best scholars it could find to staff the new institution.

There was, for example, the French diocesan priest Henry Hyvernat (1858–1941), the first faculty member to be appointed at the Catholic University of America. He had studied at the Sulpician seminary at Issy, outside Paris, under the renowned Scripture scholar Fulcran Vigouroux, S.S. (1837–1915), who had recommended him for the new university[3] (Lagrange had been in the same class). Hyvernat specialized in Christian Arabic studies and founded what is now the Catholic University of America's Department of Semitics and Egyptian Languages and Literatures. Charles Grannan, mentioned already as a consultor to the Biblical Commission, had been a seminarian in Rome and studied Scripture in Bonn and Leipzig before coming to Washington in 1891.

Sulpicians were prominent among this group of priest-scholars. They included the Irish-born John Hogan (1829–1901), who had taught at Issy and who, although not strictly a biblical specialist, influenced younger Sulpicians who were. Francis Gigot (1859–1920) and Joseph Bruneau (1866–1933), two French Sulpicians who spent most of their lives in the United States, had been seminarians at Issy. Subsequently, at the Institut Catholique in Paris, Bruneau was taught by Alfred Loisy, a diocesan priest who was, with Lagrange, the major Catholic biblical scholar of the day. Bruneau seems to have been Loisy's American literary agent at least until 1903.[4] Bruneau's confrere, James Driscoll (1859–1922), a native of Vermont who had studied in Canada and Paris, also had connections with Loisy, extending him moral support and once offering his services as a translator.[5] During the early years of the century, Gigot and Bruneau were professors at the New York archdiocesan seminary dedicated to St. Joseph, in the Dunwoodie section of Yonkers, where Driscoll was rector from 1902 until 1909.

The Westphalia-born Jesuit Anthony Maas (1858–1927) taught at Woodstock College.[6] By contrast with others mentioned here, Maas had a very different, highly negative attitude to higher criticism that he aired in

---

[3] See C. Joseph Nuesse, *The Catholic University of America: A Centennial History* (Washington, D.C.: The Catholic University of America Press, 1990) 57.

[4] Michael DeVito, *The New York Review, 1905–1908,* United States Catholic Historical Society Monograph Series 34 (New York: United States Catholic Historical Society, 1977) 199.

[5] Ibid., 210.

[6] See, for example, Gerald P. Fogarty, *American Catholic Biblical Scholarship: A History from the Early Republic to Vatican II* (San Francisco: Harper & Row, 1989) 40.

the pages of *The American Ecclesiastical Review.*[7] Henri A. Poels (1868–1948) was a diocesan priest from the Netherlands who had studied at Louvain. He taught Old Testament, particularly the Pentateuch, at the Catholic University of America from 1904 until 1910. By that time he had fallen foul of Maas and other Jesuits and of a 1906 "response" of the Biblical Commission on the Mosaic authorship of the Pentateuch. Poels's departure from the Catholic University of America resulted from a particularly egregious example of priestly politics. By far the most colorful member of this group of biblical scholars was Gabriel Oussani (1875–1934), a Chaldean Catholic from Baghdad. Oussani had studied classical Arabic, Syriac, Turkish, and French at the Patriarchal Seminary in Mosul, near ancient Nineveh. One of his main interests was archaeology. After extensive travel through the Levant and studies and ordination in Rome in 1900, he undertook further research in Semitic Languages at Johns Hopkins University before moving to Dunwoodie in 1904.[8] There he taught until his death in 1934.

All these professors came equipped with a basic seminary training in dogmatic theology, which made them appreciate the importance of coming to understand how God communicates divine truths to historically-bound humanity. Thus, they asked questions such as, what is the relationship between Scripture and divine revelation? Furthermore, if God is the "author" of Scripture, how is the work of the human authors to be understood? How does inspiration work? In what sense is the Bible inerrant? In their work as seminary professors and scholars, some (Bruneau and Driscoll, for example) continued to focus mostly on such theological questions and to introduce to American audiences the discussion that was already going on in Europe. Others became interested in archaeology, other cultural aspects of the ancient Near East, or the biblical text itself.

The work was not without its dangers: the Italian exegete and modernist Giovanni Genocchi noted the link that some were making between critical biblical studies and Americanism, which Leo XIII had censured in 1899.[9] (Americanism was an excess of enthusiasm in adapting Catholicism to the American legal and religious situation.) The connection was that both biblical scholars and "Americanists," in trying to give human realities their due, were regarded as not taking sufficient account of the divine element. (Grannan, for example, wrote an article entitled "The Human Element of

---

[7] This journal was entitled *The Ecclesiastical Review* between 1901 and 1943.

[8] E. Harold Smith, "Recollections of the Aftermath," *Continuum* 3 (1965–66) 236; Thomas J. Shelley, *Dunwoodie: The History of St. Joseph's Seminary, Yonkers, New York* (Westminster, Md.: Christian Classics, Inc., 1993) 127–8 and n. 20.

[9] Fogarty, *American Catholic Biblical Scholarship,* 67.

Scripture" in the *Catholic University Bulletin* for April 1898.) This approach made nervous a papacy that had already lost most of its territory and felt threatened, sometimes with good reason, by the trajectories of modern thought.

Sulpician John Hogan was one who connected the two worlds of "Americanism" and biblical studies. His letters show that he gave "strong endorsement of almost all aspects of the Americanist cause."[10] As the director of Divinity College (i.e., of the priest students in residence at the Catholic University of America), Hogan had worked closely with Bishop John Keane, the first rector, who had been abruptly dismissed in 1896 because he was seen as too liberal. In addition, though, Hogan had retained contact with the biblicist Alfred Loisy after the 1893 controversy that had led to Loisy's removal from the Institut Catholique and to Leo's encyclical *Providentissimus Deus*. Loisy did not become any more tractable in the closing years of the nineteenth century and the opening of the twentieth. Many in Rome regarded his espousal of religious and political autonomy as increasingly dangerous, for France was moving toward the separation of Church and state that eventually took effect in 1905, with painful consequences for the Sulpicians (and many other Catholics) there. Unsurprisingly, the Sulpician superior general who took office in 1901 soon ruled that publications by American members could no longer be censored locally but must be sent to Paris. These were difficult days to be teaching Scripture in the east coast seminaries, at least if one wanted to publish.

Yet seminaries (and the Catholic University of America, which also educated seminarians) were the only institutions in the United States where serious Catholic biblical scholarship was to be found in 1900. Thus, at the turn of the century, all of the Catholic biblical scholars in this country were priests who worked in institutions staffed almost entirely by priests, and whose students were either seminarians or (at Catholic University of America) priests undertaking graduate studies.

In the 1890s such scholars had published freely. Mostly they produced works for their students to use, for there was very little available in English. Thus, Bruneau produced a *Harmony of the Gospels* (1898). Between 1896 and 1906 Gigot wrote a number of textbooks for seminarians. His two-part *Outlines of the Life of Our Lord* appeared in 1896 and 1897. It was followed by similar outlines of Jewish and of New Testament history (1897 and 1898) and three volumes of introduction to the study of

---

[10] Christopher J. Kauffman, *Tradition and Transformation in Catholic Culture: The Priests of Saint Sulpice in the United States from 1971 to the Present* (New York: Macmillan, 1988) 169–70.

Scripture (1900, 1901 and 1906). Gigot's projected fourth volume, on the New Testament, did not appear for reasons that will soon become clear. In 1898 Hogan published *Clerical Studies*. Intended to advance the intellectual and spiritual life of seminarians and young priests, this book presents Hogan's understanding of the various elements of the seminary curriculum, from the natural sciences to biblical studies. Its chapters had originally been articles in the *American Ecclesiastical Review* which, along with other periodicals such as the *Catholic University Bulletin,* was an important vehicle for the exchange of ideas about the intellectual components of Catholicism, including biblical issues.

There were also attempts at introducing to the wider Catholic public the developments in the study of Scripture. Gigot published *Biblical Lectures: Ten Popular Essays on General Aspects of the Sacred Scriptures* (Baltimore and New York: John Murphy, 1901). The series opened with "The Bible as Literature," included essays on historical, dogmatic, moral, and liturgical aspects of the Bible, then dealt with specific topics: theocracy, the miraculous, the "popular mind," and the Bible as the inspired word of God.

Much more ambitious was the initiative taken in the first few years of the new century by a highly dynamic and talented group of faculty from the seminary at Dunwoodie. In 1905 they founded a bimonthly periodical called *The New York Review*. The leaders in this enterprise were the New York priests Francis P. Duffy (later chaplain of New York's famed Sixty-Ninth Infantry Regiment) and John Brady. Their Sulpician rector, James Driscoll, and five of his confreres also lent their enthusiasm and talents. At the same time, though, the Sulpician leadership in the United States made it clear that the society was not responsible for The New York Review. Officially, it came under the jurisdiction of the archbishop of New York, John M. Farley. He, however, seems to have had little idea of what was going on until shortly before he suppressed the review in 1908.[11]

Despite its short life, *The New York Review* is of great significance. In particular, it shows how sophisticated the best of American Catholic biblical thought was during the first decade of the twentieth century. It was unlike the other Catholic journals available in the United States at that time. *The New York Review* was subtitled *A Journal of the Ancient Faith and Modern Thought.* The first of its five specified objectives was "to treat in a scholarly fashion, yet in a manner intelligible to the ordinary cultured mind, topics of interest bearing on Theology, Scripture, Philosophy and

---

[11] By 1908 Dunwoodie was no longer a Sulpician seminary, for in January 1906 five of the six Sulpicians there (all except Bruneau) left the society and transferred to the archdiocese, in effect taking the seminary with them.

the cognate Sciences" (1:1 [June–July 1905] 132). Here, readers could learn from some of the best scholars of the day, American and European, on topics ranging from the Fathers of the Church to moral theology and beyond. The aim was, as the third "object" specified, "to secure the united efforts of the most eminent Catholic scholars, lay and clerical, throughout the world, for the discussion and solution of problems and difficulties connected with Religion" (ibid.). The editors delivered on this promise.

As befitted the times, articles on scriptural issues were numerous, up-to-the-minute, and written mostly by priests concerned to integrate their scholarly training and their position as seminary professors. Lagrange had an article in volume III. The Dunwoodie faculty contributed massively. Thus, readers could learn about the Code of Hammurabi, the interpretation of Genesis 14, or "The Story of Assyro-Babylonian Explorations" from Gabriel Oussani, who had direct experience of all three. They could allow the ever-careful Francis Gigot to introduce them to higher criticism, first by means of a general explanation, and then by using it to explicate the synoptic gospels and the books of Isaiah, Job, and Jonah. They could learn about "Recent Views on Biblical Inspiration" from James Driscoll or about "The Sacrifice of Christ" from Bruneau. These men and others also wrote numerous book reviews informing readers about the latest (mostly European) publications. The context for all of this was supplied by the "notes" in which Duffy kept the Catholic of "ordinary cultured mind" supplied with current information about people, pronouncements (of the pope and the Pontifical Biblical Commission, for example), and politics.

The review, and the relatively unrestricted cultural and ecumenical contacts that went with it, lasted only a few years. Its demise came soon after the publication, in 1907, of the anti-modernist decree *Lamentabili sane exitu* and the encyclical *Pascendi Dominici gregis,* and the ensuing climate of suspicion of "advanced" ideas and those who held them. Most of the Dunwoodie group were sent to other assignments. Those remaining at the seminary, notably Gigot and Oussani, were (each in his own way) exceedingly circumspect thereafter. The former seems to have accepted complete submission as the price of remaining what he had always been, a seminary professor. Thus, the little that Gigot published after 1908 expressed views that were quite different from those in the books he had written around the turn of the century. Oussani, an altogether more robust character, took a different tack. According to the witness of E. Harold Smith, after 1908 Oussani

> no longer prepared his lectures but talked from his acquired knowledge. He always offered excellent and up-to-date bibliographies; was not only willing but desirous to devote as much time to answering questions as the semi-

narians wished. These queries did not have to be kept within range of the class subject. Probably he did more to stimulate minds and scholarly interest by his asides than he did by his formal lectures.[12]

Smith reports student conversations with Oussani that demonstrate his independence and integrity of mind in scholarly matters (including the fourteen restrictive "responses" that the Pontifical Biblical Commission had issued between 1905 and 1915). For Oussani as for others, though, "the thought of withdrawing from the Church was not even a remote temptation."[13] On the other hand, although they continued to teach and to develop their thought, he and many others in the same situation took care not to publish during these years.

There were many other casualties of the Roman fear that "secular" approaches to knowledge would imperil the Church's understanding of Scriptures. They included seminary professors who lacked Oussani's liberty of spirit and replaced intelligent teaching with some combination of wooden certainties and pious irrelevancies. Thomas J. Shelley[14] mentions one Joseph Nelson, a teacher at Dunwoodie, as an example of this type. The deleterious effects spread widely, as such "professors" deprived generations of seminarians of a biblical formation that could have opened the Scriptures to them and those to whom they later ministered. The breakthrough would not come until 1943, when Pius XII's encyclical *Divino afflante Spiritu* made clear (among other things) the importance of understanding the human aspects of the biblical text.

The Silent Time

Throughout the 1920s and 1930s, the scholarly study of Scripture was scarcely detectable in Catholic circles. Nevertheless, there were always some priests, diocesan and religious, who were sent to study ancient languages and biblical archaeology; indeed, the Roman authorities actively encouraged it. For Americans, the most accessible place for such study was Hyvernat's department of Semitic and Egyptian Languages and Literatures in Washington. Others went to Rome or Jerusalem to study at the Pontifical Biblical Institute or the Ecole Biblique.

At a less exalted level, there were also religious educators for whom reading the Bible (but in a non-critical way) was an essential part of the program. This was the exception rather than the rule, since most Catholic colleges based their courses on texts in which Scripture was not prominent:

[12] Smith, "Recollections of the Aftermath," 236–7.
[13] Ibid., 237.
[14] Shelley, *Dunwoodie*, 192.

handbooks of apologetics or (in the case of Dominicans) Walter Farrell's *Companion to the Summa*. It was, however, otherwise with the undergraduate religious studies at the Catholic University of America, particularly during the tenure of William H. Russell, a priest of the archdiocese of Dubuque, who taught there from 1931 until his death in 1952. According to Patrick Carey, Russell emphasized the centrality of the Bible much more than did his longer-serving and better-known colleague John Montgomery Cooper. Carey notes that Russell's use of the Bible was essentially formational: he wished his students to come to know Jesus from the Gospels.[15] At the time, this approach was criticized for having little intellectual challenge or content, chiefly by Dominican friars who served on the faculty of numerous women's colleges. Yet at least it familiarized generations of students with Gospel stories. There is also evidence that students in many high schools, particularly those run by religious, were given significant exposure to the Bible (and especially the New Testament) in this manner. So life in the Church went on, although its academic component either was not high or was kept safely away from the Bible as it affected contemporary experience.

The Awakening

Into the midst of all this, in 1936 came a proposal from the American hierarchy to make a new translation of the New Testament that would replace the Rheims-Challoner version then in use. This initiative came from Bishop Edwin V. O'Hara of Kansas City, the chair of the Episcopal Committee on the Confraternity of Christian Doctrine (CCD). He gathered a group of Catholic biblical scholars. At the suggestion of Romain Butin, a Marist who had taught with distinction at the Catholic University of America since 1912, these priests then formed themselves into the Catholic Biblical Association of America (CBA). It probably was not at all evident at the time, but far-reaching changes were about to occur.

The establishment of the CBA was undoubtedly of central importance for Catholic biblical scholarship in this country. In particular, it made possible the consolidation of the Church's already substantial (although largely unrecognized) resources in the area of scriptural understanding. The aim of the association, to promote Bible study, was fulfilled in two main ways: by publications and by enabling its members to give one another "encouragement and support."

---

[15] Patrick W. Carey, "College Theology in Historical Perspective," *American Catholic Traditions: Resources for Renewal,* ed. Sandra Yocum Mize and William Portier, Annual Publication of the College Theology Society, vol. 42 (Maryknoll, N.Y.: Orbis Books, 1997) 251.

The publications sponsored by the CBA are many and varied. Of primary importance are the biblical translations, produced in association with the CCD, for liturgical, devotional, and scholarly use. By the time the completed New American Bible appeared in 1970, the association's respected journal, the *Catholic Biblical Quarterly,* was in its thirty-first year and the *Jerome Biblical Commentary* (1968) testified further to the high level of scholarship among CBA members. A fresh translation of the New Testament came out in 1986, the *New Jerome Biblical Commentary* in 1990, and a revision of the Psalms in 1991. The work continues with the ongoing revision of the Old Testament. By-products of these enterprises range from scholarly monographs (in which young scholars can publish their research), through biblical abstracts (an important tool for technical work), to *The Bible Today,* which aims at making the fruits of such work accessible to non-specialists.

Equally important was the impetus that the CBA gave to the growth and strengthening of the Catholic biblical scene by enabling the personal contact and interaction of its members. Some aspects of this have been constant. For example, since 1936 the association has held annual meetings (with the exception of 1943), and regional meetings take place in many parts of the country. The CBA now also sponsors visiting professorships to the Ecole Biblique and the Pontifical Biblical Institute, supports some archaeological research, and offers stipends and scholarships to biblical students. Some of its early initiatives (including summer Bible institutes, workshops, Bible weeks, and public lectures) were later taken over by other groups or institutions.

From the 1940s onward, the CBA was a forum in which biblical scholars who were not Catholic could experience (often to their surprise) the high level of expertise of their Catholic counterparts. The prime example here is William F. Albright, of the prestigious Oriental Seminary of Johns Hopkins University. Albright, a biblical archaeologist of world renown, addressed the association at its 1944 meeting and was voted to honorary life membership in it. He had already (in 1942) been impressed by his first Jesuit graduate student, Roger T. O'Callaghan. Later, he would mentor a significant number of Catholic priest-scholars, some of whom (including Joseph A. Fitzmyer, s.j., and the late Raymond E. Brown, s.s.) became recognized as biblical scholars of the first rank. For several years, Albright also arranged for Patrick Skehan, a priest from the archdiocese of New York who taught in the Catholic University of America Semitics Department, to substitute for him at Hopkins during his archaeological expeditions. As Gerald P. Fogarty, s.j., notes,[16]

---

[16] Fogarty, *American Catholic Biblical Scholarship,* 243.

Albright "was the key figure in gaining recognition of American Catholic biblical scholarship in Protestant circles."

The Breakthrough: *"Divino afflante Spiritu"*

Pius XII's 1943 encyclical *Divino afflante Spiritu* (DAS) is rightly regarded as the watershed of Catholic biblical scholarship. Published to commemorate the fiftieth anniversary of Leo XIII's *Providentissimus Deus,* the encyclical made clear that Catholic biblical scholars could, indeed should, use the historical method as an important component of their investigations. So those already doing so, notably many graduates of the Pontifical Biblical Institute and the Ecole Biblique, now had papal support for their practice. The pope praised highly the activities of such scholars, which he specified in detail and recognized as being in essential continuity with those of the most honored of scriptural interpreters in the Church's earlier centuries. He urged that others in the Church judge their work "not only with equity and justice, but also with the greatest charity," and refused to allow "that intemperate zeal which imagines that whatever is new should for that reason be opposed or suspected" (DAS 47). Basic to the encyclical is a vivid awareness that biblical interpretation exists to bring to others "the treasures of the word of God" (60) so that it "might daily be more deeply and fully understood and more intensely loved" (49). In other words, expositions of Scripture were intended to "help all the faithful to lead a life that is holy and worthy of a Christian" (24).

Although the biblical guild was immensely encouraged by the papal letter, not everyone was so enthusiastic. Indeed, many professors of dogmatic theology on all the continents refused to hear what it said, because of an antagonistic attitude to critical study that is (with some reason) deeply embedded in the Church's ways of thinking and operating. There was a genuine fear that the historical method laid the Church open to the prevalent academic climate of anti-religious rationalism, which had no place for anything that could not be explained in terms of science or history. Such an attitude was, of course, quite alien to the members of the CBA. They were nearly all priests who were responsible to their bishops or religious superiors responsible to their institutions (mostly seminaries) and to the welfare of the Catholic community at large, including its academic component. On the other hand, their willingness to include a "scientific" approach to the Scriptures and their increasing contact with others in the academy caused some in other disciplines to react defensively—to put it politely. So for several decades, both in European countries and the United States, there were repeated crises of greater or smaller magnitude, when opponents of biblical criticism would attempt to drive from the field those who worked according to the terms of the encyclical.

In the United States, for example, CBA members experienced much trouble from Msgr. Joseph Clifford Fenton, a professor of sacred theology at the Catholic University of America who edited the influential *American Ecclesiastical Review.* Fenton made effective use of his friends. These included Giuseppe Cardinal Pizzardo, prefect of the Congregation of Seminaries and Universities and, later, secretary of the Holy Office; Alfredo Cardinal Ottaviani, another secretary of the Holy Office; Egidio Vagnozzi, apostolic delegate to the United States from 1958 until 1967; and William J. McDonald, the rector of the Catholic University of America from 1957 until 1967. There was a major incident in 1961, when the CBA protested repeated attacks on American biblical scholars, the last straw being a Marquette commencement address by Vagnozzi that the *American Ecclesiastical Review* published. Then, in the following year, Edward Siegman, C.PP.S., was compelled to resign his position at Catholic University, ostensibly on grounds of poor health. There are, however, grounds for concluding that Fenton's long-running public opposition to Siegman as a biblical scholar (and, in particular, Siegman's direction of a doctoral dissertation on the Lucan annunciation narratives) had much to do with what took place.

Despite such setbacks, *Divino afflante Spiritu* has marked an irreversible point in the papacy's attitude to Scripture. It removed the blocks to using the historical critical method and, indeed, encouraged its use, although always within the context of the wider tradition. The encyclical was noteworthy in the way it drew attention to the existence of different (and, obviously, ancient) literary genres in the Bible and connected this with the notion of what the author had intended to say in any particular passage (DAS 35–9). So what were clearly errors of historical fact (a sensitive topic earlier in the century) could, in some instances, be merely the result of "those customary modes of expression peculiar to the ancients [and] . . . sanctioned by common usage" (DAS 38). Vatican II, in its Dogmatic Constitution on Divine Revelation *(Dei Verbum)*, would take that a step further: Scripture teaches "solidly, faithfully, and without error that truth which God wanted put into the sacred writings *for the sake of our salvation*" (DV 11, emphasis added). These developments, which had in large measure been worked out by Lagrange, were immensely liberating to anyone who realized the need to understand the biblical books in the light of their own history.

The momentum that *Divino afflante Spiritu* generated would be maintained by a series of official (or, in the first case, quasi-official) pronouncements from the Pontifical Biblical Commission. In 1955 two periodicals, one of Benedictine and the other of Franciscan editorship, carried two separate but substantially similar reviews of the same book, one in German and the other in Latin, signed respectively by the commission's secretary and undersecretary. The reviews, in effect, repealed the fourteen restrictive "responses" that the commission had put out between 1905 and 1915 by distinguishing between those relating to faith and morals (which none of them did) and those that dealt merely with matters that were literary or historical. Positively, the commission issued in 1964 an Instruction on the Historical Truth of the Gospels, *Sancta Mater Ecclesia,* that encouraged the use of form criticism and redaction criticism, and set out the three stages of the gospel tradition (the time of Jesus, the time of the apostles and disciples after the resurrection, and the time of the evangelists) that would be taken up in Vatican II's *Dei Verbum.* More recently, in 1993 the Pontifical Biblical Commission marked the centenary of *Providentissimus Deus* by issuing a document whose English title is The Interpretation of the Bible in the Church. In its opening chapter, the "indispensable" historical critical method is surveyed and assessed, along with numerous other modern methods. The remaining three chapters consider hermeneutical questions, characteristics of Catholic interpretation, and the interpretation of the Bible in the Church. As has become typical of such documents, it tried to be even-handed in its treatment of the human and the divine aspects of the Scriptures.

That balance has been hard to maintain throughout the century. It is, indeed, arguable that it has never been fully achieved, at least for more than a fleeting moment. At the start, the Church's stress was on the God-given aspect of the Bible; this was necessary to counter tendencies to see it simply as a human text. From the time of *Divino afflante Spiritu* onward, however, although the official documents always gave due weight to the human and divine aspects of the Bible (often likening the situation to that of the incarnation), scholars tended to hear more clearly their call for using modern methods of biblical criticism and the encouragement to make Scripture available to non-specialists. This, too, is quite understandable. At the same time, though, this somewhat selective reading of Church documents sowed the seed of problems that would gradually become apparent.

These problems are of two main types. The first comes from the radical break between historical critical exegesis and the centuries of pre-critical exegesis that preceded it and on which the Church's theology has always been based. Admittedly, Church teaching from the Roman See since *Divino afflante Spiritu* has strongly emphasized the continuity between the work of modern exegetes and their (pre-critical) forebears. Yet that still leaves scholars to work out exactly how, in practice, the present situation relates to the Church's past use of Scripture. The second problem concerns the future direction of biblical understanding in the Church: what kinds of contributions can critical biblical scholarship make? That is to say, to what extent can (or should) it be expected to ground a theology that will express and help to develop the community's self-understanding? Let us look at each of these problems in turn.

In the first case, the difficulty is that the historical method, like modernity itself, tends to present itself as the only intellectually respectable way to study the Bible. Anything that is pre-critical is liable to suffer by comparison with it. This is because the older approaches are often regarded as relevant only to people already committed to the truths that they produce. By contrast, critical methods present themselves as "neutral." Those who use them often think (quite falsely) that they are working without presuppositions and, therefore, that their conclusions are in principle available to anyone able to use his or her reasoning capacities.

There are various practical consequences of this. For example, to the extent that biblical criticism is thought to exclude the possibility of other kinds of knowledge (itself a presupposition), it separates exegetes from the faith tradition in which they are based. If nothing before the Enlightenment can be taken seriously by intelligent people who do not want to be deceived, exegetes risk losing contact with their co-religionists (theologians and ordinary Christians) who remain in closer contact with the larger tradition. That loss would be a major disaster for a biblical scholar who views the Bible as foundational to Christian self-understanding and practice. For the theologians and the ordinary Church members are precisely the ones whom the exegete is attempting to serve: biblical scholarship that does not help them has lost most of its *raison d'être*. At the same time, though, there are ecumenical consequences. Because the critical method enables contact across and beyond denominational lines, it has allowed (and, in some cases, virtually compelled) Catholic exegetes to be in dialogue with those of other traditions and with the academy at large. This freedom, which Catholic biblical scholars struggled hard to attain, has produced many benefits for the Church, although it has also involved some scholars in conversations that are of doubtful religious relevance in the long term.

The second problem has proven to be no less refractory. For recent gains in biblical understanding, although of intrinsic interest to scholars, have often turned out to be scant fare for sustaining the life of the religious communities to which those scholars belong. This is not necessarily evident in the work of the exegetes themselves. It often is, though, when their ideas and methods are taken up by those with less knowledge or pastoral sensitivity. Thus, anyone can now amass large amounts of very interesting information about the ancient Near East, the composition of the Gospels, or the social situation presupposed by a particular Pauline letter, for example. Yet when the acid of criticism destroys traditional views, it leaves (at least initially) only the rather meager "historical facts" that our sources allow us to "know" with a greater or lesser degree of certainty. Sometimes such knowledge can be contextualized within the life of the community: the many different forms taken by the death-and-resurrection paradigm in the New Testament, for example, can vastly increase people's ability to make sense of certain aspects of their lives. Often, though, attempts at updating people's biblical understanding have left them with mere information that unsettles without providing a new synthesis. The "so what?" question is prominent.

It probably did not have to be that way. For, as Denis Farkasfalvy has noted,[17] between *Divino afflante Spiritu* in 1943 and Vatican II in the early 1960s, there were Catholic theologians and exegetes who tried hard to find a grounding for Catholic exegesis in a clearer understanding of inspiration, canonicity, hermeneutics, and the patristic heritage. Among their number were Henri de Lubac, Karl Rahner, Yves Congar, Hans Urs von Balthasar, Pierre Benoit, and Luis Alonso Schökel. Yet, on the whole, their work was largely bypassed by exegetes, particularly in the United States. Perhaps that was, in part, because the American exegetes' colleagues, the systematic theologians, were so focused on the relatively unbiblical systems of Rahner and Bernard Lonergan.

Another part of the answer seems to lie in the wide range of options (John Donahue has aptly termed it "a dazzling kaleidoscope") opened up by Vatican II. No longer restricted to seminaries, biblical studies grew suddenly, as it was undertaken by much larger numbers of Catholics, clerical and lay. To a large extent, the different religious traditions were either lost sight of or deemed irrelevant, as students joined with those of other denominations to learn biblical languages and the historical critical method. At the same time, though, they became aware of the contextual nature of knowledge. So they researched with great diligence and success the historical and cultural background of the biblical texts. They became conscious of their own social locations (or, at least, of some aspects of them) and opened up the Bible to groups that had previously not found much of a voice there. They showed how Scripture could be a valuable resource in the Church's mission to relieve human oppression. They wrote books, articles, and pamphlets; gave innumerable workshops, talks, retreats, classes,

---

[17] Denis Farkasfalvy, "A Heritage in Search of Heirs: The Future of Ancient Christian Exegesis," *Communio* 15:3 (Fall 1995) 505–19.

and (if they were priests) homilies; joined task forces and seminars; trained the next generations of students. The positive consequences of all this are obvious: the Bible became a vital force for many Catholics, often for the first time. Catholic biblical scholarship became academically respectable. Biblical scholars were providing many fascinating insights for popular audiences and their intellectual peers. This process still continues apace, particularly at the level of ordinary churchgoers, many of whom have a sense of the Bible's importance and a hunger for coming to understand it better. There are some excellent resources available to them.

At the same time, however, there has been a strong tendency for biblical studies to go its own way, even to build its own mini-universe, in isolation from broader theological or ecclesiological issues. Like all academic disciplines, the study of Scripture has become increasingly diverse and specialized. In consequence, an exegete's conversation partners are much more likely to be scholars from other Christian denominations or from the secular academy than the theologians from his or her own tradition. For a while, this was not perceived as a problem, and for many it still is not. There is, though, a growing consensus that, if pursued in a theological vacuum, biblical studies run the risk of losing touch with the Church's broader self-understanding. For example, it is frustrating to Catholic exegetes that, although those responsible for articulating the Church's official positions acknowledge the need for historical exegesis, they mostly make little use of it themselves; the *Catechism of the Catholic Church* (1994) is a case in point.

It is perhaps even more problematic that the specialization within the exegetical enterprise leaves exegetes unable to engage with the fundamental theological questions underlying the place of the Bible in Christian life. This is all part of a wider, societal situation that results from the fragmentation of disciplines. It also results more specifically from the changed demographics within the Church. Unlike the most prominent of their predecessors, younger biblical scholars are much less likely to be ordained men who belong to a residential religious community. So, although the new generations may be very well educated by the standards of the academy, their experience is less likely to include an extended education in philosophical and theological disciplines that is integrated into the community's apostolate and the Church's liturgical life and structures. Certainly, biblical scholars talk to one another, but what is less evident is serious, productive dialogue between them and theologians in other branches (including patristics scholars) for the sake of the wider Church. It seems obvious that this lack must somehow be supplied.

In Conclusion

The situation at the close of the twentieth century was, therefore, strikingly different from that at its beginning. In the United States today, biblical scholars in the Catholic tradition are numerous and varied. White male clerics are probably still the most influential group. Yet the field has been greatly enriched by the inclusion of large numbers of women, along with a growing contribution from those whose cultural roots are in Latino, African American, Native American, or Asian expressions of Catholicism. Gone are the old certainties whereby Catholics had degrees from seminaries and Catholic graduate schools, Lutherans from Lutheran schools and seminaries, and so on. It is now taken for granted (and, indeed, found to be most enriching) that they should be interacting with those of other faiths and none. In addition, their partners in conversation have extended beyond the philologists, archaeologists, and historians who were involved at the turn of the twentieth century. Now, those from a much wider range of disciplines are involved, including social scientists, literary critics, and philosophers of language. It is important to ensure that all who wish to participate may do so.

Yet, important though all that may be, it is not sufficient. The task now is to ensure that a further integration take place: with the Church's theological tradition. That will entail bringing the current situation into dialogue with, on the one hand, certain relevant aspects of the past and, on the other, the more seriously theological aspects of the present. In this process, the historical critical method will continue to play a necessary part in biblical studies. Throughout the twentieth century it has proved to be an excellent tool. It is, however, only one of many.

I should like to thank Paul Zilonka, C.P., and Gerard S. Sloyan for their comments on earlier drafts of this essay. —P.McD.

Ecumenism: From Isolation to a Vision of Christian Unity

Jeffrey Gros, F.S.C.

It is amazing when we look back to the turn of the twentieth century to see where we are moving at the dawn of the third millennium with our fellow Christian churches, Protestant, Orthodox, and Anglican. In looking ahead to the twenty-first century, Pope John Paul II called Catholics to focus on Christian unity, saying: "Among the most fervent petitions which the Church makes to the Lord during this important time, as the eve of the new millennium approaches, is that unity among all Christians of the various confessions will increase until they reach full communion" *(Terio millennio adveniente)*.

This is all the more marvelous when we recall the history of this century. It began with a condemnation of Anglican orders under Leo XIII in 1896, with condemnations of modernism and Americanism, and with an Austrian ambassador able to veto a papal election. During the course of the century we were able not only to come into dialogue with Anglicans, but by 1994 to conclude that sufficient work had been done together on Eucharist and ordained ministry; in 1995 John Paul II offered to reform the exercise of his office in the service to the unity of the churches, with an invitation to ecumenical advice on how to do so; by 1998 we moved toward putting aside differences on the issue of justification with the Lutherans; and we are committed to religious liberty as a Church. Indeed, not only does the Austro-Hungarian Emperor, or any other head of state, no longer have influence in papal elections and appointment of bishops, but only two countries in Europe, Monaco and Malta, have the Catholic Church as the established state church.

Yet the transition to a Church committed to full communion from a Church in defensive reaction against the revolutions of Europe, Enlightenment thought, the idea of religious liberty and pluralism, is so dramatic as to have stunned both Catholics, who lived through the conciliar era

(1959–65), and our fellow Christians who knew the Church before and after Pope John's great idea and the beginnings of the conciliar reforms, shepherded by Popes Paul VI and John Paul II.

We remember "mixed" marriages—i.e., with Protestants—occurring only in the sacristy or rectory. Today young people wonder why there would be any concern about a Mass in such a wedding, which church should be used, or what would be entailed in discerning if the Protestant spouse would receive communion. We remember when we did not go into Protestant churches except for funerals and weddings. Today we are encouraged to share regularly in ecumenical prayer and worship, and are often invited to speak in others churches.

We remember in the 1954 when Catholics were forbidden to attend the World Council of Churches meeting in Evanston, even as press. Today there is no meeting of the World Council that does not have full Catholic participation at some level. Almost sixty bishops' conferences around the world belong to their national councils. Over half of the dioceses in the United States belong to state or local councils.

Those of us who recall the 1950s or before realize that Catholics were cautioned about association with Orthodox and Protestants. Yet by 1987 the Catholic bishops of England and Wales could articulate with their fellow Christians: "It is our conviction that, as a matter of policy at all levels and in all places, our churches must now move from cooperation to clear commitment to each other, in search of the unity for which Christ prayed in common evangelism and service of the world."

From his very first encyclical through his twelfth, *Ut unum sint,* in 1995, Pope John Paul has made it clear that the unity of the churches, for him, is "a pastoral priority."

As we recall the history of the Holy Year Jubilees, from their founding under Boniface VIII in 1300 through those celebrated by Pius XII, there was always a great emphasis on a centralized papacy, pilgrimages to Rome, and promotion of indulgences. Although Roman hospitality, a modest indulgence, and papal initiatives are not absent, they are very muted in John Paul's 1994 letter initiating Jubilee preparations, On the Threshold of the Third Millennium. His focus on the biblical Jubilee theme (Leviticus 25), with its emphasis on liberation of captives, remission of debt, and sabbatical for the land, put forward social justice themes in remarkable contrast to the genesis of the Holy Year idea. John Paul's emphasis on repentance, calling conferences on the Holocaust and on the Inquisition, calling the Church to beg pardon for the sins of her members in the past, and pledging the Church to promote unity among Christians and outreach to the other world religions was bracing, even for some Catholics.

This development from a resistive, defensive, and anti-ecumenical Catholicism of the first half of the century to a Catholic identity with zeal for the unity of Christians at its center did not emerge over night. Indeed, it is the careful attention to prayer and the urging of the Holy Spirit that were the core of the conversion which has begun to overtake Christians, Catholics among them, so that they see coming closer to Christ as entailing coming closer to one another and therefore building solidarity toward the day when full communion can emerge among the churches.

In this brief essay we will review the early decades of this century. We will note the leadership of the Church and the stirrings that gave rise to the ecumenical impulse. We will then recount the mid-century shift, indicating how the dramatic story of the council and its aftermath unfolded. Then we will recount the developments since the council and the hopes that Catholics bring to the new millennium.

A Defensive Church and a Return to the Sources

The Church as an institution had suffered greatly in the eighteenth and nineteenth centuries as a result of the French revolution, with its anti-clerical and secularizing militancy. Catholicism came into the twentieth century with the trauma of the loss of the papal states in 1870 and the pope being virtually a prisoner in the Vatican. In Europe, Catholic countries such as France had expropriated the property and institutions of the Church and expelled religious.

While Pius IX had condemned religious liberty and democratic forms of government, the Church in the United States was thriving. However, as a collective of predominantly immigrant communities, often confronting overt Protestant prejudice, the Catholic Church of necessity was given to developing its internal identity and institutions, with little opportunity or invitation to ecumenical outreach. While Americans prospered under the regime of religious liberty and effective use of democratic institutions, this experience was not yet of use to the Church universal.

While the church in Europe was struggling for survival and the church in the United States was sinking roots in new soil, other movements were emerging in the churches that were to shape a more open and reconciling future. In the United States, the Episcopal Church made an initiative in 1886 which would become part of worldwide Anglicanism's basis for Christian unity at Lambeth in 1888, the so-called Chicago Lambeth Quadrilateral. In this they invited unity among the Christian churches on the basis of Scripture, the classical creeds, the two sacraments of baptism and Eucharist, and a ministry including bishops in the apostolic succession. In the United States, reformed theologian Philip Schaff founded the American Society of Church History in that same year, with the intent to recapture, in a Protestant context, the catholic and ecclesial dimensions of the Christian faith through the study of history, including pre-Reformation Church history.

The mid-nineteenth-century Oxford Movement in England, but with significant influence around the world including the United States, brought a more sacramental and historical center to Anglican and other Protestant thinking on the Church and an openness to Roman Catholicism, if not its Marian and papal claims of the period. From the Anglican Oxford Movement, Catholics received John Henry—later Cardinal—Newman. His influential book *Essay on the Development of Doctrine,* along with the Tübingen School of German theologians, revived an interest in history, development, and the organic and sacramental character of Catholicism and the Church. These theological developments laid the ground work for Protestants, Anglicans, and Catholics reviving interest in one another and developing common approaches to the doctrine of the Church.

At the turn of the century Leo XIII encouraged the study of Scripture, the renewal of Catholic social teaching, and a return to St. Thomas Aquinas in his original texts. The nineteenth century had begun to see an increased interest in the history and renewal of worship among Catholic and Protestant scholars and in certain Benedictine monasteries around the world. The scholarly, ecumenical, and monastic interest in liturgical reform began to influence the Catholic Church when Pius X lowered the age of First Communion and encouraged the renewal of liturgical music in the early twentieth century.

At the same time, Protestant and Anglican missionaries were seeing the absurdity of competing Christian claims in facing the non-Christian contexts of Asia and Africa. The churches came together in Edinburgh in 1910 for a World Mission Conference, which would provide the stimulus for the formation in 1948 of the World Council of Churches. While Catholics were not involved in Edinburgh, the Anglican and Protestant churches were very sensitive to recognize that Latin America was not to be seen as a missionary field because of the presence of the Catholic Church there.

Two other movements, one for theology and the other for social service and action, developed after the Edinburgh Conference: Faith and Order, and Life and Work. From its very beginning, Faith and Order felt the need to bring together not only Orthodox, Protestant, and Anglican church representatives, but also to involve the Roman Catholic Church. As a result there was correspondence as early as 1914 with the Vatican Secretary of State Pietro Cardinal Gasparri, who responded most graciously on behalf of Benedict XV. Anglican Bishop Charles Brent visited with Benedict after the First World War, in 1919, as the first World Conference on Faith and Order was being planned.

The ambivalence of the Catholic Church to the ecumenical movement during that period is nicely captured by the report of the American ecumenical delegation headed by Bishop Brent:

> The contrast between the Pope's personal attitude towards us and his official attitude towards the [World] Conference was very sharp. One was irresistibly benevolent, the other irresistibly rigid. The genuineness of the Pope's personal friendliness towards us was as outstanding as the positiveness of his official declination of our invitation.[1]

The pope could affirm the impulse to Christian unity. The Catholic position at that time was that all Orthodox, Anglican, and Protestant Christians must "return" to Roman Catholicism. Obviously, the same delegation of ecumenists received more favorable receptions in the Orthodox patriarchates of Constantinople, Alexandria, Damascus (for Antioch), and Jerusalem.

Of course, the Catholic Church had always acknowledged that by baptism there is a relationship among Christians and that the Eastern churches—Assyrian, Oriental, and Eastern Orthodox—have a valid ministry and sacraments and therefore are properly called "churches," in the theological sense. However, the practice of "conditional" rebaptism was still widely practiced.

Even though the Catholic Church during this period was not able to see itself free to participate in the movement for unity among Christians, Pope Benedict committed himself to prayer on behalf of the Orthodox, Anglican, and Protestant Christians in their efforts to seek the unity that Christ desires for the Church. In 1928 Pope Pius XI issued the encyclical *Mortalium animos,* which was intended to promote Christian unity, but today appears as a cautionary rejection of the modern ecumenical movement. Anyone wishing to document the contrast between early-twentieth-century Catholicism and the Church today will want to read this encyclical along side John Paul's *Ut unum sint* of 1995 to see how far we have come in this century!

From 1921 to 1925 there were informal, but papally approved, conversations held between Anglicans and Catholics in Malines under the sponsorship of Belgium's Désiré Joseph Cardinal Mercier. While these conversations did not materialize into concrete proposals, they established a certain level of goodwill between the two churches. Out of these conversations came the principle for Anglican-Catholic relations, "united but not absorbed," which began to articulate the move away from the "return" theology.

---

[1] Ruth Rouse and Stephen Neill, eds., *A History of the Ecumenical Movement* (Geneva: World Council of Churches, 1986).

In the mid-twentieth century, before the council, important developments on the official level began to lay the ground work for what was already going on among the theologians and the People of God. Pope Pius XII's two important encyclicals—*Divino afflante Spiritu* (1943), which encouraged modern biblical scholarship, and *Mystici corporis* (1943), which emphasized the organic and spiritual character of the Church—laid a ground work for the ecumenical movement. In Germany the *Una Sancta* movement began to nourish Catholic leadership committed to the unity of the Church. In France Abbé Couturier and in the United States Fr. Paul James Wattson of the Graymoor Franciscan Friars of the Atonement began to promote prayer for Christian unity, which evolved into what we celebrate today as the Week of Prayer for Christian Unity, usually in January. By 1940, early in the war, the cardinal of Westminster and archbishops of Canterbury and York, along with other religious leaders, were able to issue a pastoral on peace. In 1950 the Catholic Conference for Ecumenical Questions was founded, which produced many of the leaders who would serve the Church when the council opened, among them Johannes Willebrands.

As Catholic scholars began to read and work with Protestant scholars of the Bible, more common ground and understanding were created. As Catholics in the pews began to study the Bible they came to develop a common vocabulary and appreciation for Protestant biblical piety. As the Church began to see itself in more spiritual and sacramental terms, the institutional and centralizing tendencies of earlier centuries began to be balanced by an understanding of the Holy Spirit's action in history. A renaissance of Catholic-Luther scholarship in Europe gave Catholics a new appreciation of the positive aspects of the Reformation and of the genuinely religious character of the Reformer's contribution.

During this same period, liturgical reforms in Catholic worship began to open Catholics to what they shared with Protestant and Orthodox and to draw on the ecumenical liturgical scholarship of the previous decades. Lay movements, collaboration of Christians during the difficult times of World War II, and increased interchurch marriages all created a sense that new relationships were possible with fellow Christians in different churches.

Monumental Catholic scholarly studies by Yves Congar, George Tavard, and Josef Lortz made important contributions to an understanding of the Church and of history that created the ground work for new attitudes and new, authentically Catholic, appreciation of Orthodox, Anglican, and Protestant contributions to a common understanding of Church. Catholic theologians followed the studies of the World Council of Churches with appreciative analysis.

Thus, in spite of what seemed to be a continuing defensiveness and closed attitude toward ecumenism, as the Church moved into mid-century, there was already a great deal of ground work for launching the Catholic Church officially into the fullness of the modern ecumenical movement.

A Church in Transition from Isolation to Openness

When during the Week of Prayer for Christian Unity 1959 Pope John XXIII announced at St. Paul's Outside the Walls that there would be an ecumenical council for the Catholic Church, many were stunned, few were hopeful, and even fewer knew the preparatory work Pius XII had put in place for such a council or what might be an appropriate outcome of such a historic gathering. However, the bases had been laid in theology, liturgical renewal, relationships with other Christians, and revival of various aspects of Catholic life.

Already in 1949 the Holy Office—now Congregation for the Doctrine of the Faith, earlier the Inquisition—had put out an Instruction on Catholic participation in ecumenical meetings. While cautious, it was positive and enabled a growing number of Catholics to take part in the study of ecumenical questions and to be in dialogue with ecumenical partners. In 1957 Bishop John Wright, then of Worcester, Massachusetts, encouraged Frs. John Sheerin, C.S.P., and Gustave Weigel, S.J., to participate in a Faith and Order ecumenical meeting in Oberlin, Ohio.

Between the announcement of the council in 1959 and its opening in 1962 it was not at all clear that Pope John's hope for renewal and ecumenical openness would have a way of coming before the bishops. The original drafts of the various documents were drawn up by the traditional leadership from the Roman Curia. Meanwhile, Pope John called out of retirement a trusted biblical scholar, Augustine Cardinal Bea, S.J., to set up a Secretariat for Promoting Christian Unity—a new idea and a new office, with no precedent in the long history of the Roman Curia and no detailed game plan for its role in the Church.

Some felt the Secretariat would be a public relations arm of the Church for "external relations," to be closed when the council finished. In fact, it began its own work in preparing some documents to be presented to the council fathers, though some in the Curia doubted its right to do so. When the three thousand bishops met in the fall of 1962, it was still not clear that they would be able to exert any more leadership than to rubber stamp documents prepared for them. In fact, the first two sessions were only able to produce two documents, those on the liturgy and on the media.

Early in the course of the first session it was clear that the bishops were not at all satisfied with the draft documents they were given and did not have the means to revise them in the direction they wished. A close vote rejecting the draft on Divine Revelation led John XXIII to draw in the Secretariat for Promoting Christian Unity to work with the Theological Commission to develop a draft acceptable to the majority in the council.

Pope John was succeeded by Pope Paul VI during the months following session one. Pope Paul decided that the council would continue and that it would take the course of the majority of bishops, with its emphasis on internal renewal of the Church, its collegiality and increased role for the laity; on an openness to the world and the Church's mission of evangelism, justice, and peace; on the renewal of the biblical and theological life of the Church; on its outreach to the religions of the world; and on its commitment to ecumenism including the visible unity of the churches.

From the beginning Pope John had wanted ecumenical observers from the Orthodox, Anglican, and Protestant churches. These observers made important contributions to the discussions and drafting of texts, as well as helping to interpret the council and Catholicism in their churches back home. With the help of the World Council of Churches and the other observers, many of the bilateral relationships—that is, between two churches—and conciliar relationships that were to flower among Catholics after the council were initiated. Even before the bishops left Rome in 1965, they had begun to establish national ecumenical committees and reach out to the churches with whom they lived in their home countries.

While the Secretariat and the Theological Commission were working on the Decree on Divine Revelation, there was extensive ecumenical discussion on the same theme. While the council was meeting, but in recess, in 1963, the World Council held a major Faith and Order Conference in Montreal, where Catholics were represented for the first time. A young Fr. Raymond E. Brown, the biblical scholar, delivered a significant paper. That conference produced the ground-breaking study on revelation titled *Scripture, Tradition and the Traditions.* Many of the observers and some of the Catholic experts from the council were in Montreal. Their influence on both this World Council study and the Council's Decree on Divine Revelation shows the maturity which had already been reached in the ecumenical movement, just as the Catholic Church was coming on board.

In the end the council promulgated documents on Divine Revelation, the Church, Religious Liberty, and the Church in the Modern World, all of which laid the ground work for understanding the Catholic Church in a new way, both by Catholics and their ecumenical partners, and for reaching out with a new common ground. The council also promulgated documents on ecumenism and on the eastern churches which give specific mandates for ecumenism at the center of Catholic identity.

The Secretariat for Promoting Christian Unity was influential throughout the council itself. Afterward it supported the Church in setting up dialogues, providing support for the dioceses around the world in their ecumenical initiatives, and developing ecumenical policies for Catholicism. It is now called the Pontifical Council for Promoting Christian Unity and is headed by Edward Cardinal Cassidy.

I remember, as a high school biology teacher in St. Louis in 1963, reading in *Time* magazine that the Catholic Church is now to be ecumenical. I went across the street to a local seminary, Concordia Lutheran. I had a chance to meet a scholar, Dr. Arthur Carl Piepkorn, who was interested in Catholicism, liturgical renewal, and the history of the Church. Little did I know that, by 1966, he would become part of a dialogue, Catholic and Lutheran, that would produce agreements on the Eucharist, ordained ministry, papacy, infallibility, Mary and the saints, and contribute to a Joint Declaration on Justification by Faith, approved by the Holy See and the Lutheran World Federation in 1998. Even more surprising was the possibility to go into doctoral studies, in 1965, to study the Church. Before the council non-ordained Catholics, even religious, did not go on for doctoral studies in theology. Today, of course, the majority of Catholic scholars are laity, as the council has encouraged.

The council was a time to begin the shift:

- from defining the "one true Church" as the Catholic Church to saying that the "one true Church" subsists in the Catholic Church;
- from a sectarian standoffishness to a conversion to Christ's will for the unity of Christians;
- from looking at other ecclesial communities—in particular Protestants—as groups of individual Christians to recognizing them as instruments of Christ's salvation for their members;
- from an ecclesiology of "return" to a common Christian search for God's will for the Church in his manner and in his time, coupled with internal repentance and renewal;
- from a papacy of centralized control to a collegiality of all bishops, with the bishop of Rome serving the unity of the Church, both among Catholics and among Christians;
- from a claim to be the established church where politically possible to an affirmation of religious liberty and a support of freedom of conscience for all;
- from an ecclesiology centered on the institutional form of present-day Catholicism to a recognition of the real, if imperfect, communion among all Christians.

All of these shifts set the stage for a pilgrimage for the Catholic Church and all Christians which begins with the concrete conversion and reception of the ecumenical impulse.

The Beginning of a Pilgrimage Toward Full Communion

After the close of the council in 1965, the Church worldwide faced the enormous challenge of implementing the sixteen documents of the council: a new understanding of the "way the Church works" in terms of collegiality and correspondibility; the massive liturgical, biblical, and social justice reforms; renewing our theological understanding of the sacraments, divine revelation, the nature of the Church and its mission; the incorporation of laity into leadership at all levels of Church life; and reaching out in interreligious dialogue. Every year since the council, dioceses, bishops conferences, and the Holy See have provided documents, texts, and directives to enable the reforms to be received in the concrete lives of our people.

The ecumenical program of the council was no exception: the new understanding of the Church, of our relations with other churches, of how the Catholic Church needs to organize and educate itself for ecumenism, of how to enter into dialogue with other churches with the goal of better understanding, of moving toward full communion. This is a fascinating pilgrimage, just begun in these short thirty years since the council. In this section we will review the developments since the council as they touch on internal Catholic life and the results of the dialogues to which the Church is committed.

One would not expect the worldwide reception of the Vatican Council, and its ecumenical initiatives, to be uniform. For example, religious liberty—the necessary foundation before any ecumenical initiatives could be credible—came easily in the United States, where such important initiatives had been made in the council itself. By contrast, it took from 1965 to 1973 for the bishops to come to one mind on what religious liberty might mean in Spain. It was only in 1980 that a new agreement (concordat) was approved there, five years after the death of Generalissimo Francisco Franco. Since then, and for the first time since King Ferdinand and Queen Isabella in 1492, the Church is free to appoint its own bishops unhindered, Protestants are free to worship without sanction, and religious pluralism is possible.

Another example was Eastern Europe, where Christian education was not permitted. Religious and ethnic tensions were common. Some countries, such as Romania, did not even allow their Catholic bishops to attend the council. Accordingly, many of the elements of conciliar renewal and education were able to be begun in earnest only after 1989, and then often under the most trying circumstances.

On the more positive side of the reception of the council, let us look at some concrete examples.

In the Diocese of Memphis in the early 1970s, when we were preparing the first class of permanent deacons for their internships after two years of class and a year before ordination, we selected mentors for their service component with great care. It was important to place the candidates with ministers who had a deep faith, an articulate sense of vocation, and skill in the social ministry to which they were committed. Many were placed with sisters and priests in diocesan or parish work.

However, we did want to place one or more with a sister working in an ecumenical housing ministry in north Memphis. That would provide the opportunity for some members of the class to be working in the African American community with ministers who were representative of the Protestant as well as Catholic churches there.

Another placement was with a Southern Baptist minister serving at Shelby County Penal Farm. We did this not just because he would provide a good ecumenical experience for the deacon-candidate, an experience that would be shared in our theological reflection group. More important, Rev. Ben Bledsoe had the best reputation in town for ministering to the inmates. Reception of the ecumenical movement has entailed supporting this sort of collaboration at every level of Catholic life.

When I was director of religions education in St. Augustine's parish in the South Bronx in 1970, we wanted to devise a culturally sensitive confirmation preparation that would serve the young black and Puerto Rican confirmands in their Christian militancy in a context of competition with the Black Panthers and Puerto Rican gangs. When the bishop came for the celebration, we invited all of the ministers who were connected in any way to the parish to be in the sanctuary. We had worked with them as sponsors for some of the service projects, such as the Methodist soup kitchen. Other Protestant clergy were members of the neighborhood organization with the Catholic clergy, or were pastors of some of the non-Catholic parents. We did not know exactly whether or not Communion for them was possible. Of course the council had articulated the two principles: (1) the Eucharist is central in building up the unity of the Church and (2) the Eucharist is the sign of unity achieved among Christians. As the director of religious education I wondered how to advise the pastor. There were no precise Vatican guidelines at the time. (As I recall, I think I advised caution because the bishop was celebrating—not to bring the subject up with the clergy and not to refuse them if they came forward.)

By 1973 the Holy See had issued guidelines authorizing the bishop to oversee questions of sacramental sharing. In 1983 the new Code of Canon Law, amplified in the 1993 ecumenical directory, authorizes the *Catholic minister* to carry out this discernment in the light of diocesan guidelines. In the 1970s, also, Lutheran and Anglican agreements on the Eucharist emerged, followed in 1982 by the World Council of Churches text *Baptism, Eucharist and Ministry,* and convergence statements with Methodists and Presbyterians in the later 1980s. Today Catholics have many more resources than were available to us in the years immediately after the council.

Another example recalls the development in ecumenical sensitivity in Catholic sacramental practice. My colleague at work is an active member of Holy Trinity parish, Georgetown. He came into the office fuming one day. He stated that he had practically run down the aisle, barring the way of some of the candidates who had been called up to receive the Word of God (Bibles) in one of the rites of initiation and were being dismissed from the Eucharist with the catechumens. When he calmed down, it became clear that a mistake had been made in the parish. Baptized candidates for full communion were being subjected to the catecumenate and its rites. These are designed for the uncatechized and the unbaptized.

In many parishes, candidates for full communion and bona fide unbaptized catechumens were mixed together. This is a counter witness to Catholic theology. It is a confusion for the congregation and a violation of the directives of the Rite of Christian Initiation for Adults (RCIA) itself.

However, we have a successful catechetical renewal in the RCIA development. We find coming to us Catholics who are baptized and uncatechized, Christians who are baptized and uncatechized, Christians who are firm believers but seek full communion with the Catholic Church, and even Christians who want to "transfer" to the Catholic Church, but who do not see the need for initiation. We have had to learn how to deal with this much more complex world with ecumenical sensitivity. Every stage of liturgical renewal, from the 1960s until today, has entailed new ecumenical understandings and new challenges for our lives as Catholic parishioners.

An instance of the educational challenge the council has provided can be illustrated by a seminary experience. When I was teaching Church and Sacrament to a class at Memphis Theological Seminary in 1974—the class was composed of several Catholics who were candidates for the Master of Arts in Roman Catholic Studies as well as the regular Protestant students—we were challenged to find materials that gave an ecumenical view of the sacraments and the Church. We had a great time looking at one anothers' liturgical books, exploring how we told the story of the Reformation differently, how we understood the Church and its unity, and especially how the Protestants were able to profit by an ecumenically sensitive Catholic explanation of the "other five" sacraments.

By 1975 the World Council of Churches (WCC) had published, with full Catholic participation, its vision of a united Church titled "Conciliar Fellowship (Communion)," further elaborated by 1991 in the text *The Church as Koinonia: Gift and Calling.* During the 1970s both Anglicans and Lutherans developed agreements with Catholics on baptism and Eucharist. Important progress has been made on ordination. By the 1990s all the major Western churches, Catholic and Protestant, had renewed their liturgical texts so that parallel eucharistic prayers can be found in most of our worship books, grounded in a common theology. In the 1980s convergence positions emerged between Catholics and Methodists and Reformed, and the World Council of Churches published its historic *Baptism, Eucharist and Ministry,* to which more than two hundred Orthodox, Protestant, Anglican churches and the Catholic Church responded.

There are now also dialogues with Pentecostals, Baptists, and Evangelicals that touch on some of these issues. For every doctrinal course a Catholic might take—such as the one I taught on Church and Sacraments—there are ample resources in the bilateral dialogues (theological agreements between two churches) and the multilateral dialogues (dialogues between several churches, for example, within the World Council) to inform our understanding of the Catholic tradition and of the ecumenical progress to date.

Today Church and Sacraments can be easily taught in an ecumenical context, recognizing commonalities of doctrine and practice, respecting differences, and noting progress toward full reconciliation.

These examples, about collaboration in service, sharing Eucharist, baptismal practice and teaching Catholic doctrine, are all cases where the Church's life has begun to be transformed by the ecumenical developments within Catholicism. We have begun to receive the vision of our Church as in real, but imperfect, communion with all Christians, of our Church as committed in every aspect of its life to serve the unity of the churches, and of our Church as on a pilgrimage of conversion, self renewal and responsiveness to God's call to unity.

In 1993 the various postconciliar directives and the conciliar theological vision were brought together by the Holy See into the *Directory for the Application of Principles and Norms on Ecumenism,* and in 1995 John Paul II celebrated the irreversible commitment of the Catholic Church in his encyclical *Ut unum sint.*

In addition to the internal renewal necessary for ecumenism, the Catholic Church also began dialogues toward full communion with a host of churches, East and West. The Orthodox churches were slow to engage in theological dialogue, and the relationship has been even more strained since the opening of eastern Europe in 1989, even though during the council the mutual condemnations of 1054 were "consigned to oblivion" by Pope Paul and Patriarch Athenagoras, and there began a *dialogue of love* with annual exchanges of delegations on the feasts of Saints Andrew and Peter. Only in 1980, however, was a *dialogue of truth* able to be initiated, with the goal of restoring full communion.

Dialogues with the Oriental Orthodox churches—Indian Syrian, Armenian, Egyptian Coptic, Ethiopian, and Syrian—have taken place between the Holy See and the individual churches with remarkable success. The divisions over the person and nature of Christ, dating from 451, have been virtually resolved. With the Syrian Churches we even have agreements on mutual eucharistic hospitality. By 1994 the disagreements of Ephesus (431) between Catholics and the Assyrian Church of the East were resolved.

With the churches of the Reformation there are more challenges, because we do not yet recognize the ordinations and Eucharist in any of these churches. Yet more theological progress has been made because we have developed within the same Western culture similar thought patterns and similar methods of studying Scripture and Christian history. Likewise, in the wider context, where many churches come together in the search for unity, as in the Faith and Order Commission of the World Council of Churches, much progress has been made. The Catholic Church has been a full member of WCC Faith and Order since 1968.

There is also a host of dialogues with particular Reformation churches: Anglican, Lutheran, Methodist, Reformed (Calvinist), Disciples, and Baptist. John Paul II is particularly concerned that we make these results central to Catholic life. "At the stage which we have now reached, this process of mutual enrichment must be taken seriously into account, . . . a new task lies before us: that of receiving the results already achieved" which "must involve the whole people of God." Results are not to remain "statements of bilateral commissions but must become a common heritage" (*Ut unum sint,* 80, 87).

When I was living in Good Shepherd Parish in north Manhattan, I came to the 9:30 Spanish Mass one Sunday in August to find Paulist Fr. Paul Rospond preaching on the Gospel text about Peter (Matt 16:13-23). As you may recall, this text includes the confession of Peter in Christ's divinity, the promise of the "keys," and Christ's rebuke of Peter as "Satan."

Father Paul's homily was on the ambivalent role of Peter—and of his papal successors—as both foundation stone of faith and stumbling block toward unity. He quoted extensively in Spanish from agreed Lutheran Catholic statements on papal primacy and infallibility. His preaching was adapted to the audience, most of whom did not have even a high school education. However, he made clear the importance of the pope among the bishops of the Church. He emphasized his ecumenical service and the open discussion of the papacy among Christians.

He went on further, and simply, to distinguish between our Lutheran and other ecumenical colleagues, and the Pentecostal storefront churches in the neighborhood, the people who might be ringing our Catholic door bells to invite us to evangelical Protestant services. This good preacher was able to articulate, in the context of the Gospel reading, both Catholic affirmations and some of the ecumenical progress. He was able to clarify, in a direct and uncomplicated manner, the distinction between different churches. He explained the importance of different, but positive relationships. This is but one example of the multiple ways in which these positive results become part of Catholic life.

Catholics not only relate to Christians whose churches are open to the pilgrimage toward full communion with us, we also reach out to fellow Christians who may themselves not be open to the ecumenical movement. In 1965, when the Second Vatican Council was wrapping up its deliberations, I took a group of young brothers in formation to worship with a local Pentecostal Church of God congregation at the bottom of the hill from our novitiate in Glencoe, Missouri. We were initially unnerved by the animation of the worship, since in those days we were only used to a prefabricated Latin worship. When the congregation accepted our return invitation to worship with us during the week of prayer for Christian unity, they were wide-eyed at the crucifix and statues in our chapel. (We decided to worship in the music room with piano rather than organ!) Many of these young men continued to visit this Pentecostal church and made friends there as part of the spiritual discipline of their novitiate.

One could not imagine in 1965 that by 1970 there would be a fullblown Catholic charismatic movement, that by 1975 there would be a scholarly society with full Catholic and Pentecostal participation, that by 1980 there would be a productive dialogue between the Vatican and Pentecostals, and that by 1998 the Vatican/Pentecostal dialogue would publish an agreed text: *Evangelization, Proselytism and Common Witness.*

The Holy See has formal dialogues with the Baptist World Alliance, the largest member of which is the U.S. Southern Baptist Convention, with the Mennonite World Conference, with Pentecostal Christians, and with the World Evangelical Fellowship. None of these churches expects full communion with other churches, particularly with the Catholic Church.

However, the task of enhancing relationships among Christians is a priority for Catholics. Some Christians in these other communities understand the importance of deepened relationships, at least on the theological and personal, if not on the institutional level. Local Catholic relationships with Evangelicals are much more extensive than public appearances would suggest. In the United States there has been an almost thirty-year conversation with official representatives of the Southern Baptist Convention.

The decades after Vatican II have been a time of renewal, reform, and reception for the Catholic Church and for fellow Christians. Pope John Paul, in an encyclical letter, reiterated the centrality of conversion for Christians if we are to respond to Christ's prayer for unity. He moved from the language of "separated brethren" to that of "fellow Christians." He reiterated the irreversible character of the Catholic commitment to Christian unity. He emphasized in particular the importance of receiving the level of reconciliation already achieved.

Catholic Challenges on the Threshold of the Third Millennium

When I began teaching in 1959 at St. George's in Evanston, I was criticized for teaching my freshman religion class that they might possibly, some day, celebrate Mass in their own language. I responded to that criticism (in a rather politically incorrect way!) that my students could see Mass celebrated in the vernacular, Arabic and occasionally English, three stops down on the "L" at St. George's Melkite Church. I said that there they could also receive Communion in the body and blood of Christ—and that they should! And, of course, we did eventually take them down for just such a celebration.

I used to ask whether or not my students were prepared for the coming of the good Pope John's council and its renewal of our liturgical life. Now, of course, few Catholics remember when Latin prevailed in those days before the conciliar reforms, and when we even taught that it would not be possible for the Church to change its form of worship.

Catholics today have an impatience for the unity of the Church. They can develop the knowledge to equip them for deepening the bonds of our parishes, dioceses, and churches as we seek to realize God's will. We are preparing to live, work, and pray with fellow Christians with whom we already share more than divides us.

Pope John Paul has continually reminded us that we share more with fellow Christians than divides us. In speaking in 1994 of the ordination of women in the Anglican Communion he was most clear that we should neither be surprised nor deterred from the goal of full communion by new challenges or obstacles. After all, ecumenism is the work of the Holy Spirit!

Indeed, central to Catholic identity is the zeal for the unity of the Church. As we celebrate two millennia of Christianity there are challenges before us. Pope John Paul recognized this when in the service of unity he opened his own office to reform, with the help of Protestant, Orthodox, and Anglican church leaders and their theologians.

We also recognize that the Catholic Church, the largest Christian community in the world and the largest church in the United States, is a particular challenge for our ecumenical partners. Protestants, Anglicans, and Orthodox had forty years of dialogue and discussion, as well as institutional relationships around the world, before Roman Catholics became ecumenical partners after 1965. With the theological tradition, the authority claims, and the sheer numbers and cultural diversity of the Catholic Church, councils of churches would be overwhelmed by a Catholic presence in numbers reflecting their membership. Furthermore, not all Catholics have the ecumenical formation to be effective partners, and therefore internal ecumenical formation becomes a major priority if Catholics are to be effective ecumenical partners and fulfill their responsibilities. We have special responsibilities for the unity of the Church and for providing resources for the ecumenical movement. Since the Catholic Church is the largest partner, we should provide more staff and financial resources to enable the unity of the churches. We need to come to know one another. We need to celebrate the gifts we receive from one another and to be generous in sharing the heritage with which the Spirit has gifted us with our fellow Christians.

We are challenged to help all Catholics see that commitment toward Christian unity is central to their spiritual life, in prayer, dialogue, study, and collaborative action in the world. We have to find ways of helping the results of the dialogues become a "common heritage" by translating the technical theological agreements into material that is preachable, teachable, and prayable. We need structures, as Catholics, that hold our leaders and decision-making bodies responsible to the level of communion we share and the levels of agreements we have achieved.

In all of this as we move from the twentieth to the twenty-first century, we recognize the role of the Holy Spirit as Pope John Paul says:

> With the grace of the Holy Spirit, the Lord's disciples, inspired by love, by the power of the truth and by a sincere desire for mutual forgiveness and reconciliation, are called to re-examine together their painful past and the hurt which that past regrettably continues to provoke even today. All together, they are invited by the ever fresh power of the Gospel to acknowledge with sincere and total objectivity the mistakes made and the contingent factors at work at the origins of their deplorable divisions (*Ut unum sint*, 2).

Social Justice: Catholic Teaching Goes Global

John C. Cort

By the year 1999 the people of eleven European nations had voted into power governments controlled by socialist parties. In two more countries socialists were part of coalition governments. The only two countries not governed by socialist parties or by coalitions in which socialists were prominent were Spain and Ireland. A fair conclusion would be that the people of Europe, the motherland of Christianity and the Catholic Church, had voted for socialism—democratic socialism, that is, as defined by the Socialist International, to which all those parties belonged.

Could it also be said that the Catholic Church, such a formidable enemy of socialism at the beginning of the century, had also come around to voting for socialism at its end? It seems not, judging from the last social encyclical of Pope John Paul II, *Centesimus annus,* published in 1991. Since most people, including Catholics, tend to take the statements of the current pope as the official position of the Church, they also tend to assume that the latest statement on any subject thereby displaces or nullifies all previous papal statements.

With the collapse of communism as a serious threat either politically, economically, or intellectually, there remain only two movements competing for political and economic dominance in the world today: capitalism and democratic socialism. How the Catholic Church and its teaching on these two movements relate and respond to this new situation has to be of major interest to any student of world affairs, but especially to those who see the Church as God's instrument of choice to bring peace and justice to a troubled world.

The words *Centesimus annus* are Latin for "one hundredth year," that is, the one hundredth anniversary of the publication of Leo XIII's *Rerum novarum* in 1891, which set the stage for Catholic teaching on social justice in the twentieth century.

From Leo XIII through Pius XI, John XXIII, Paul VI, and Vatican Council II, continuing on through the first two social encyclicals of John Paul II, *Laborem exercens* and *Sollicitudo rei socialis,* the development of the Church's social teaching was consistently critical of capitalism to the point of hostility. Although it started as equally hostile to socialism, which by 1891 had come under the domination of Marxist atheists, Pius XI, John XXIII, and, in particular, Paul VI progressively softened the opposition to socialism to the point of Paul's saying in effect in *Octogesima adveniens* (1971) that if "careful judgment" were exercised, Catholics might well join socialist parties (31).

The discussion of "socialization" in *Laborem exercens* (1981) does not include a reference to socialism, but the thrust was so leftward that Fr. David Hollenbach, S.J., of Boston College, an astute student of papal teaching, concluded, "It really looks like the Pope's criticism of capitalism and collectivism argues for a form of democratic socialism."[1] Nicholas von Hoffman, writing in *The New Republic,* characterized John Paul's position as "a form of soft, non-Marxist socialism."[2]

Sollicitudo continued this leftward movement, faulting both communist and capitalist societies with equal severity, noting, for example, that Communist societies put "everyone in a position of almost absolute dependence, which is similar to the traditional dependence of the worker-proletarian in capitalism" (15).

Inflamed Conservatives

This reduction of both communism and capitalism to a kind of moral, or immoral, equivalence inflamed conservative laymen in the American Church. William F. Buckley Jr., the prolific right-winger, wrote that *Sollicitudo* "makes Christian blood boil with indignation."[3] Joining Buckley on the TV show *Firing Line,* Michael Novak of the American Enterprise Institute, a conservative think tank, agreed that the encyclical was "a disaster . . . inexcusable. . . . The Pope is just miserably misinformed."[4]

Novak, by his own admission, set out to inform the pope, and later reported that he had had some success. When *Centesimus* then came out, Buckley hailed it as "a firm affirmation of capitalism" and felt emboldened to dismiss as "suddenly obsolete" the U.S. Bishops' 1986 pastoral on the

---

[1] *Religious Socialism* (Winter 1982) 3.
[2] Ibid.
[3] *Cross Currents* (Spring 1993) 141.
[4] Ibid.

economy, *Economic Justice for All: Catholic Social Teaching and the U.S. Economy.*[5] Writing in the *Wall Street Journal,* Fr. Richard Neuhaus, a Catholic convert for only nine months, seconded both Buckley's accolade and his rebuke to the bishops, who were now "unrepresentative of the Church's authoritative teaching."[6] Novak, more deeply moved, "heard in [his] heart . . . the surging sound of a Te Deum."[7]

To describe Novak's achievement as "some success" is an understatement. He succeeded brilliantly. But how? How was it possible to bring about such a result, so that two encyclicals written by the same pope could produce in the same knowledgeable American observers two such radically different reactions? How was it possible at the same time to switch John Paul II from the winning side to the losing side in Europe?

Let us hazard a possible strategy: (a) you raise no objections as more progressive members of the encyclical-writing team repeat the principles, alarums, and caveats that have marked previous encyclicals and the statements of Vatican Council II; (b) you then concentrate on persuading the pope to include the following:

(1) Two definitions of capitalism on the if-but-if formula. If capitalism limits itself to the free market, the right of private property, "the positive role of business" and "free human creativity," this is good and should be approved. But if it becomes "a system in which freedom in the economic sector is not circumscribed within a strong juridical framework which places it at the service of human freedom in its totality . . . the core of which is ethical and religious" (42), then it is bad and should not be approved. The catch here is that capitalism in the United States qualifies under both definitions, so that neither definition is really accurate. The question is: Which definition is more descriptive of the actual situation, which capitalism is dominant? Previous popes, and previous encyclicals of John Paul II himself, have tended to see capitalism as coming *more* under the second definition and have therefore rejected it. This encyclical refuses to make a judgment, and therefore leaves it to those readers who see capitalism through rose-colored glasses to make a favorable judgment.

(2) A sharp, extended critique of "the so-called 'welfare state': on the ground that it too often violates the principle of subsidiarity, thereby leading to an 'enormous increase in spending'" and justifying "very harsh criticisms." The Holy Father concludes that "needs are best understood and satisfied by people who are closest to them" (48).

---

[5] Ibid.
[6] Ibid.
[7] *National Review,* Special Supplement, S-11.

Welfare states have not been beyond criticism, either harsh or gentle, but what stands out is the heavily negative nature of the pope's analysis. It is a far cry from Leo XIII's clarion statement of another fundamental principle of Catholic social teaching in *Rerum novarum:* "If, therefore, any injury has been done to or threatens either the common good or the interests of individual groups, which injury cannot in any other way be repaired or prevented, it is necessary for public authority to intervene" (52).

This also rests on the selfsame principle of subsidiarity, namely, that higher organs of society should perform functions that cannot be, or are not being, performed by lower organs. Since capitalism is marked by a chronic failure to satisfy many basic human needs and to respect many basic human rights, the intervention of public authority in the form of the welfare state has periodically become necessary.

(3) An extraordinary statement that "exploitation, at least in the forms analyzed and described by Karl Marx, has been overcome in Western society" (41). Marx, whatever his faults—which were many and great—did have a sharp eye for forms of exploitation, forms that still remain recognizable today.

In the pope's defense it might be said that he is more familiar with the welfare states of Western Europe than that of the United States. One set of comparative statistics only: Germany had double-digit unemployment in the early 1990s, but its child poverty was in the single digits, while child poverty in the United States, with much lower unemployment, was well over 20 percent and even 40 percent for African American children. Clearly, the Christian Democrats of Germany have been more moved by papal teaching than the Christian Republicans, or the Christian Democrats, of the United States.

(4) A total identification of socialism with Marxist-Leninist communism. The Socialist International, which ought to know, has repeatedly denied that communism has any claim to the name "socialism," insisting that the latter cannot exist without political and economic democracy. Communism is not "real socialism," as the pope calls it in this encyclical, but rather false socialism (56). The fact that communists of the former Soviet Union, China, Cuba, etc., also claimed, or claim, to be socialists does not make them socialists.

Some Clarification

At this point we must clarify our discussion with some definitions and background information. This may help to explain why the political conversion of Western Europe to socialism should concern Catholics in the

United States. European ideas and European movements take some time to cross the Atlantic, but the lesson of history is that they eventually do.

In 1951 the Socialist International, which was originally organized in 1864, reconstituted itself at Frankfurt, Germany. The first European socialists, back in the 1830s and 1840s, were more likely to be Christians than Marxists, but the Marxists did eventually prevail. At Frankfurt, for the first time, the Socialist International welcomed socialists who were "inspired by religious or humanitarian principles."[8] More recently, in Stockholm in 1989 the Socialist International deleted all references to Marxism from its new declaration and repeated its insistence on democracy, a mixed economy, private as well as public ownership and control of production, cooperatives, free competition, and markets that are regulated in the interests of the common good. Its only reference to sexual or reproductive questions was a call for "family planning."[9] In effect it declared socialism to be almost synonymous with Catholic social teaching.

Judging only from the text of *Centesimus annus,* nobody in the Vatican has ever read either the Frankfurt or Stockholm Declarations of the Socialist International, which now dominates the European continent. Only such ignorance could explain the caricature of socialism that appears in its pages.

The Frankfurt Declaration includes this sentence, and the substance of it is repeated in the Stockholm Declaration: "While the guiding principle of capitalism is private profit, the guiding principle of socialism is the satisfaction of human needs."[10]

Substitute "Catholic social teaching since Leo XIII" for the word "socialism" in that sentence and you have a perfectly true statement, at least until *Centesimus annus.* Capitalism can most accurately be defined as a system that is concerned primarily with the interests and the profit of those who own and control "capital," its root word. The root word of "socialism" is the Latin word *socius,* which means "common" as in common good or "common" as in the satisfaction of common human needs.

There is no truer statement, no sounder measurement of private virtue or public good than the Bible aphorism "By their fruits shall ye know them." By this measurement the most socialist society, the most socialist economy in the world today is that of Japan, which happens to be governed by the conservative Liberal Democrats, who say they are wedded to

---

[8] Frankfurt Declaration of the Socialist International, *The New International Review* (Winter 1977) 7.

[9] Stockholm Declaration of the Socialist International (Maritime House, Clapham, London SW40JW, U.K.) §72.15.

[10] Frankfurt Declaration, §3-1.9.

capitalism. But despite U.S. pundits' glee over an alleged Japanese recession, child poverty in Japan is less than half what it is in the United States, unemployment is about the same as in the United States, there is no inflation, workers' wages and job security are superior, ditto education and public safety, and there is a much more equitable distribution of wealth and income. In short, the Liberal Democrats are wedded more to "the satisfaction of human needs" (socialism) than they are to "private profit" and the interests of those who own capital (capitalism). This is so probably due to the fact that so many bright, energetic people are crowded into a very small mountainous space and they had to be socialist in this sense or die. Either that or the fact that they take their Buddhist/Shinto/Confucian religions more seriously than Americans take their Christianity. Or both.

Conclusion: as the wise old Pope John XXIII said about socialism in *Pacem in terris,* and as one might also say about capitalist socialism in Japan: "Besides, who can deny that those movements, insofar as they conform to right reason and are interpreters of the lawful aspirations of the human person, contain elements that are positive and deserving of approval" (159).

The Loaded Gun

We return now to number 5 in "a possible strategy," the successful effort to include in *Centesimus annus* a one-sentence loaded gun: "The state could not directly ensure the right to work for all its citizens unless it controlled every aspect of economic life and restricted the free initiative of individuals" (48).

There are several extraordinary things about this sentence. One is that it concerns the most basic human right, the right to life, for without work and a decent wage for that work no life that is worthy of the name is possible. Some people live off the work and wages of others, but we are speaking here of the ordinary person who does not have such a source of income. We are also speaking of the psychological as well as the physical damage that unemployment inflicts on a normal human being. Unemployment is a killer, a killer of the body and a killer of the spirit.

Gustavo Gutiérrez, the Peruvian founder of liberation theology, somewhere makes an eloquent protest against what he calls "premature, unjust death." Poverty and unemployment kill prematurely and unjustly. Why unjustly? Because they are preventable, especially here in the United States, where there is more than enough money, brains, and material resources to employ every one who wants a job and to pay them a living wage. And where there are far more than enough useful things for them to do while earning it. It is purely a question of political will.

What this sentence in *Centesimus* is saying is that government can never guarantee this basic right without "controlling every aspect of economic life, etc."

Since World War II the demand for economic rights in general and the right to work in particular have swept around the world. In his State of the Union Message of 1944, Franklin D. Roosevelt, noting that our Bill of Rights has "proved inadequate to assure us equality in the pursuit of happiness," called for a new economic bill of rights that would include "the right to a useful and remunerative job."[11] Even his Republican opponent that year, Governor Thomas E. Dewey of New York, echoed Roosevelt's call for a federal job guarantee. How times have changed!

In 1948 the new United Nations voted without dissent for a Universal Declaration of Human Rights that included the following language: "Everyone has the right to work . . . and the right to just and favorable remuneration ensuring for himself and his family an existence worthy of human dignity."[12]

John Paul II himself in this same encyclical, *Centesimus annus,* quotes Leo in *Rerum novarum:*

> Pope Leo XIII affirmed the fundamental rights of workers. Indeed, the key to reading the encyclical is the dignity of the worker as such and, for the same reason, the dignity of work, which is defined as follows: "to exert oneself for the sake of procuring what is necessary for the various purposes of life and first of all for self-preservation" (6).

How else can one read that but as an affirmation by both pontiffs that the right to work is a fundamental right intrinsic to, and identical with, the right and duty of self-preservation? Leo notes that "to preserve one's life is a duty common to all individuals," adds that "to neglect this duty is a crime." and concludes, "hence arises necessarily the right of securing things to sustain life and only a wage earned by his labor gives a poor man the means to acquire these things" (62).

How else can one read these texts, together with Section 52 of *Rerum novarum* quoted above, but to conclude that government has a right and duty to intervene to protect, promote, and, if need be, insofar as it is able, to guarantee the economic right to work for a living wage?

Novak has written that "the extensive effort to commit the Church to 'economic rights' has the potential to become an error of classic magnitude."[13] Would this protest include the Church's defense of the economic

---

[11] Philip Harvey, *Securing the Right to Employment: Social Welfare Policy and the Unemployed in the United States* (Princeton, N.J.: Princeton University Press, 1989) 3, 4.

[12] Universal Declaration of Human Rights, art. 23.

[13] Michael Novak, "Economic Rights: The Servile State," *Catholicism in Crisis* (October 1985) 10.

right of private property and private ownership of the means of production? It seems unlikely.

The Church has insisted, of course, that the right to private property is not absolute. In the next great social encyclical *Quadragesimo anno* (1931), Pius XI wrote that "it is rightly contended that certain forms of property must be reserved to the state, since they carry with them an opportunity of domination too great to be left to private individuals without injury to the community at large" (125). He thereby took another step closer to the Socialist International's stand, opting for some degree of public ownership in a mixed economy.

Paul VI, quoting from Scripture, one of the early Fathers, and Vatican Council II, expanded further on the limitations to the right of private property in *Populorum progressio* (1967). This is such a fine summary of Catholic teaching on social justice over the centuries that we quote at length:

> The recent council reminded us of this: "God intended the earth and all that it contains for the use of every human being and people. Thus, as all men follow justice and unite in charity, created goods should abound for them on a reasonable basis." All other rights whatsoever, including those of property and of free commerce, are to be subordinated to this principle . . . (22).
>
> "If someone who has the riches of this world sees his brother in need and closes his heart to him, how does the love of God abide in him?" (1 John 3:17). It is well known how strong were the words used by the Fathers of the Church to describe the proper attitude of persons who possess anything toward persons in need. To quote St. Ambrose: "You are not making a gift of your possessions to the poor person. You are handing over to him what is his. For what has been given in common for the use of all, you have arrogated to yourself. . . ." That is, private property does not constitute for anyone an absolute and unconditioned right (23).

What Do We Mean by "Rights"?

Before we go further, we should come to an understanding of what we mean by "rights." The word did not become popular until the eighteenth century, but the reality behind it is as old as humankind. A right is no more or less than a moral claim, a claim that somebody else has the duty, the moral obligation, to satisfy. Moral claims and obligations have existed from the very moment God created men and women and placed in their souls a conscience and the universal rule: "Whatever you wish that others would do to you, do so to them."[14] This is a fundamental law of

---

[14] Matt 7:12.

human nature, natural law in the sense defined by Thomas Aquinas: "the participation of the eternal law in rational creatures."[15] That participation was confirmed by Jesus when he added to the above rule, "for this is the law and the prophets" (Matt 7:12).

Justice is therefore defined, as in the ancient Justinian Code, as "the constant and perpetual will to render to everyone his [or her] due,"[16] that is, to satisfy all moral claims (rights) that he or she may have upon you.

The Church's commitment to economic rights, from the beginning of the twentieth century, and its commitment to government's duty to protect and, when necessary, to enforce those rights, was clearly set forth in *Rerum novarum* when Leo XIII wrote: "It is within the competence of the rulers of the State that, as they benefit other groups, they also improve in particular the condition of the workers. Furthermore, they do this with full right and without leaving themselves open to any charge of unwarranted interference" (48).

We have already quoted a similar passage in Section 52. There are passages on the evils of child labor, the imposition of unsuitable, oppressive work on women, Sunday work, even upon the work and conditions imposed on strong men such as miners. There are passages on the economic right of workers to organize in trade unions so that they might be able to fight for and protect their rights even before government is compelled to intervene, for, as Leo quotes from Proverbs, "A brother that is helped by his brother is like a strong city" (70).

In the encyclicals of Pius XI, John XXIII, and Paul VI, in *Gaudium et spes,* Vatican Council II's Pastoral Constitution on the Church in the Modern World, and, finally, in the first two social encyclicals of John Paul II there are similar variations on the same declarations of economic rights made by Leo XIII in *Rerum novarum.* Therefore, only those that differ from or add to those declarations will be mentioned hereafter.

The Technical Question

In *Quadragesimo anno* Pius XI says that "the Church . . . can never relinquish her God-given task of interposing her authority, *not indeed in technical matters, for which she has neither the equipment nor the mission,* but in all those that have a bearing on moral conduct" (39, emphasis added). But John Paul writes that "the state could not directly ensure the right to work for all its citizens unless it controlled every aspect of economic life and restricted the free initiative of individuals" (48).

---

[15] Thomas Aquinas, *Summa Theologiae* (Britannica Great Books, 1990) 18:209.

[16] David Miller, ed., *The Blackwell Encyclopedia of Political Thought* (New York: Basil Blackwell, 1987) 260.

Of course, every intervention of government to protect any kind of right automatically "restricts the free initiative of individuals" who are violating, or who would like to violate, that right. So that part of the pope's concern can safely be ignored. The other part, the part about "controlling every aspect of economic life," is a technical question that would seem impossible to prove unless you could point to several democratic countries operating under free market economies that had "ensured the right to work," but only by controlling every aspect of economic life. Obviously, they could not do so without destroying the free market. Pointing to the rigid economic controls of communist dictatorships such as that of the old Soviet Union is not going to prove the point. In any case, it remains a technical question, and Pius XI has said that the Church has no competence in that area. In the other area, that of "moral conduct," John Paul is on record as insisting that every effort must be made by government to promote and protect the right to work at decent wages.

We do have the testimony of an economic expert on the need for a federal job guarantee in the United States and on its feasibility without controlling every aspect of economic life. Lester Thurow, professor of economics at MIT and former dean of its Sloan School of Management, is the author of *The Zero-Sum Society,* a popular book on economics. In this book Thurow writes:

> Whatever the reasons, we need to face the fact that our economy and our institutions will not provide jobs for everyone who wants to work. They have never done so, and as currently structured they never will. . . . Since we regard the United States as a work ethic society, this restructuring should be a moral as well as an economic goal. We consistently preach that work is the only "ethical" way to receive income. We cast aspersions on the "welfare society." Therefore we have a moral responsibility to guarantee full employment. *Not to do so is like locking the church door and then saying that people are not virtuous if they do not go to church* [emphasis added].[17]

Although Thurow is a technical economic expert, he makes a point on moral conduct that, with all due respect, John Paul II might well consider.

Fascism or Economic Democracy?

In *Quadragesimo anno* Pius XI, harking back to the medieval guilds, called for "the reestablishment of vocational groups" (89). This plan, about which much controversy and confusion have raged and rambled, was actually the brainchild of the German Jesuit Oswald von Nell-Breuning

---

[17] Lester Thurow, *The Zero Sum Society* (New York: Penguin Books, 1980) 203–4.

(1890–1990), who was the main author of the encyclical. He in turn got it from his mentor, a fellow German Jesuit, Heinrich Pesch (1854–1926), who was the first world-class Catholic economist. Pesch called it "solidarism," and its thrust was both anti-capitalist and anti-Marxist. The idea was that a just and successful society could not be built either upon the notion of a relentless class warfare that would eliminate the capitalist class, as the Marxists would have it, or on "free competition alone" (94). Although class struggles might be justified whenever one class or the other is attacked or oppressed, the ideal was a system that would bring together capital, labor, consumers, and government in each industry, and in the national economy as a whole, for mutual benefit, cooperation, and regulation.

Unfortunately, almost as soon as the proposal was made it began to run off the track. Nell-Breuning later revealed that the only independent contributions of Pius XI to the text were sections of paragraphs 91ff., which said "some ambiguously favorable things about Mussolini's fascist order."[18] Although *Quadragesimo* immediately added a criticism of Mussolini's scheme as being too authoritarian, state-controlled, and "excessively bureaucratic and political" (102), the fat had slipped into the fire. Pesch's plan, which he and Nell-Breuning saw as a form of economic democracy, was tagged as "corporatism," which in turn was tagged as "fascism" by all of the Church's enemies and even some of its friends.

Dollfus in Austria, Franco in Spain, Salazar in Portugal, Pétain in France all followed Mussolini in trying to hitch their Fascist and semi-Fascist tails to the papal kite. In the swirl of negative opinion several things have been overlooked. One is the failure to note that the CIO (Congress of Industrial Organizations), the more militant wing of the American labor movement during the 1930s, 1940s, and 1950s, at every convention between 1941 and 1955 unanimously endorsed an "Industry Council Plan" that was based on the vocational group plan of Pius XI in *Quadragesimo anno.*

This was acknowledged by different parties who were in a position to know. One was Philip Murray, a devout Catholic and one of America's most popular labor leaders, who was president of the CIO from 1940 until his death in 1952. At a communion breakfast of the Association of Catholic Trade Unionists (ACTU) in New York City in 1942, Murray said that a critic "charged that I had taken the plan—body, boots and britches—out of the encyclicals." Murray acknowledged that this charge was "almost completely true."[19]

---

[18] John Coleman, "Development of Catholic Social Teaching," *Origins* (January 4, 1981) 38.

[19] *The Labor Leader* (ACTU newspaper), March 16, 1942, 3.

ACTU newspapers strongly promoted the CIO's Industry Council Plan as an excellent application of *Quadragesimo anno* to the American scene. Another body that was even better qualified to make a judgment was the National Catholic Welfare Conference, forerunner of the U.S. Conference of Catholic Bishops, which in 1948 took the position that the phrase "industry councils" was an accurate way "to designate the basic organs of a Christian and American type of economic democracy" derived from the encyclical *Quadragesimo anno.*[20]

A fascinating footnote: in that same year of 1948, well into the Cold War, *The Daily Worker,* official newspaper of the Communist Party, labeled the plan "the ACTU Industry Council Plan," called it "'fascism' and simply an American incarnation of Mussolini's and Franco's 'corporate state.'"[21] The only difficulty with this verbal gas attack was that all the Stalinist delegates to all the CIO conventions since 1941 had voted for it. In fact, William Z. Foster, Communist Party Chairman, had himself in 1942 written that "the Murray Plan of industry-labor-government councils in the various industries offers a practical means to accomplish the indispensable end of speeding up production by giving labor a real voice in war industry."[22]

Strange that between 1942 and 1948 "a real voice for labor" had somehow taken on the scary sound of "FASCISM!"

In the years leading up to 1986 and the U.S. Bishops' pastoral Economic Justice for All, we find Michael Novak introducing himself into this question of the Church and economic democracy, once again in a negative role. Even before the bishops had issued the first draft of their pastoral, Novak had organized a lay commission of Catholics, consisting mostly of corporate executives, which published a statement defending U.S. capitalism from anticipated attack by the bishops.

Calling attention to our founding fathers' experiment in political democracy, the first draft of the bishops' letter had included this excellent sentence: "We believe the time has come for a similar experiment in economic democracy: the creation of an order that guarantees the minimum conditions of human dignity in the economic sphere for every person."[23]

After the draft was made public in November 1984, the McNeil-Lehrer TV program invited Archbishop Rembert Weakland, chairman of the bishops' committee, and Novak to discuss it. McNeil pressed Novak for

---

[20] "The Christian in Action," Nov. 21, 1948, *Pastoral Letters of the American Hierarchy, 1792–1970,* ed. Hugh J. Nolan (Huntington, Ind.: Our Sunday Visitor Press, 1971) 411.

[21] George Morris in *The Daily Worker,* January 8, 1948, 6.

[22] William Z. Foster, *Labor and the War,* 1942, pamphlet published by Foster and the Communist Party.

[23] John C. Cort, *Christian Socialism* (Maryknoll, N.Y.: Orbis Books, 1988) 331.

specific criticisms of the draft, which was mainly critical of the U.S. (Capitalist) economy. Finally, Novak singled out the appeal for "economic democracy" and added, "That's an Olof Palme phrase,"[24] by which he meant a socialist phrase, since Palme was then the socialist prime minister of Sweden and a top leader of the Socialist International.

As we have shown, it would have been more accurate to say, "That's a Catholic phrase." Nonetheless, in the final draft the bishops deleted their excellent sentence and substituted, *"We believe the time has come for a similar experiment in securing economic rights: the creation of an order, etc."* (95, emphasis in the original). If the bishops thought to placate Novak and friends with this substitution, he disabused them in October 1985, with his public statement that the Church's commitment to economic rights "has the potential to become an error of classic magnitude."[25]

But the bishops held firm for economic rights, as the substitution itself also shows, and their final draft, judged by that standard, can only be characterized as an indictment of the U.S. (capitalist) economy, although it nowhere uses the word "capitalist" or "capitalism." They were especially critical of the failure of the U.S. economy to provide jobs for all at decent wages, leaving as it has so many millions of men, women, and children, including working men and women, mired in poverty.

This pastoral in turn left Novak, Buckley, and Neuhaus in a depressed condition that was only aggravated in 1987 by John Paul II's *Sollicitudo rei socialis,* to be relieved in 1991 by John Paul II's *Centesimus annus.*

How About the Practice?

So much for the tangled tale of the Church's teaching on social justice in the twentieth century. We come now to the question: What did American Catholics, lay and clerical, do to implement that teaching, to apply its principles and its mandates to the practical problems of life in the United States?

By the year 1900 immigrants from Catholic countries and areas of Europe—Ireland, Italy, parts of Germany, etc.—had produced a working class that was largely Catholic and poor. The Irish had the advantage of a familiarity with English and quickly became leaders in the growing labor movement. The Irish clergy, mostly sons of poor workingmen and women, had every reason to support the workers' struggles. And they did. Most prominent was James Cardinal Gibbons of Baltimore (1834–1921), who entered the century with a well-established reputation as a champion of labor.

[24] Ibid.
[25] Novak, "Economic Rights," 10.

In 1886 he had headed a group of bishops who succeeded in persuading Leo XIII not to extend the condemnation of the Knights of Labor from Canada to the United States, as desired by conservative Archbishop Michael Corrigan of New York.

Among the lower clergy one of the first was Fr. Peter Dietz (1878–1947), first to be given the title "labor priest," first to write extensively about labor problems, mainly in German Catholic periodicals, and first to attempt to organize an association of Catholic trade unionists. He did this at the American Federation of Labor (AFL) convention in 1910 and called it the Militia of Christ for Social Service. It consisted mostly of top union officials, but his plans for AFL backing were rejected and the group never comprised more than a few hundred members, mainly in Midwest cities like Milwaukee, Chicago, and St. Louis, where German Catholics were numerous.

The second was Msgr. John A. Ryan (1869–1945), who after Heinrich Pesch became not only the most famous Catholic economist of the modern era, but in his dual influence on the U.S. bishops and President Roosevelt became easily the most influential. Fr. Charles Coughlin, the anti-Semitic radio priest, called him "Right Reverend New Dealer" in a sarcastic attack, but the title had a basis in fact. His major work, *Distributive Justice: The Right and Wrong of Our Present Distribution of Wealth* (1916), highlighted an intellectual conviction that he carried through the Great Depression, namely, that recessions and depressions are caused primarily by the maldistribution of wealth as between the rich and the poor. Although he was the first editor of the *Catholic Charities Review,* he once said that "charity is a poison when taken in substitute for justice."[26]

In 1919 Ryan put together a Program for Social Reconstruction for the post–World War I era. With few revisions it was adopted and published by the Administrative Board of the U.S. Bishops in 1920. By more than fifteen years it anticipated New Deal legislation that provided protection of labor's right to organize, minimum wages, maximum hours, social security, abolition of child labor, public housing, unemployment, and health insurance. Upton Sinclair called it "a Catholic miracle."[27] Miracle or not, it served notice to the world that the U.S. Bishops had entered the public arena as champions of labor and meant to remain there, exercising a consistently "preferential option for the poor."[28]

[26] Jeffrey M. Burns, "Ryan, John Augustine," *The New Dictionary of Catholic Social Thought* (Collegeville: The Liturgical Press, 1994) 852.

[27] Ibid., 853.

[28] This phrase first became popular following the meeting of the Conference of Latin American Bishops (CELAM) at Medellin, Colombia, in 1968.

From 1919 to the year before his death in 1945, Ryan served as director of the Social Action Department of the National Catholic Welfare Conference. He was ably assisted by Fr. Ray McGowan and in his last years by the young man who was to become the preeminent "labor priest" of the century, Fr. George G. Higgins. Among them they kept the Church in the forefront of the major struggles for social justice.

Among the laity the standout has to be Dorothy Day (1897–1980), an ex-socialist/communist convert who for her first thirty years led the life of a Greenwich Village bohemian. Until she founded the Catholic Worker Movement in New York City in the Depression year of 1933, most of the agitation for social justice had come from the ranks of the clergy. The power of her writing, her personality, and her example of voluntary poverty in service to the poor inspired and continues to inspire hundreds of lay leaders in the fields of trade unionism, journalism, scholarship, and the practice of the Works of Mercy in soup kitchens and Houses of Hospitality around the country and around the world. Among her more prominent disciples have been Ed Marciniak, Bob Senser, Eileen Egan, Catherine de Hueck, John Cogley, Jim O'Gara, Peter and Margaret Steinfels, Betty Bartelme, Jim Forest, Tom Cornell, and Michael Harrington, who became America's leading socialist.

Ironically, Dorothy received her own inspiration from a French hobo philosopher named Peter Maurin (1877–1949), who preached a gospel that was authentically Catholic in faith, but quite at odds with the thrust of the encyclicals. He was a radical agrarian-anarchist, anti-union ("Strikes don't strike me"), and taught that the best way to eliminate poverty and unemployment was to abolish the industrial system and get everyone back to the land and making things by hand. He did, however, have a great gift for forceful simplification of Gospel truths as well as agrarian phantasies, and these, reduced to free verse *Easy Essays,* he published in *The Catholic Worker* and influenced many of its readers for both good and ill.

Despite Peter's anti-unionism, Dorothy's left-wing background would not allow her to turn her back on the labor movement, not in the turbulent 1930s when millions of workers were on the street, desperate for jobs, and those who were still working had no hope or help except from the likes of John L. Lewis and his brash new CIO. She visited the scene of steel and auto strikes and wrote in the paper:

> When workers are striking, they are following an impulse, often blind, often uninformed, but a good impulse—one could even say an inspiration of the Holy Spirit. They are trying to uphold their right to be treated not as slaves but

as human beings. They are fighting for a share in the management, for their right to be considered as partners in the enterprise in which they are engaged.[29]

This had an authentic encyclical ring, anticipating John Paul II's *Laborem exercens* and his call for every worker "to consider himself a part-owner of the great work shop wherein he is working with everyone else" (14).

With Dorothy's encouragement, a group of trade unionists, meeting around the kitchen table at the Catholic Worker, founded the ACTU in 1937. Unlike Father Dietz's Militia of Christ, this was predominantly a rank-and-file organization. It spread from New York to most of the major industrial cities, organized hundreds of labor schools, fought oppressive employers, corrupt labor racketeers in the old AFL, and Communist influence in the new CIO. It also published influential newspapers: *The Labor Leader* in New York and *The Wage Earner* in Detroit. Among its more effective leaders were Martin Wersing and George Donahue of New York, Paul Weber of Detroit, and the patriarch of all ACTU chaplains, Msgr. Charles Owen Rice of Pittsburgh, who in his nineties is still speaking out for justice for workers and the poor. A typical activity of the early ACTU:

In 1937 the CIO organized the clerks at Woolworth stores in New York. Barbara (Babs) Hutton, the Woolworth heiress, came under attack in the press and a society columnist defended her and noted that she had given eleven million dollars to charity. Meeting at the Catholic Worker, we voted to support the strike and marched on the picket line with a sign that read: "Babs Gave $11 Million to Charity, But 'The worker is not to receive as alms what is his due in justice'—Pope Pius XI."[30] Since this was the first time a pope had appeared on an American picket line, it made quite a stir, even among the jaded lefties in nearby Union Square.

The ACTU was controversial and made enemies. And times changed. Labor became better established, though it has lately become somewhat disestablished. The Catholic population, even Catholic workers, has become more middle class in its attitudes. Labor education has been taken over by the unions and universities. Of the hundreds of labor schools organized and run by ACTU and by the Jesuits, only the school run by the Labor Guild of Boston and Fr. Ed Boyle, S.J., remains alive and well. One Jesuit has been immortalized in film. Fr. John Corridan, assistant to Fr. Philip Carey at the latter's labor school in New York City, was the inspiration for the priest in the award-winning *On the Waterfront*.

---

[29] *Dorothy Day, Selected Writings: By Little and Little,* ed. Robert Ellsberg (Maryknoll, N.Y.: Orbis Books, 1983) 241.

[30] The papal quote is from the 1937 encyclical *Divini redemptoris* (New York: Paulist Press) 21.

The ACTU itself faded away in the late 1960s. By then its role as a defender of honesty, democracy, and fair dealing within the union movement had been taken over by a secular organization, the Association for Union Democracy. During the 1990s, a more ecumenical time, the ACTU's role as a religious organization working in support of the labor movement has been taken over by the National Interfaith Committee for Worker Justice. Under the dynamic leadership of Kim Bobo, a sort of Protestant Dorothy Day, this committee has brought together forty-eight organizations in twenty-five different states and begun to play a major role in the renewal of religious effort to reverse the decline in labor's strength and effectiveness. Catholic bishops, priests, and lay men and women are active in its leadership.

Dorothy Day's influence remains strong long after her death in 1980, as witnessed by one hundred Catholic Worker Houses and a variety of newspapers that don't always agree with each other, but agree on loyalty to what they perceive as her legacy. In September 1998 Cardinal John O'Connor of New York journeyed to Rome to initiate her cause for canonization. As a retired admiral and chaplain of the U.S. Navy, he saw nothing incongruous in his advocacy of one of America's foremost pacifists. "If anybody in our time can be called a saint," he said, "she can."[31]

In 1924 a Belgian priest, Canon Joseph Cardijn (1882–1967), journeyed to Rome to defend before Pope Pius XI his Young Christian Workers (YCW) from attacks by Belgian employers and conservative clergy. This was the occasion when the Pope said, "At last some one speaks to me of the working class." He also said to Cardijn, "The great scandal of the nineteenth century was that the Church lost the working class."[32]

The Church lost the working class to Marxism and to Leninism, in Europe but not in the United States, thanks to sympathetic bishops, priests, and lay activists like Dorothy Day and those whom she inspired in ACTU, the YCW, and similar organizations. Today Leninism is virtually dead, but Marxism, though severely wounded, staggers on and actually shows signs of a desperate vitality at meetings of the Socialist Scholars Conference.

Within Catholic circles Marxism has since the 1960s made some inroads among intellectuals through the writings of liberation theologians in Latin America, who have used Marxist analysis in their praiseworthy efforts to align the Church behind "the preferential option for the poor."

One challenge today in the United States is to replace Marxism, a hopelessly flawed system, as the predominant ideology of the left, of all those who work and write and fight for social justice. Catholic social

[31] *The New York Times Magazine,* November 8, 1998, 44.
[32] Cort, *Christian Socialism,* 304.

teaching, emanating from the Vatican, cannot do it. What might do it is an effort to persuade the left to read and adopt the teachings of the Stockholm Declaration of the Socialist International, written mainly by Michael Harrington, an apostle of Dorothy Day. This declaration, which almost no American socialists have ever read, is grounded in a set of political and economic principles that are, as we have shown above, virtually identical with the predominant Catholic social teaching.

As Europe has gone socialist, it has also gone Catholic in its political and economic thinking, although few people, including those in the Vatican, seem to realize it. This may be the real "Catholic miracle."

Physician, Heal Thyself

St. Basil, the fourth-century champion of the poor, quoting Plato, once wrote, "This is the last extreme of injustice: 'To appear to be just without being so.'"[33]

This charge has been leveled at the Catholic Church in America because of the anti-union activities of management in a number of Catholic institutions such as schools, colleges, and hospitals. Our bishops and our popes, from Leo XIII up to and including John Paul II, have proclaimed the right of workers to organize, free from any kind of intimidation. John Paul has written that unions are "indispensable" and "are indeed a mouthpiece for the struggle of social justice" (*Laborem exercens,* 20).

Despite this some Catholic administrators have been guilty of the most blatant anti-unionism, hiring notorious union-busters as consultants and attorneys. In his excellent book *Organized Labor and the Church,* Monsignor Higgins deals with this sad story from his perspective of more than fifty years of intimate involvement with the Church and labor. One positive story from the book:

> At the end of a 1990 labor dispute, the hospital association in New York City, including the Catholic hospitals announced that workers who had gone on strike would not get their jobs back. In effect, the hospitals were going to fire the strikers. [Cardinal] O'Connor, however, stepped in and ordered Catholic hospitals to break ranks with the association. "There will be no firing of strikers in this archdiocese," was his message. He told the Church-related institutions to negotiate a separate agreement. They did, and by doing so put pressure on other New York hospitals to follow suit.[34]

---

[33] St. Basil, "On Reading Greek Literature," *The Wisdom of Catholicism,* ed. Anton Pegis (New York: Random House, 1949) 16.

[34] George G. Higgins with William Bole, *Organized Labor and the Church: Reflections of a "Labor Priest"* (New York: Paulist Press, 1993) 182.

A splendid example for other bishops and archbishops.

Another positive development: the National Interfaith Committee for Worker Justice, mentioned above, has proven its worth by bringing together union representatives, healthcare administrators, and religious leaders to work out a consensus on *Guidelines for Unions and Management of Religiously-Sponsored Healthcare Institutions* (1020 W. Bryn Mawr Ave., Chicago, IL 60660).

Involvement in this effort moved Sr. Doris Gottemoeller, president of the Sisters of Mercy of the Americas and chair of the Catholic Health Association of the United States, to make a significant concession. When asked about the guidelines' advice about not hiring anti-union consultants, she said, "I suspect that's a good position to take. I have no problem with that."[35]

And that's good advice for other administrators who want to be faithful to Catholic teachings on social justice. The last thing the Catholic Church would want as it enters the new millennium is to appear to be just without being so.

---

[35] *Our Sunday Visitor* (October 11, 1998) 21.

Money and the Faith: Is Mammon an Ogre Still?

John C. Haughey, S.J.

This will be a somewhat personal account of the Catholic faith and money in the twentieth century. Proceeding narratively seems necessary because of the bulk of the material and its complexity. I invite readers to do their own autobiography of money while they read my account. I believe they will find such an exercise as enlightening as I have.

Early Emotions

My mother and father were Irish immigrants who bore me in 1930 with two of my siblings already in this world and four more still to come. My earliest recollection of money was that we didn't have anywhere near enough of it at any time in my growing up years. I think the reason why I find myself even now connecting money with my emotions, both positive and negative, is because of those early years. Connected with this memory of far-too-little was an almost daily exhortation about the virtue of industriousness. Frugality, on the other hand, was an involuntary condition of our lives; no exhortation to its virtue was necessary. Depression was an omnipresent reality in my parents' consciousness and in many of the town's families—and in those days it wasn't a clinical term. Although the country had several economic downturns in the first three decades of the century, the Depression brought many to their knees, both knees in both senses.

I vividly remember embarrassed, able-bodied men coming to the back door of our house asking for a sandwich. Our house was near a railroad and many of them would be hobo-ing their way through Pennsylvania in search of work. My mother never turned any of them aside, even though we denizens would feel the effects of her charity at lunch time that day or the next. I never got to ask her why she was so spontaneously compassionate (she died when I had just turned fourteen), but her very strong

Catholic faith almost certainly connected their indigence with the christo-
logical reminder: "When I was hungry you gave me to eat."

December 7, 1941, changed several things. It brought millions work,
many of them women. And it brought millions into the armed services.
But in the world of very micro-economics, unbeknownst to Emperor Hi-
rohito and Adolph Hitler, Pearl Harbor made it possible for me and my
brother to be welcomed for work at a nearby farm and at a farther away
orchard. I mention this because these few dollars made a big difference to
our family's fortunes, or so our parents made us think. But in culturally
more significant ways, people's needs and the one-to-one acts of compassion that had attempted to meet those needs began to be dealt with by national, state, and local social programs. The New Deal programs, begun
during the 1930s under Franklin Delano Roosevelt's leadership, were the
beginning of this transformation in the American way of dealing with
hunger, unemployment, and lack of shelter. Although ever changing, this
social interventionist feature of our democracy did not cease in all the subsequent decades of the twentieth century.

I mention these personally-experienced moments to introduce the
subject of the Catholic faith and the financial condition of the faithful because they are still impacting my understanding of our faith. Most of us
are not in a situation of want at present. But the simple act of charity is no
longer simple, is it? It is now seen as part of a larger, more complex picture that is inextricably entwined with income taxes, welfare, addiction,
rehabilitation institutions, and, of course, politics. Even begging has become more sophisticated and professionalized. No less complex has the
individual's money become with stock offerings, 401k plans, pension
plans, IRA accounts, re-mortgaging, mutual-fund investing, health and life
insurance, savings accounts, etc. Even the elemental matter of food is different. At least half of what we ate as kids, it seems, came from our own
garden. I haven't eaten anything grown by me or my family since I was
thirteen years old. Like so many Americans my family moved from a
small town to an urban area at that time. The whole country has shifted
from rural life with its farms feeding their families and the local population to mass production of food and manufacturing. New technology and
a rapid growth of the professions and the service industry drastically
changed the employment picture in the course of the twentieth century.

It would be hard to exaggerate the degree of change Americans and
American Catholics have undergone in this past century in our relationship to money. Most of us have gone from a simple life which was family
centered and self-reliant and religiously defined, to a much more complex
life that is still interdependent but, unfortunately, less and less dependent

with and on each other. Rather, we are interconnected to larger impersonal mechanisms that we are beholden to, uncertain of, and feel powerless to effect. It would be consoling if we could name the problem as capitalism pure and simple and begin to undo it. But it's difficult to indict the capitalism you are in bed with, especially when you are as much the beneficiary of it as the victim of it.

The impression that has been left on my consciousness about these earlier years of both my life and of our country's life in the first five decades of the twentieth century is that faith was usually associated with money in the sense that if you did your part by hard work, God would not leave you bereft. God was the rock on which one could stand. But in the last five decades, partly because our life expectancy increased by almost thirty years since the beginning of the century, something else came between the foot of believers and the rock on which they stood. I am referring to the nest egg. It's hard to stand on or trust both one's nest egg and God. I think of the Gospel warning that one cannot serve or give yourself to God and Mammon at the same time (Luke 16:13). Mammon is an Aramaic word and means that in which you put your trust. Jesus is saying that one cannot have two competing objects of trust.

This impression about how faith and money connected in the past is followed by a judgment. The judgment is that we have been increasingly privatizing our financial condition in the course of these past decades, privatizing in the sense of taking care of ourselves with more and more sophistication and letting those who can't take care of themselves be cared for by the institutions which are set up to do that kind of thing. How else can we explain that the vast network of institutions established and maintained by the Church in the last 150 years out of the pockets of usually poor Catholics are being closed with greater and greater frequency for lack of financial support, while the Catholic population is increasingly upper middle class with not a few of them among the wealthy of our society? Granted there are many factors that could be taken into account to mitigate this judgment, such as the diminishing numbers of priests and nuns who once staffed these institutions for a pittance, as well as the undesirable location of many of these institutions in situations of urban blight. But even this last factor could be analyzed as evidence of the same problem of privatizing wealth.

Things are doubtless a lot more subtle than I am expressing. To chew on one of these subtleties: the number of institutions created by religious women, women vowed to poverty, in these years boggles the mind. The pittance they received for their unceasing labors paid the bills for their congregations while they were numerous enough and young enough to continue "manning" (I know . . . but live with it) these institutions. According to the U.S. Catholic Conference's Sr. Janet Roesener, as quoted in Charles Morris' book *American Catholic: The Saints and Sinners Who Built America's Most Powerful Church* (New York: Times Books, 1997), "the total unfunded retirement liability for American religious orders is calculated at more than $7 billion" (311). The faithful at present are being requisitioned yearly to help pay for this now largely aged, infirm, and dying population. And since the faithful are coming through to the tune of about $30 million a year, a major embarrassment to the Catholic Church has been somewhat averted, though this sum is just a drop in a very big bucket.

The further we Catholics grew into the warp and woof of the culture, the more we took our cues about our money from the culture rather than the Church. A culture is a teacher and the Church is a teacher, but the lessons each teaches are not the same. What has the teaching Church been teaching in the course of the past century about doing justice with the money we have, both the money we have as a nation and the money we have as individuals and families?

Money and Norms

The hierarchy of the Catholic Church in this country has had something important to say about money understood in terms of economic justice on three separate occasions in the twentieth century, the first in 1919 and the last two in the last fifteen years. On the first occasion, a year after the end of World War I, the National Catholic Welfare Council (precursor to the U.S. Catholic Conference) issued a statement known as the Bishops' Program of Social Reconstruction. It didn't address our personal use of our resources, but our government's use of the financial resources with which we provided it. And it wasn't a critique of capitalism as such but of the distribution of its fruits. On the basis of their reading of the Gospel, the bishops called for sweeping changes in the government's role in improving the condition of people by advocating such things as labor's right to organize and bargain collectively and government-backed insurance to protect against unemployment, illness, accident, and problems of old age.

The bishops' document was met with scorn by many, including the president of the National Association of Manufacturers who deemed it "socialistic propaganda." But as it turned out the document proved prescient since many of its recommendations would be enacted into law during the New Deal years. In this document the government is seen as the primary instrumentality for implementing economic justice. The bishops' understanding was that the role of the Church was to speak truth to power, and the role of power (the state's) was to shape its policies according to truth about economic justice, distributive justice in particular.

The bishops' 1919 letter cannot be mentioned without citing the genius behind its authorship. It was that of John A. Ryan, a Minnesota farm boy, who as a seminarian and priest of St. Paul steeped himself in the Catholic social thinking, particularly that which was coming from the pen of Pope Leo XIII. Ryan saw its relevance for the conditions of working Americans more deeply than any of his contemporaries and was the main influence on Catholic social thought from the first decade of the twentieth century through the 1930s. A decade before the 1919 letter, Ryan had set out and promoted in his writings a number of legislative reforms that he saw as essential for economic justice in American society: (1) a minimum wage; (2) the eight-hour work day; (3) protective legislation for women and children; (4) legislative protection for peaceful picketing and boycotting; (5) unemployment insurance; (6) provision against accident, illness, and old age. He enjoyed the epithet which someone accurately attached to him in the 1930s of "Right Reverend New Dealer."

But some voices soon began to be raised from within the Catholic community which were much more critical of capitalism as such. Not steeped in the natural law tradition of Catholic social thought, these voices supplied a much more radical way of looking at the economy and our relationship to it. For example, Dorothy Day, Peter Maurin, and the Catholic Worker Movement practiced voluntary poverty and refused to be under the hegemony of the Capitalist economy. They wanted to keep neighbor-care more local, more personal, and closer to home. We could characterize this kind of voice as prophetic. It speaks truth to the Church, and a listening Church appropriates the prophecy and, in turn, speaks the deepened truth it has come to understand to the power it addresses. Prophets of justice have not been wanting since Dorothy Day. I think of Cesar Chavez and the National Farm Workers Association, of numerous labor priests who galvanized the will of countless workers to stand up for their rights, Dr. Martin Luther King Jr. and the Civil Rights movement, Helen Prejean and the growing movement to eradicate capital punishment—but these last two move us beyond the matter of economic justice and the just distribution of wealth, personal and national.

As with so many other things in the life of the Church of the twentieth century, the Second Vatican Council was a major influence on individual Catholics and their leaders. The Pastoral Constitution on the Church in the Modern World, *Gaudium et spes,* was particularly clear that the human person was "the source, the center, and the purpose of all socio-economic life" (GS 63). It criticized the fact that in economically-developed areas far too many of the citizenry "seem to be hypnotized, as it were, by economics, so that almost their entire personal and social life is permeated by a certain economic outlook" (GS 63.) "Man" is very close to being made for the economy rather than the economy for "man." Of course, "economic activity is to be carried out according to its own methods and laws but within the limits of morality, so that God's plan for mankind can be realized" (GS 64). Individuals were reminded by this pastoral constitution of the "universal purpose for which created goods are meant . . . [they are, notwithstanding one's ownership of them, to be regarded] as common property in the sense that they should accrue to the benefit of not only himself but of others" (GS 69). And, finally, "the right to have a share of earthly goods sufficient for oneself and one's family belongs to everyone" (GS 69).

A second major moment in the century's understanding of wealth in this country, as the Catholic Church views it, took place in 1986 with the bishops' pastoral letter on the economy: Economic Justice for All. It was the first time in the entire history of the United States that a religious body undertook to subject the country's economy to a moral critique. The document was five years in preparation and its several drafts evoked many reactions—positive and negative—both within and outside the Church. Bishop James Malone from Youngstown, Ohio, told me an amusing but telling incident that happened the morning the letter was overwhelmingly passed at the annual bishops conference in Washington. One of the network anchor's shoved a microphone in Bishop Malone's face and asked disarmingly: "So what am I supposed to do, given this document that all you fellows have worked so hard on and signed today?" To his great consternation, he was not able to answer the simple question. I mention this incident because the strength of the document was its comprehensiveness. But its weakness was also its comprehensiveness. It presented a definite world view of economic justice, but one that was difficult to translate into pulpit material and personal choices. It addressed public policy more clearly than it did personal use of one's financial resources.

As was usual with Catholic social teaching, the bishops' pastoral used both scriptural resources and natural law reasoning as it attempted to address both Catholics and "men of good will." I wondered out loud to the drafting committee, which was interviewing a number of us about what direction it might take before it set about in the direction it did, whether the scope of such a projected letter might be a case of running before one learns to walk. Should not Catholics be addressed first and foremost, I asked the committee, in ways that might enable the faithful to be wise in their personal interaction with the economy and leave for a second letter something that addressed the country's economic policies? My small voice not having been successful, I decided to write what I thought was the direction the pastoral should have gone. *The Holy Use of Money: Personal Finances in the Light of Christian Faith* (Garden City, N.Y.: Doubleday, 1986) was the fruit of my mild protest.

It would take us far afield if I were to spell out the contents of the pastoral, so let me settle on one metaphor as a way to communicate its contents. It was a call to all, our government in particular, to overcome the economic apartheid that we have all too comfortably settled into in our country. The left-behinds are being left more and more behind and the ever-widening chasm between them and the rest of us needs to be bridged by a more just distribution of the benefits of our economy. Between the time of the letter's publication and this writing, the Clinton administration's welfare reform program has been passed and implemented. It places the onus on welfare recipients to be more industrious and warns them that their window of opportunity between "the dole" and self sufficiency is a short five years. Although many have gotten off the welfare rolls, the program gets mixed reviews. The burden for meeting the needs of those who are falling between the cracks of this welfare program is increasingly falling on private groups and churches.

Catholic Giving

The third effort by the Catholic Church in the twentieth century to address us on the subject of money was done in 1992 and was entitled "Stewardship: A Disciple's Response." Since I was part of the committee that prepared the U.S. Bishops' pastoral letter on stewardship, I can speak with some authority about it. There was a split in the committee on what we thought should be done. Several of the bishops and I thought we should be meditative and theological and avoid anything exhortative or quantitative. But the rest of the bishops were much more pragmatic about it. Their financial needs were growing and they needed a document with some teeth in it to establish the particulars that would evoke a greater response from the Catholic faithful for sustaining the institutions they oversaw. I don't think either side was wrong, but the combination was difficult to pull off. The result satisfied neither side.

We agreed that the pastoral should spell out the meaning of stewardship in terms of discipleship. For far too long Catholic giving was pre-Gospel in its rationale, a combination of we have bills to pay so let's meet them or you have an obligation to "contribute to the support of your pastor." Being a steward of the goods one has access to is what any disciple of Christ has to be. A steward is put in charge of what the master owns and

manages it according to the mind of the master, never forgetting it is entrusted to, not owned by, the steward. Translated, each of us is responsible
for bringing increase to what we have and to see these as gifts God has
given us. This way of understanding stewardship went far beyond financial resources and evoked a total worldview which included ecological
concerns, work, abortion, the arts, and so forth, not to mention the tired
troika of time, talent, and treasure. We discussed tithing at some length
and decided against making it or any other quantitative measure our way
of determining what constituted acceptable giving, to the disappointment
of the advocates of tithing. Archbishop Thomas Murphy, the chair of the
committee, thought the best way of proceeding was to begin with a more
theological document and each year to follow up with more pragmatic,
motivational materials. As far as I know such a follow-up process has not
been implemented since the publication of the pastoral, perhaps because
of Archbishop Murphy's subsequent illness and death.

Before and after this stewardship pastoral, voices have been raised
about the reason for the well-documented decline in Catholic giving patterns and the unfavorable comparison between Catholic giving and that of
other churches. The clearest of these voices is that of Fr. Andrew Greeley,
who uses his sociological instruments and sociological data to prove to his
own satisfaction that the reason for the downturn in Catholic giving can be
traced to Catholic anger at not being given voice in general and at the hierarchy's positions on sexual ethics, plus the 1968 papal encyclical *Humanae
vitae* in particular. To explain why this giving downturn has not been accompanied by any increased defection from the Catholic Church, Greeley
weaves a complex thesis of the compatibility between alienation on the one
hand and Catholic loyalty on the other—again to his satisfaction.

I don't have any proof that he is wrong, but I think the matter is much
more complex than this. Some of my hypotheses for making it more complex are: (1) with the increasing insecurity about the financial stability of
the country/world there is a felt need to hold on to a greater percentage of
one's income than previous generations had done; (2) greater affluence
brings with it need for a greater expenditure to retain the lifestyle affluence
has made one accustomed to; (3) Catholic philanthropy is going more to
causes than to sustaining traditional Catholic institutions; (4) being Catholic is only a part of my identity or one could say "the world is too much
with us"; (5) a vote of non-confidence about the direction the Church has
been taking about who should be ordained; (6) given our increasing
longevity, we have many more years to cover than we had in the past.
Whatever the explanation the downturn in Catholic contributions is un-
mistakable and troubling.

Three legitimate questions arise from the above Church teachings. Have they been taught? How have they affected the economic attitudes of Catholics? What is the actual behavior of Catholics about Church giving? The reader can answer the first question. My suspicion is that a rare reader will say that they have. I have not been able to find any good data on the second of these questions about the economic attitudes of Catholics, but a recent study by Dr. Lawrence Iannaccone in *The Journal of Economic Literature* (September 1998) about the faiths of Americans and their attitudes toward the economy and money confirms my own anecdotally-arrived-at hunches. His findings are that "people's religious affiliation or degree of religiosity seems not to influence their attitudes concerning capitalism, socialism, income redistribution, private property, free trade and government regulation" (1477). His main reason for thinking the influence from their faiths is slight is because "within virtually every religious tradition or denomination, one finds a bewildering variety of economic statements emanating from the representative bodies and leading thinkers of most denominational families" (ibid.). The faithful of each of the religious traditions find so much variation in their leaders' and members' attitudes about the subject that there is, "enough ambiguity to justify any number of economic positions" (1479).

Ambiguity, of course, is in the eye of the beholder and can be generated either out of one's desire to leave things ambiguous or because one's social location has a stronger influence than one's faith. Nevertheless, Catholics have less reason to be ambiguous about this subject matter than other denominations since their leadership has been much more articulate and clear about it. But ambiguity there is. For example, a lay letter responding to the bishops' pastoral Economic Justice for All ("Liberty and Justice for All," published by the Brownson Institute) was one long hiss against the document. Those who put together that vigorous demur were successful business types. The primary author and main spokesman was Michael Novak. Their major complaint with the bishops' pastoral was that wealth was treated merely in distributive terms rather than in the generative terms it deserved. The capitalism these entrepreneurs had operated out of and succeeded in mastering was, therefore, not seen as problematic. The lay letter itself was evidence enough that the bishops' pastoral was not going to change the economic attitudes of the letter's authors or those whose social location mirrored theirs. And as the twentieth century closed, there was little reason to believe the economics pastoral will change many, because it seems that most of our economic attitudes are determined more by our social location than by our faith.

I believe that the national economic climate which had made the bishops determined to do an economic pastoral in the first place was the recession of 1981–82. Things seemed ominous then even though there was a bit of a demand-side recovery in 1983–84. But these ups and downs were accompanied by a maelstrom of downsizing and mergers and acquisitions that rendered more and more workers and their families insecure about their future financial condition. At the moment of this writing, however, much has changed. We are nationally as far from a recession as from inflation. Our economy has seldom been more robust, with unemployment at a thirty-year low and an overall economic growth of 0.6 percent in 1998. Although there are always storm clouds, they are at this moment still small and from nations far away.

The third question: What is the relationship of Catholics to Church giving since the pastoral on stewardship? To my great disappointment, I find that there has been no comprehensive amassing of information on actual giving by Catholics to date. Three comments have been made to me by the leadership of the organization most up on the matter, the National Catholic Stewardship Conference in Washington, D.C., that pique my interest in awaiting this information. The first of these is that some dioceses and parishes have been hugely successful in turning around the giving patterns of their people. The second comment is that where this success has been most notable is where there is a deep taking of ownership of the parish by the parishioners. This, in turn, usually occurs as a response to the style of leadership being exercised in the parish, part of which shows itself in the giving patterns. The third comment is that a celebration of the tenth anniversary of the stewardship pastoral is being planned for 2002 in which there will be up-to-date information on stewardship since the issuance of the pastoral. It is to be hoped that it will include data that contrasts the before and after picture.

Going Global

One last item that must be included in this twentieth-century picture is the growing globalization of the economy. We are only at the beginning of this phenomenon as economic parameters are extending out further and further, drawing us into a oneness that will affect all of us in most personal ways. I think of my niece in the third year of her marriage. She spends most of her working week/life in London, while her husband is in Hong Kong months at a time. I don't know who waters the plants in their home in New Jersey or when, or if, children will be part of their future. Sensitive uncles don't ask such questions. I think, too, of my Jesuit confrere who works in the Philippines and speaks of the deep disrespect he finds in the young in his rural parish for anything that comes from their immediate culture since they are enthralled by any American thing to which they can gain access: the music, food, entertainment, clothing, basketballs. Certainly imperialism is no one's intention, but the globalization of the economy makes many more losers abroad than winners. The conquered, oddly, seem to want to be conquered while to the victors belong the spoils of monotonous monoculturalism. The media accelerate the globalization with paradoxical consequences, like greater knowledge of savagery where savagery would otherwise go unnoticed and unaddressed, but at the same time the media give greater exposure to the baser aspects of human nature which seduce and bring out the worst in all of us.

I do not want to end this essay predictively, but with a macroeconomic retrospect. We will not be prepared for the global economy of the twenty-first century unless we have a better grasp of what it was that triggered the rise and fall of the market economy of this country in the early part of the twentieth century. I borrow from Karl Polanyi's still unsurpassed classic *The Great Transformation* (New York: Farrar & Rinehart, Inc., 1944) for this analysis. He observed the beginnings of a virtually global economy in nineteenth-century England with its theory and practice of economic liberalism, in particular with its free, self-regulating market system which began to shape the political order of not only England but gradually Europe and eventually the United States. Gain was the new principle which grew into the controlling principle that recontoured what more local power and their politics had previously determined. When this nascent, almost-global economy of the earliest years of the twentieth century dissolved, the Great War ensued (1914–18).

The post-war League of Nations made the reconstruction of this same economic liberalism primary so there was a return to the international currency, credit, and gold standard components that had created the pre-war system of *haute* finance. The stabilization proved utopian and premature. Just as the restoration of the gold standard both held together and symbolized the global solidarity that had been reached, so also its abandonment by Great Britain and the United States in the early 1930s symbolized the dissolution of the solidarity. The result was the collapse of the League of Nations in the 1930s, which led to a process of adversarial nationalism and the reversion to the power game. Enter World War II.

The global market economy that is in full swing now has its roots in the market economy of the beginning of the twentieth century. While a national market economy organizes our humanity nationally, a global market economy organizes social interaction globally. When gain and profit determine us rather than the other way around, *homo oeconomicus* is born. A humanity that becomes subordinate to the free market isn't free anywhere. In all previous ages and cultures, their always-more-local economies were submerged in and emerged from the social relations of human beings. People produced for use not for gain. (In the first chapter in his treatise *Politics,* Aristotle deemed production for gain "not natural to man.") Social anthropology describes the economic systems of peoples prior to the twentieth century as a function of their social relations. Markets there were, but they were local and national. The idea, then, of an unregulated or self-regulating market had hitherto been unthinkable since it commodified not only the products of the laborers but the laborers themselves. If wages buy them, are they not, in effect, for sale? A self-regulating market economy would have its minions (us) put our trust in this complex economic mechanism that makes people (us) the means to an end: gain!

There always was a countervailing dynamism, of course, attempting to restrict the ever-expanding free market mechanism. Hence, there were innumerable national interventions with social legislation seeking to redress the wrongs being incurred by the market; there was the federal reserve system; there were trade unions, regulations, and tariffs, and eventually international treaties, trade agreements, and the GATT (the General Agreement on Tariffs and Trade). But the impact of these restrictive interventions seems to be diminishing rather than increasing as national boundaries, more permeable to the laws of supply and demand, are becoming like unobtrusive points of entry and exit of trade rather than the cultural and political demarcation points they had been. The question facing us leaving the twentieth century was thus the same as the one that faced us at its beginning: is the basic principle governing our social organization—whether interpersonal, local, national, or international—to be material gain as that is determined by the market, or human flourishing as that is determined by ourselves and those who represent our better selves?

Who represents our better selves? For the last twenty-two years my candidate is Pope John Paul II. On the subject of globalization, he comments in his January 22, 1999, document *Ecclesia in America* that if it is

> ruled merely by the laws of the market applied to suit the powerful, the consequences cannot but be negative. These are, for example, the absolutizing of the economy, unemployment, the reduction and deterioration of public services, the destruction of the environment and natural resources, the growing distance between rich and poor, unfair competition which puts the poor nations in a situation of ever increasing inferiority (20).

The Holy See is increasingly conscious of the negative ecological consequences on all of us of any "absolutizing of the economy." The global economy must be subordinated to the good of the planet.

John Paul II calls upon the church in America to "promote greater integration between nations, thus helping to create an authentic globalized culture of solidarity, but also to cooperate with every legitimate means of reducing the negative effects of globalization such as the domination of the powerful over the weak especially in the economic sphere" (55).

***

In a sense all of the information in this chapter provokes a challenging question: Since "money talks," are we going to be satisfied with having money talk to us without our talking back? We talk back to money by having it do our bidding, thus keeping it firmly in the order of means to the good ends we espy in faith and humanly pursue.

Church and State: Large Issues Resolved, Large Issues Pending

James Finn

"Congress shall make no law respecting an establishment of religion
or prohibiting the free exercise thereof."

When George Bush was on the presidential campaign trail, someone asked him what went through his mind when, during World War II, his plane was shot down and he was plunked into the sea. His response:

> Was I scared floating around on a little yellow raft off the coast of an enemy-held island, setting a world record for paddling? Of course I was. What sustains you in times like that? Well, you go back to fundamental values. I thought about Mother and Dad and the strength I got from them, and God and faith—and the separation of Church and state.

We are entitled, I believe, to a skeptical smile at that last phrase. Can we really believe that George Bush, bobbing around on his little raft, gave a moment's thought, under those conditions, to the relation of Church and state? But, if not, why then did he say something so improbable?

My own speculation is that having invoked the moral strength he received from his family training, from God and faith—a fairly common reaction of those in roughly similar situations—he was suddenly struck by a campaign fear that he had crossed some invisible line, that voters might believe his religious beliefs would impinge unacceptably on political issues. He then hastily threw out the phrase "separation of Church and state" as a fire wall against such an interpretation of his position.

But why did that particular phrase seem to come to mind ready-made? Because, I suggest, it has become shorthand for what many people believe best describes the relation of Church and state in this country. The late William Bentley Ball, a passionate defender of religious liberty who argued a number of cases before the Supreme Court, put it this way: "The American Constitution, in its First Amendment, had been wisely designed as a wall against unlimited state power affecting religion. Its Establishment

Clause barred the setting up of a state church. Its Free Exercise Clause forbade government to prohibit the observance of religion."[1]

Yet when we look back at the First Amendment there is no reference to the state. It is Congress, only one agency of our state, that is mentioned. And grammatical propriety would dictate that the "clauses" be described as phrases of a simple sentence and to recognize that both are governed by the single use of the word "religion." The difference in how the amendment is read has significant consequences.

The religion portion of the First Amendment has been invoked in issues that range from life and death issues (abortion, euthanasia, assisted suicide, war and conscription, the death penalty) to quotidian issues (taxes, prayer in public schools, at a commencement address, or before an athletic event). On particular understandings of the amendment, a state Supreme Court dismissed a murder sentence because the prosecutor had cited a biblical text in his summation, a primary-school teacher told her students to strike out the word God in the class textbooks because it was, she said, illegal to mention God in a public school, and a fourth-grade teacher told a girl in her class that she could not wear a cross on her necklace.

The Supreme Court has ruled that a commencement address in which a rabbi invoked God was unacceptable because it offended a young graduate and her atheist parents, but a school board could insist, over his parents' vigorous objection, that a student could be obliged to read a book filled with curses, the frivolous use of "Jesus Christ," and evaluations of sex that ran counter to the religious beliefs of the student and his parents. Through a variety of rulings the Supreme Court has affected the gradual extrusion of religious practices, teachings, symbols, and references from the nation's public schools. The attentive reader will have noted that the Supreme Court, as well as Congress, has been credited—although credit many not always be the appropriate word—for many of the changes wrought in our national life by the government's understanding of the First Amendment.

If a traveler were to start a trek from the beginning of the twentieth century to the present, attempting to observe along the way significant events in Church-state relations—both large and small, political and legal, moral and cultural—that have brought us to our present condition, what would the traveler find? Before starting the march that traveler might be tempted, first, to glance back to see what was being left behind. Traveler, as we will call him—Ms. Traveler having declined to make this trip—could glance far back at a country and a time when settlers, overwhelmingly

---

[1] William Bentley Ball, *Mere Creatures of the State?* (Notre Dame, Ind.: Crisis Books, 1994) 11.

Protestant, had formed colonies in which Catholics were a small minority. He could see, however, that by the 1840s Catholics outnumbered any single Protestant denomination. Many of them had come as immigrants, fleeing hunger and starvation at home, to find that their new home was marked by a Protestant hegemony and a deep hostility to Catholicism. ("No Irish need apply" was a common code to express that sentiment.) Amid scurrilous phrases and epithets hurled at the immigrants, there sometimes appeared more elegantly phrased bigotry. For example, the Rev. Lyman Beecher warned that "the Catholic Church holds now in darkness and bondage nearly half the civilized world. . . . It is the most skillful, powerful, dreadful system of corruption to those who wield it, and of slavery and abasement to those who live under it."[2]

Traveler, even though he was much closer to that time than we are, could not fully grasp the intensity of the anti-Catholicism of the period. The smoke from the Ursuline convent burnt down in 1834 had almost completely drifted away and the noise of religious riots in Philadelphia a decade later had faded into the further distance. Some of the most bitter differences, however, had yet to be fully engaged, let alone resolved. Protestants and Catholics agreed, for example, that a good moral education could not be separated from specific doctrinal teaching. They differed, however, on the specifics, including which version of the Bible, which prayers, which hymns, almost all of which in the common schools that were developing were Protestant, virtually as a matter of course. Failing to ensure that the schools would be religiously acceptable to them, and unable to secure federal funding, Catholic leaders instituted what became the remarkable system of parochial schools. (Much of this was accomplished by the redoubtable Bishop John Hughes of New York, whose religious militancy was matched by a political insensitivity that led him to anticipate publicly the ascendancy of Catholicism over a declining Protestant influence.)[3]

The last decade of the 1800s saw the emergence of what has been termed the "Americanist crisis" within the Church—a term used to describe the conflict between Catholics shaped by traditional European models of the Church and those whose models were strongly influenced by the political and religious culture of the United States, including the separation of Church and state. Erroneous reports about the conflict reached Rome.

In 1895 Pope Leo XIII praised the accomplishment of the church in America but warned that the separation of Church and state, American style,

---

[2] A. James Reichley, *Religion in American Public Life* (Washington, D.C.: The Brookings Institution, 1985) 203.

[3] This story is very well told in Vincent P. Lannie, *Public Money and Parochial Education* (Cleveland: Case Western Reserve University, 1968).

was not a model for other countries. His 1899 encyclical *Testem benevolentiae* was read as a condemnation of "Americanism," and the "progressive" Americanists were squelched.[4] "American Catholics had known an inchoate moment of native constructive theological thought. They now slipped more or less peacefully into a half century's theological hibernation."[5]

Hibernation did not appeal, however, to the activist spirit of Catholics in other spheres. They began to move rapidly up the ladder of political and financial achievement. During World War I Catholics served in the military forces in numbers disproportionately higher than their total in the general population. The Church established for the first time in the United States an organization committed to political and social action, The National Catholic War Council (NCWC). (Renamed the National Catholic Welfare Conference in 1922, it vigorously applied Catholic social doctrine to American society.) Catholics and Protestants worked together effectively during the war and, with no public or government objections, mingled church and government funds in joint ventures.

Traveler would carry as baggage some of these memories, but as he turned his face toward the future and the terrain that lay before him, he noticed an odd phenomenon. Aside from an odd bump or two in the path immediately ahead, it was relatively smooth and straight until, in the distance around the milestone of the 1940s, it seemed to twist and turn and bristle with unfamiliar structures. Before he reached there, about a quarter of the way through the twentieth century, Traveler encountered two quite different but instructive events. The first he thought he might even pass by since it provoked only narrow if intense interest.

In 1922 Oregon had adopted by referendum a law that would render subject to arrest and prosecution parents who sent children between the ages of eight and sixteen to other than public schools.[6] The law, sponsored by Scottish Rite Masons, was contested by Society of Sisters of the Holy Names of Jesus and Mary and a secular military academy. Posing the issue as starkly as possible, the counsel for the state argued that "between church and state we insist that the state has the prior and paramount right to direct the education of the children of the state." On that understanding

---

[4] The encyclical was directed to Cardinal Gibbons, who replied: "This doctrine, which I deliberately call extravagant and absurd, this Americanism as it has been called, has nothing in common with the views, aspirations, doctrine and conduct of Americans." Quoted in John Tracy Ellis, *Documents of American Catholic History* (Milwaukee: Bruce Publishing Co., 1962) 534.

[5] James Hennesey, *American Catholics: A History of the Roman Catholic Community in the United States* (New York: Oxford University Press, 1981) 203.

[6] Ball, *Mere Creatures of the State?* 12–14.

private schools were judged to be not only unnecessary but divisive. In 1925, the court found for the order of nuns, stating: "The child is not the mere creature of the state; those who nurture him and direct his destiny have the right, coupled with the high duty, to recognize and prepare him for additional obligations."

The *Pierce v. Society of the Sisters* case is significant for its findings that the state has a proper regulatory but narrow role over schools, that it does not have an educational monopoly, and that both the rights and obligations of educating children belong to their proper guardians.

Before Traveler went much further in his chronological passage he encountered another national issue plainly marked "religious." Alfred E. Smith was a four-term popular governor of New York, an undeniably urban Irish politician, derby, cigar, accent, and all. He was also Catholic, and when he became the Democratic candidate for the presidency of the United States the full weight of religious bigotry and reasonably expressed concern fell upon him. Above hectic and often vitriolic exchanges two documents stand out. Charles Marshall, a lawyer and an Episcopalian, brought together many of the serious charges and published in *The Atlantic Monthly* "An Open Letter to the Honorable Alfred E. Smith."[7] Replete with quotations from *The Catholic Encyclopedia,* encyclicals, and a number of popes, Marshall's letter drove to the conclusion that "there is a conflict between authoritative Roman Catholic claims on one side and our constitutional law and principles on the other," and respectfully asked Smith how, if he accepted both teachings, he would reconcile them.

It was reported that Smith's first reaction was to ask, "What the hell is an encyclical?" but he then prepared a measured and reflective response in his own open letter, which the editor entitled "Catholic Patriot: Governor Smith Replies."[8] Relying upon his own convictions, his political record, and learned counsel his sober reply reassured some, but he lost the election, badly. How much religion was a factor was uncertain, but that it was a factor was beyond doubt.

Traveler was led to reflect on this event. He knew that Article VI of the Constitution stated that "no religious Test shall ever be required as a Qualification to any Office or public Trust under the United States." Yet Smith had been asked to reassure not only bigots but other Americans that his religion would not interfere with his political office if he were elected president. A Church-state issue? Although both were involved, the state

---

[7] Peter H. Odegard, ed., *Religion and Politics* (New York: Oceana Publications, 1960) 49–62.

[8] Ibid., 62–74.

did not pose the question, nor did the Roman Catholic Church, the institution to which Smith owed allegiance, offer the response. No, it was better described, Traveler realized, as a religion-society issue. There was no separation here, nor should there be. He agreed with a speaker who asserted that one of the more enduring fictions in American history is that religion had been separated from politics. From the very outset "religious convictions intermixed with perceived interests and ethnic loyalties in political parties."[9]

He realized that once Smith became a candidate for public office any beliefs or principles that large numbers of his fellow citizens thought might influence his political judgment would come under scrutiny. Furthermore, it would be up to the candidate and his supporters to respond as they thought best. Whatever it might mean to its many interpreters, that famed "wall of separation" did not and could not come between religion and society.

Although there were occasional side paths that tempted him, Traveler encountered his first cluster of Supreme Court rulings on Church-state issues in the 1940s. Three decisions of the Supreme Court directly involved Jehovah's Witnesses, but the findings had serious implications for other religions as well. Because of a slight altercation as they proselytized on the streets, Jehovah's Witnesses were charged and convicted in Connecticut courts but appealed to the Supreme Court. On the basis of free exercise of religion, in a unanimous decision, the court sided with them. The *Cantwell* case, as it is named, stands out as the first in which the actions of a state were invalidated by the Supreme Court on the basis of religious liberty. The court made explicit by this ruling that the First Amendment regarding free exercise applied to the individual states as well as to Congress. In the century and a half before the 1940s, all of the claims based on religion—there were less than a dozen—were brought against the federal government. With *Cantwell* the flood gates began to swing open and the level of cases against individual states to build up.

In another court case in 1940, the Supreme Court found against Jehovah's Witnesses and ruled that a school board could enforce its mandate and require school children to salute the flag. Commenting on this case, the *Christian Century,* a liberal Protestant publication, noted that the decision came when there was war in Europe and sensitivity to patriotic loyalty at home. "Not for a moment is it to be assumed that the decision of

---

[9] John F. Wilson, "The Religious Clauses and Modern American Experiences: Seeking Out New Bottles for Old Wine," Presented at a National Symposium on the First Amendment Religious Liberty Clauses and American Public Life sponsored by The Williamsburg Charter on April 11–13, 1988.

the court was influenced by the popular mood. Such a suggestion would be righteously resented."[10]

Traveler was skeptical about this sentiment. He asked himself whether the Supreme Court should be responsive to public opinion, or should it rest satisfied with its own decision even when that turned on a five to four vote with strong minority dissent? Traveler decided to hold that judgment in suspense.

Three years later, a similar case was brought by Jehovah's Witnesses and the Supreme Court found for them: their children did not have to salute the flag. In delivering the opinion of the court, Justice Robert H. Jackson noted that "this case calls upon us to reconsider a precedent decision as the Court throughout its history often has been required to do."[11] In their concurring decision Justices Hugo L. Black and William O. Douglas noted that "long reflection convinced us that although the principle [previously invoked] is sound its application in the particular case was wrong."[12]

Traveler was struck by the willingness of the court to reverse an earlier opinion, but even more by Justice Frankfurter's dissenting opinion, in which he expressed the strong need for judicial self-restraint. The issue to be decided, he wrote, came before the court with the full authority of the state of West Virginia. The framers of the Constitution could have assigned some share in the legislative process to the court. But they did not. They shielded the judiciary from the legislative function. He continued: "If the function of the Court is to be no different from that of a legislature . . . then indeed judges should not have life tenure and they should be made directly responsible to the electorate."[13] Well, Traveler mused, another view of the shifting roles of the court, legislation, and public opinion!

Those judgments, too, Traveler decided were matters for reflection as he trekked onward. He did not leave the 1940s, however, before he encountered even graver issues of Church-state questions. The first of these arose when the New Jersey policy of funding the transportation of pupils to and from public and parochial schools was challenged as a violation of the no-establishment provision of the First Amendment. By a five to four vote the court found that such public funding was not unconstitutional. Traveler learned that the *Everson* case, as it was labeled, became a landmark decision for several reasons. First, it established that the no-establishment as well as

---

[10] Editorial, "The Flag Salute Case," *The Christian Century* (June 19, 1940). Quoted in Terry Eastland, *Religious Liberty in the Supreme Court: The Cases that Define the Debate Over Church and State* (Washington, D.C.: Ethics and Public Policy Center, 1993) 37.

[11] Eastland, *Religious Liberty in the Supreme Court,* 41.

[12] Ibid., 47.

[13] Ibid., 51.

the free exercise provision of the First Amendment applied to the states as well as to the federal government. Second, it was the first clear effort by the court to determine squarely the intended meaning of "an establishment of religion." What did "no establishment" mean? Third, it attempted to establish the method by which its own interpretation was determined. As a firm basis for their opinions, all nine of the justices turned to history and to the efforts of Thomas Jefferson and James Madison to secure religious liberty—but they read that history differently. In his majority opinion Justice Hugo L. Black asserted that the establishment of religion clause meant that neither a state nor the federal government "can pass laws which aid one religion, aid all religions, or prefer one religion over another."[14] Then he added that the clause was intended, in the words of Thomas Jefferson, to erect "a wall of separation between church and state."[15]

[Jefferson's famed metaphor appeared, not in an official document, but in a letter he wrote to the Baptist Association of Danbury, Connecticut, on January 1, 1802. After quoting from the First Amendment he added, "thus building a wall of separation between church and state."]

The court assimilated that metaphor in its conclusion: "That wall must be kept high and impregnable. . . . We have not breached it here."[16]

All of these major findings and opinions and a number of lesser ones, Traveler vowed to keep in mind as he forged onward. He noted before he left this case, however, that a dissenting opinion put forth by Justices Robert H. Jackson and Felix Frankfurter asserted:

> It is no exaggeration to say that the whole historic conflict in temporal policy between the Catholic Church and non-Catholics comes to a focus in their respective school policies. . . . Our public school, if not a product of Protestantism, at least is more consistent with it than with the Catholic culture and scheme of values.[17]

That judgment, too, Traveler tucked into the back of his mind, but it reinforced his decision to focus on school-related issues.

No more than a year later the Supreme Court ruled on what was termed a "release time" program, in which teachers from different religious affiliations could offer religious instruction in the public schools for an hour a week. Students could elect to attend one of those classes or to continue their regular classes. The teachers were subject to approval but were not paid by the state. The case made its way up the judicial ladder to

[14] Ibid., 64.
[15] Ibid., 65.
[16] Ibid., 67.
[17] Ibid., 67–8.

the Supreme Court. Referring to its findings in the *Everson* case, the court judged by a vote of eight to one that the program violated the no-establishment provision. Traveler's attention was arrested briefly by a statement in the majority decision and by another in the minority. Justice Robert H. Jackson, regretting that the court did not circumscribe its findings, wrote that, in effect, it would "ban every form of teaching which suggests or recognizes that there is a God."[18] And after saying that almost everything in our culture that gives meaning to life is saturated with religious influence, that separating the secular from religion in education is a task of the utmost delicacy, that neither the Constitution nor any other legal source provides guidance to the court, he concluded that the judges are left only with their own prepossessions. That seemed a properly modest acknowledgment of judicial limitations. The second statement he noted was that of Justice Stanley F. Reed, who said that "the wall of separation" did not exclude religious education from the university Mr. Jefferson had founded and that "a rule of law should not be drawn from a figure of speech."[19] The apparent disjunction between Jefferson's declarations and his practice was not the last of the anomalies Traveler was to encounter as he followed Supreme Court decisions.

Four years later, another release-time program was considered by the court. In this instance the religious instruction was not given on public school property, it did not draw upon public funds, nor, the majority opinion found, was there any coercion involved. Writing for the five to four majority opinion, Justice William O. Douglas said that within its scope the separation of Church and state is absolute. But, he wrote, the First Amendment does not posit such a separation in every respect. Neither the First Amendment nor the finding in the *McCollum* case "mean that public institutions can make no adjustments of their schedules to accommodate the religious needs of the people. We cannot read into the Bill of Rights such a philosophy of hostility to religion."[20] He also wrote a statement that became one of the most quoted and contested opinions in constitutional debates: "We are a religious people whose institutions presuppose a Supreme Being," an assertion that his own judicial opinions years later would throw into doubt.

Entering more fully into the 1950s, Traveler turned his attention to other than court cases to consider the role of religion in American society. He was led to reflect once more on the variety of ways in which American citizens put their religious beliefs into practice, often affecting public issues

---

[18] Ibid., 91.
[19] Ibid., 95.
[20] Ibid., 107.

and policies. Further, he immediately saw that the believing citizen could be at once a member of an organized religious grouping—a church or synagogue—and at the same time an elected or appointed political agent. As such he could understand himself to be performing religious and political functions simultaneously when he ministered directly or indirectly to the poor, the hungry, the homeless, the sick, and the oppressed. There was, in other words, no necessary opposition between religion and government—which did not mean there were no problems regarding the role of religion in society, particularly in a religiously pluralist society such as that of the United States. The question—really a series of shifting particular issues—was and is how that role is to manifest itself.

He turned to consider several ways in which the social order was being shaped by a mixture of political and religious concerns. In World War II Catholics once again served in the military in numbers disproportionate to their percentage of the population. After the war, large numbers of Catholic veterans took advantage of the G.I. Bill of Rights to attend religious-based colleges, which they permanently altered. (Some years later the Catholic community realized that in return for government subsidy American Catholic higher education had been noticeably secularized.) After the war, many Catholics became strongly anti-Communist, opposing Communist influence in, for example, labor unions, education, and foreign policies. Into the political climate characterized by charges of Communism, anti-Communism and anti-anti-Communism stepped Joseph R. McCarthy, the junior U.S. Senator from Wisconsin. Wielding a blunt but powerful political machete, he attacked a large number of political figures as Communists or their dupes. At the peak of his influence, support for the senator was considerable among Catholics and Protestants, with Catholic support running 7 to 9 percent ahead. Catholic publications were largely favorable but the leading Catholic lay-edited journal, *Commonweal,* consistently opposed him.

Divisions between Catholics and Protestants widened, old stereotypes were revived and burnished anew, and cooperative religious ventures established during the war began to fall apart. In 1949 Paul Blanshard, a harsh critic of Catholicism, published the book *American Freedom and Catholic Power,* which argued that the two were inevitably inimical. Within half a year it went into its sixth printing, evidence that there was a large receptive audience for his message. The newly formed Protestants and Other Americans United for the Separation of Church and State took as its prime concern and target the Catholic Church. Leading Protestants, fearing a McCarthy run for the presidency, demanded that the Catholic bishops repudiate him. (Were these the same people, Traveler wondered, who expressed fear that the Catholic Church would dictate to Catholic politicians?) Swept up into the acrimonious exchanges were particular matters such as Myron Taylor's mission to the Vatican. Taylor, a Protestant and former board chairman of U.S. Steel, was appointed personal representative by President Franklin Roosevelt and given the status of ambassador. And once again, or still, federal aid to education was placed on the national agenda.

Later in the decade Traveler was an observer at meetings in New York where such matters were discussed in more civil and nuanced terms. The occasion was a seminar on religion in a free society. Approximately one hundred persons gathered for a week; the principal speakers included John Courtney Murray, Reinhold Niebuhr, Leo Pfeffer, Will Herberg, Abraham Joshua Heschel, and Paul Tillich. Speaking from within different traditions, they often disagreed with each other, frequently diametrically. Locked together in argument—a definition of civilization—the boundaries of which were largely set by Father Murray, they debated the nature of political community, civil society and civil religion, public affairs, religious traditions, and America's self-understanding, on which turns a sense of self-identity. In a diminished form, the loss of self-identity is, Murray asserted, insanity and "it would not be good for the American giant to go lumbering about the world today, lost and mad."[21]

Murray proposed that our pluralist society be viewed as one in which four different conspiracies interact—Protestant, Catholic, Jewish, and secularist. Stripped of invidious connotations, the term conspiracy means, he explained, a "breathing together," a concord, a unanimity of opinion. Within a single conspiracy agreement in belief and action is relatively easy to reach; between the conspiracies it can be extremely difficult. Discrepant histories, styles of thought, interior lives all form different universes of discourse. The declared search for truth and fairness often cloaks a conflict of ideas and allegiances, of power and prestige which frequently breaks through the civil veneer to reveal the true face of war. It would be utopian to hope that we can achieve a single conspiracy based on unanimous consent. But it might be possible, he concluded, to reduce the war and enlarge the dialogue, to achieve orderly conversation.

Among the various matters in which unanimity is difficult to reach, Murray named the use of tax funds and school support. The basic terms of the argument offered by Catholicism are not, Murray asserted, complex.

> Its principle is that the canons of distributive justice ought to control the actions
> of government in allocating funds that it coercively collects from all the people

---

[21] John Courtney Murray, "America's Four Conspiracies," *Religion in America,* ed. John Cogley (New York: Meridian Books, Inc., 1958) 13.

in pursuance of its legitimate interest in universal, compulsory schooling. The fact is that these canons are presently not being observed. . . . So in drastic brevity, runs the argument. For my part, I have never heard a satisfactory answer to it.[22]

Murray's projection of how that argument would be met by members of the other conspiracies was soon borne out.

Reinhold Niebuhr, a noted Protestant theologian, observed that the secularization of education is the price we pay for the separation of Church and state, which is "a gain for our public life, since organized religion is bound to be divisive," and *that* "we simply cannot afford."[23] He acknowledged that the price that Catholics pay for their separate school system, which instructed 12 percent of the nation's students, was, of course, "double taxation" for which prudential compensation ought to be made.

Will Herberg traced the reasoning behind the governmental operation of schools. It was never intended that government would preempt the field or supersede the prime right of parents to educate their children. The principles of subsidiarity and pluralism were the guides then—and should be now. "*In principle,* there is no reason why the religious school should be barred from governmental support because of what is said or implied in the First Amendment."[24] He concluded, however, that for the foreseeable future, assistance beyond present fringe benefits would be regarded as going too far.

James Hastings Nichols, a theological faculty member at the University of Chicago, differed head-on with Will Herberg. Roman Catholic controlled education, he charged, is censored education, its graduates "crippled as contributors to the great dialogue of our common life."[25] Again: To many if not most American Protestants "the expansion of Roman Catholic controlled education means a major threat to the free society." And, rhetorically: "Does distributive justice require that we subsidize his [the Roman Catholic] secession from the civic dialogue?"

Leo Pfeffer, associate general counsel of the American Jewish Congress, relying upon his reading of United States history and various Supreme Court cases, argued that the "no establishment" and the "free exercise" provisions were not separate principles but two sides of the same coin: separation guarantees freedom and freedom requires separation. On

[22] Ibid., 30–1.

[23] Reinhold Niebuhr, "A Note on Pluralism," *Religion in America,* ed. John Cogley (New York: Meridian Books, Inc., 1958) 47.

[24] Will Herberg, "Religion, Democracy and Public Education," *Religion in America,* ed. John Cogley (New York: Meridian Books, Inc., 1958) 135.

[25] James Hastings Nichols, "Religion and Education in a Free Society," *Religion in America,* ed. John Cogley (New York: Meridian Books, Inc., 1985) 163.

this reading no government support should go to any single religion, preferentially or not preferentially. Any past deviation from this he explained in historical terms. This view, he knew, was termed absolutist by some, but it was, he insisted, a fair reading of the situation.

The seminar ended, Traveler observed, with the conspiracies firmly in place, along the lines that John Courtney Murray had predicated. He noted, however, that many of the opinions and judgments were prudential, based on findings "at this time." Would they change with changing times, with different conditions?

Traveler passed rapidly from the seminar to the active political arena. In 1960 John F. Kennedy was making a run for the presidency of the United States. His Catholicism immediately served as a lightning rod for diverse and often contradictory opinions. Would his religion be a factor for those who would actually vote? Could he be elected? *Should* he be elected? Is his religion his own private business or does it have a social and corporate dimension that should be publicly examined? Some of the questions, not always polite and sometimes accusations merely disguised as questions, caused more than one commentator to say they now understood the observation that "anti-Catholicism is the anti-Semitism of the intellectual." The president of the Southern Baptist Convention, for example, asserted, "I am not a bigot," then said, "All we ask is that Roman Catholicism lift its bloody hand from the throats of those who want to worship in the church of their choice."[26] One group of Protestant ministers said bluntly that Kennedy's religion rendered him unfit for the presidency.

Other Protestant church leaders, including notably Reinhold Niebuhr and John Bennett, defended Kennedy from such charges. On Kennedy himself, however, fell the principal burden of defusing the issue. Appearing before a group of Protestant ministers he stated his views: opposed to extending government support to parochial schools; opposed to an ambassador to the Vatican; favored strict separation of Church and state; if, in a circumstance he could not foresee, there would arise a conflict between his oath to uphold the Constitution and his conscience, he would resign. When he won the election narrowly, one commentator said wryly that it proved a Catholic could be elected president—"if he went to Harvard, was a Democrat, had a rich father, a beautiful wife, a finely tuned political machine and some plain good luck."[27] Whatever the reasons, with this election the major debates about the fitness of a candidate because of his Catholicism were given an American burial.

[26] Hennesey, *American Catholics,* 308.

[27] Cushing Strout, *The New Heavens and New Earth: Political Religion in America* (New York: Harper & Row, 1974) 300. The person quoted is Daniel Callahan.

In the midst of the turbulent 1960s, Traveler broke off his observations of the public statements and marches that religious leaders—Jewish, Catholic, and Protestant—were making to combat racism, to advance civil rights, and to oppose the war in Vietnam.[28] He traveled to Rome where Vatican Council II, called by Pope John XXIII, was taking place. He was aware that John Courtney Murray had been locked in a scholarly debate with other Catholic theologians who supported what they understood to be perennial Catholic doctrine: ideally the one true religion would work with and be supported by the state, which would profess that religion. Expediency could change the practice but not the ideal. Murray's developing views headed in a different direction.

For years Murray had been forbidden to publish his work on Church-state relations and had, in fact, been uninvited to the council. But after the personal intervention of Cardinal Spellman, to whom he served as theological consultant, Murray was in Rome, and his views noticeably present in conciliar debates. With a degree of American chauvinism, Traveler took delight in seeing Murray as a concelebrant with Pope Paul VI as the council drew to its end. He drew greater satisfaction, however, from the fact that "the greatest argument on religious freedom in all history broke forth in the Church"[29] and changed definitively the way religious freedom would henceforth be considered in Church-state discussions in Rome—and back in the United States. He was also amused to see Paul Blanshard, an informal observer, looking both pleased and slightly disconcerted by the attention lavished on him by friendly nuns who surrounded him. When, later, Traveler read the council's Declaration on Religious Freedom, he noted that religious freedom was not reduced to "freedom of conscience," with its temptation to subjectivism, but was defined to mean "that all men are to be immune to coercion . . . [and] that in matters religious no one is to be forced to act in a manner contrary to his own beliefs."[30] This definition, based on the dignity of each person, Traveler believed to be perfectly harmonious with the First Amendment of the U.S. Constitution.

Traveler returned home to find a number of interesting items concerning Church-state issues. Robert M. Hutchins, a former president of the Uni-

---

[28] The views of many of these people, including Gordon Zahn, Daniel Berrigan, S.J., John C. Bennett, Dorothy Day, Richard John Neuhaus, Abraham Joshua Heschel, and James Forest, are in James Finn's *Protest: Pacifism & Politics* (New York: Random House, 1967).

[29] John Courtney Murray, "Religious Freedom," introduction to *The Documents of Vatican II*, ed. Walter M. Abbott (New York: Herder & Herder, 1966) 672.

[30] Declaration on Religious Freedom *(Dignitatis humanae)*, The Documents of Vatican II, ed. Abbott, 679.

versity of Chicago and a noted liberal educator, had published a hard-hitting article stating that "federal aid to education is an absolute necessity. But a political argument over funds for parochial schools, masquerading as a constitutional issue, bars the way."[31] President Kennedy, Hutchins added, perpetuated the masquerade. After noting the many government programs of grants, loans, and tax benefits to Church-supported institutions, Hutchins spelled out what he termed a G.I. Bill of Rights for children in primary and secondary schools.

Traveler also found that the Supreme Court, faced with a quandary concerning the definition of religion, had found an ingenious solution. The quandary: In the context of the Vietnam War, three young men claimed to be conscientious objectors but did not fulfill the accepted criteria that would earn them the congressional grace of exemption, that is, they did not come to their conscientious stance "by reason of religious training or belief in a Supreme Being." And the court was acutely aware that its own interpretation of the establishment provision forbade preference to an establishment of religion. Would they be showing a preference if exemptions went only to those with religious affiliations? What to do? Paul Tillich to the rescue, with his extremely inclusive definition of religion. Following him at some distance and possibly unaware of the theological terrain on which they were encroaching, the justices adopted a functional interpretation of religion. Exemption was granted a plaintiff, Daniel Seeger, on the basis that he held "a sincere and meaningful belief which occupies in the life of its possessor a place parallel to that filled by the God of those admittedly qualifying for the exemption."[32] Some years later the court extended that definitional umbrella to include beliefs that are "purely ethical or moral in source." Ingenious, yes, but helpful? The court then vigorously rejected exemption for a Roman Catholic who based his claim on the long tradition of just war teaching and concluded that the war in Vietnam was unjust.[33] One acute student of the First Amendment said that with these judgments the Supreme Court was risking intellectual double hernia.

Traveler learned also that in a footnote to a court case Justice Hugo Black had included in a list of religions Secular Humanism and Ethical

---

[31] Robert M. Hutchins, " Liberal Calls for Aid to Church Schools," *Saturday Evening Post* (June 8, 1963) 6–8.

[32] William Lee Miller, *The First Liberty: Religion and the American Republic* (New York: Alfred A. Knopf, 1986) 339.

[33] The politico-moral framework of such a claim is covered in *A Conflict of Loyalties: The Case for Selective Conscientious Objection,* ed. James Finn (New York: Pegasus, 1968). It contains essays by John Courtney Murray, William V. O'Brien, Michael Harrington, Paul Ramsey, and others.

Culture, groups that Traveler knew many others regarded as non-religious. His common-sense views were assailed by the court findings. The list of matters he found necessary to put aside for further reflection was growing at an alarming rate.

As he entered the 1970s his own ponderings were distracted by a court case that astounded him. Accustomed as he had grown to the court making decisions that he thought should properly be matters for the legislators of the United States, for Congress or the states, he was not prepared for the 1973 *Roe v. Wade* case. The court declared abortion to be legal and ruled that states could not prohibit abortions or make them unnecessarily difficult to obtain. In one fell decision, the various laws and restrictions concerning abortion that existed in every state in the union were swept from the books. Recalling Justice Frankfurter's insistence on judicial restraint, Traveler heard himself sigh, "Ah, Felix, thou shouldst be living at this hour."[34] Expressed negatively, the ruling removed from legal protection unborn human beings if their mothers chose to end their lives. Expressed positively, it gave mothers the right to end their pregnancies by abortion. That ruling followed an earlier decision in which the Supreme Court found a right to privacy in the "penumbras formed by emanations" of guarantees in the Bill of Rights. Traveler had privately, and frivolously he now realized, called that "the pneumatic theory of interpretation," not realizing the judicial mischief that would follow from it. Traveler decided to track the consequences of *Roe v. Wade* as that ruling wove itself into our national life. The number of abortions increased, of course, and the issue itself tore at the fabric of our society. Two sharply differing groups—self-described as pro-life and pro-choice—did not become locked in civil argument, which requires at least agreement on ground rules; instead, they became mired in crossed beliefs and attitudes. Traveler found that much of the public exchange was based on misrepresentation or actual ignorance of what the Supreme Court had ruled. This led to the accurate but odd finding that the majority of Americans say they want to keep the *Roe* decision intact, but favor specific restrictions that would eviscerate that ruling.[35]

Apart from the issue itself, Traveler was struck by the way many people, often highly educated, articulate, and politically sophisticated, related public discussion to consequent political decision. One such person,

---

[34] The issue of judicial activism and judicial restraint became a lively and often rancorous debate in the nineties. *First Things,* an ecumenical journal of religion and public life edited by Richard John Neuhaus, was a particularly active participant in the debate. A very useful compilation of various opinions, pro and con, is found in *The End of Democracy?* ed. Mitchell S. Muncy (Dallas: Spence Publishing Co., 1997).

[35] James Davison Hunter, "What Americans Really Think About Abortion," *First Things* (June–July 1992) 13–21.

Senator Edward Kennedy, posed the issue starkly. The Catholic bishops had said that to separate personal morality and public policy was not logically tenable. Placing his comments specifically in the context of their statement, Church and state relations, religious values and national decisions, the senator said in cases like abortion and prayer "the proper role of religion is to appeal to the free conscience of each person, not the coercive rule of secular law." And again: "Personal choices like abortion should be questions for public debate but in the end the answers cannot be matters for public decision."[36] Public debate but not public decision? But who then should make the decisions on abortion? On the death penalty? On the parental role in education? Nine members of the Supreme Court? The people's representatives, legislatures of fifty states, whose varied efforts to do so the court dismissed? Traveler found that an odd understanding of how democracy works, or should work. And in the case of abortion, it leaves out of the equation the role of the most vulnerable and voiceless among us, the unborn child. But he recognized that many others thought as the senator did and would happily see the Church be silent on these matters of life and death.

Traveler was also puzzled by those who stated, "I am personally opposed to abortion but I do not want to impose my view on others." He thought the absurdity of this would be evident if one substituted for "abortion" the word "slavery" or "racism" or one of many other social ills generally regarded as grievous. But he soon discovered that he was wrong. Senator Kennedy's position was also supported by those who thought that religious leaders should not intervene in politics. For example, Arthur Schlesinger Jr., who said that when they do intervene "they do so at their own risk—and at risk to their churches." Fair enough, Traveler thought, religion is not a no-risk enterprise. But the reasons the noted historian gave seemed strangely uninformed. For after denouncing religious fanaticism, Mr. Schlesinger concluded that "religion deals in absolutes: politics is compromise and adjustments."[37] There are absolutes in religion surely, but religious leaders who hold them have often proved themselves to be adept political figures of great integrity. After all, Traveler thought to himself, the great Thomas More, not an obscure historical figure, showed well how it could be done.

Not long after Kennedy's statement Traveler found a small pamphlet issued by the United States Catholic Conference, the introduction of which reads in part:

---

[36] *The New York Times,* September 11, 1984, A26.

[37] *The Wall Street Journal,* September 29, 1984. These frequently-repeated views of Mr. Schlesinger drew a forceful riposte from Michael Novak, "Relativism or Absolutes: Which Is the American Way?" *The National Catholic Register* (October 29, 1989) 5.

A notable characteristic in the 1980s has been the increasing visibility of religious questions and themes in the political life of the United States. From medical technology to military technology, from economic policy to foreign policy, the choices before the country are laden with moral content. The moral dimension arises from the human significance of these choices.[38]

Among the issues which the pamphlet addresses are abortion, civil rights, the economy, family life, human rights, capital punishment, and regional conflict in the world. The bishops had made some of these issues matters of large public debate, with special pastoral letters on nuclear deterrence and war and on the economy.

Having followed court opinion through stages in which it set down a three-fold test for statutes to be acceptable (the statute must have a secular legislative purpose; its primary effect must neither advance nor inhibit religion; it must not foster an excessive entanglement with religion), to cases where this test was disregarded, to the Tillichean definition of religion, to the so-called mystery clause in *Planned Parenthood v. Casey* ("at the heart of liberty is the right to define one's own concept of existence, of meaning, of the universe and of the mystery of human life"), Traveler believed that the court's decisions in the last fifty years rang with cognitive dissonance. The "no establishment" provision seemed lost in a thicket of judicial readings. The First Amendment now safeguards, apparently, the free exercise of philosophy, whether it is religious, anti-religious, or something in between. A mess! Or as a more sober assessment has it, on matters religious the court is "so much at odds with itself and often with history that its glosses on the Constitution sometimes may appear to sound more like glossalalia than like convincing arguments."[39]

Traveler believed that only prolonged, clear, and persuasive argument could shift our cultural patterns so religiously informed opinions could, once again, be given their due weight in the making of public policies— and judicial findings. Traveler was relieved to turn back to school-related issues to which prolonged public argument and changing cultural conditions were inspiring renewed judgment. Briefly, deficiencies of many public, that is government, schools were becoming increasingly evident; increasingly evident too was the remarkable scholastic success of parochial schools. The need for moral instruction which public schools were hobbled from providing and which parochial schools emphasized became stronger; given a choice minorities and inner city children—often

---

[38] *Political Responsibility for the Future* (Washington, D.C.: United States Catholic Conference, 1987) 1–2.

[39] Strout, *The New Heavens and New Earth*, 285–6.

the same—elected to go to parochial schools; in economic terms the cost for each child in the government schools far exceeded that for a child in the parochial schools. Those who hold monopolies are naturally reluctant to look kindly on any challenges to long-standing practices from which they benefit. Traveler was not surprised, therefore, to find that reactionary forces, teachers' unions, special interests, and simply altruistic supporters of the government schools deny, dispute, or dismiss many of these empirically based statements. The findings carry enough weight, however, so that a majority of the public is in favor of parental choice, which includes empowering them to make that choice. One commentator predicted that opponents of parental choice "place their hopes on legal challenges since public opinion polls and the shifting of legislative attitudes across the nation make it increasingly clear that democracy will prevail."[40]

Traveler was heartened at these signals of a welcome break in long-standing educational policies at the primary and secondary level, but his heart sank as he looked at Catholic education at the college and university level. Put simply, the Catholic community in America was now divided on how best to implement *Ex corde ecclesiae,* the apostolic constitution on Catholic education that Pope John Paul II issued in 1990. It goes to the very identity of the hundreds of Catholic educational institutions. What characterizes them as Catholic? As institutions operating in intellectual freedom? What is their special mission? What are the degrees of responsibility of the Catholic bishops, of theologians, of administrators and faculty, of trustees and those who bear fiduciary responsibility? Will clear Church control jeopardize entitlement to federal and state aid? Will continued acceptance of such aid lead to the "secularization" of the colleges and universities? The questions themselves seem at cross purposes.[41] Would they be resolved by the end of this millennium? No, Traveler told himself, they will extend into the indefinite future.

Weary from his long travels through the twentieth century, Traveler fell into a deep sleep and a restless dream filled with fragments of his scattered observations. He dreamed that he saw the wall of separation winding its sinuous way through the century, and as he approached it he heard alternating voices saying "something there is that doesn't like a wall" and

---

[40] David W. Kirkpatrick, "Democracy Will Prevail" (Milwaukee: The Blum Center for Parental Freedom in Education, February 1998). A full-scale treatment of the argument is provided by Quentin Quade, *Financing Education: The Struggle Between Governmental Monopoly and Parental Control* (New Brunswick, N.J.: Transaction Publishers, 1996).

[41] A very good overview of the issues is provided by *Commonweal* in a special supplement to which a half dozen writers of different professional backgrounds contribute (April 9, 1999).

"good walls make good neighbors." Close to the wall he saw that it had been constructed over time, and that it was built of good, solid, well-shaped bricks, Swiss cheese, blue smoke, and mirrors. He saw also that workers were still adding to it. Adding and taking away.

On waking, Traveler attempted to summarize the experiences he had during his long trip and his own reactions to them. Impossible! Too many, too complex, too incomplete. On the negative side he could say that John Courtney Murray's hope that our conspiracies at war with each other might be replaced with conspiracies locked in civil dialogue would also have to be pushed into the future. Our experiment in a free society was still an experiment, still developing.

Still, Traveler concluded, borrowing from the great legal scholar Judge John T. Noonan Jr., one great virtue of our free society has been preserved, even as it has been constantly challenged. "Free exercise—let us as Americans assert it—is an American invention."[42] No false modesty should cloud or obscure this distinctive historical achievement. Further, the development of free exercise had fed into the Declaration on Religious Freedom, enabling the Catholic Church to emerge as the great upholder of human rights and defender of religious freedom around the world. The twentieth was not the best of centuries. But in terms of freedom, for the Church in the world and for the Catholic Church in the United States, neither was it the worst of centuries.

---

[42] John T. Noonan Jr., *The Lustre of Our Country: The American Experience of Religious Freedom* (Berkeley: University of California Press, 1998) 2.

Communications and the Arts:
Lost: The Mind of the Church

Michael O. Garvey

A few years before my father was born, my grandfather purchased a fifteen-volume edition of the *Catholic Encyclopedia,* which I inherited a few years ago. It appeared just four years before my father did, early in this century, 1913 to be exact. I love its magisterial tone and occasionally sonorous prose, and I know that I am not alone, because late in this century, in 1995, Kevin Knight, a young man in Denver, Colorado, assembled a nationwide network of volunteers who are still in the process of transmogrifying the 1913 edition and launching it into deepest cyberspace, where most of it is available on the World Wide Web.

Knight's heavily trafficked "New Advent" website includes, among many, many other things, the Douay-Rheims translation of the Bible, the entire *Summa Theologiae,* a massive patristics library, the *Baltimore Catechism,* the more recent *Catechism of the Catholic Church,* the Code of Canon Law, most papal encyclicals, the texts of most of the Church's general councils, and links to the official website of the Holy See. Knight was inspired to undertake the project while taking part in World Youth Day in Denver in August of 1993 and hearing Pope John Paul II's appeal for a new evangelization.

It certainly seems to be the sort of project John Paul was enthusiastically approving in a 1989 letter (on World Communications Day, May 27) which insisted that

> we must be grateful for the new technology which enables us to store information in vast man-made artificial memories, thus providing wide and instant access to the knowledge which is our human heritage, to the Church's teaching and tradition, the words of sacred Scripture, the counsels of the great masters of spirituality, the history and traditions of the local Churches, of religious orders, and lay institutes, and to the ideas and experiences of initiators and innovators whose insights bear constant witness to the faithful presence in our midst of a loving Father who brings out of his treasure new things and old.

Even Catholics as gratefully docile as I ought to be forgiven for wondering what sort of response John Paul's statement might have drawn from his predecessor at the beginning of the century. Pope Pius X had little use for initiators and innovators of any kind, and in what is arguably the most readable (because arguably the most passionate) encyclical ever written, denounced them as "partisans of error [who were to be found] not only among the Church's open enemies; but, what is most to be dreaded and deplored, in her very bosom, and are the more mischievous the less they keep in the open." In *Pascendi Dominici Gregis* (On the Doctrine of the Modernists), published a few years before my grandpa's *Catholic Encyclopedia,* Pope Pius sounds less like a bishop addressing his fellow bishops, less even like a father addressing his children, than like Stonewall Jackson addressing his brigade before a battle.

He instructed his bishops:

> We order that you do everything in your power to drive out of your dioceses, even by solemn interdict, any pernicious books that may be in circulation there. The Holy See neglects no means to remove writings of this kind, but their number has now grown to such an extent that it is hardly possible to subject them all to censure. Hence it happens sometimes that the remedy arrives too late, for the disease has taken root during the delay. We will, therefore, that the Bishops putting aside all fear and the prudence of the flesh, despising the clamor of evil men, shall, gently, by all means, but firmly, do each his own part in this work. . . . Let no Bishop think that he fulfills his duty by denouncing to Us one or two books, while a great many others of the same kind are being published and circulated. Nor are you to be deterred by the fact that a book has obtained elsewhere the permission which is commonly called the Imprimatur, both because this may be merely simulated, and because it may have been granted through carelessness or too much indulgence or excessive trust placed in the author, which last has perhaps sometimes happened in the religious orders. Besides, just as the same food does not agree with everyone, it may happen that a book, harmless in one place, may, on account of the different circumstances, be hurtful in another. . . . In all cases it will be obligatory on Catholic booksellers not to put on sale books condemned by the Bishop. And while We are treating of this subject, We wish the Bishops to see to it that booksellers do not, through desire for gain, engage in evil trade. It is certain that in the catalogs of some of them the books of the Modernists are not infrequently announced with no small praise. If they refuse obedience, let the Bishops, after due admonition, have no hesitation in depriving them of the title of Catholic booksellers. . . .
>
> It is not enough to hinder the reading and the sale of bad books—it is also necessary to prevent them from being published. Hence, let the Bishops use the utmost strictness in granting permission to print. . . . We have the highest esteem for this institution of censors, and We not only exhort, but We order that it be extended to all dioceses.

It's difficult to see how any literate or even sentient Catholic could honestly lament the fact that *Pascendi Dominici Gregis* has become an anachronism in the ensuing century. The encyclical is scolding and sulfurous in tone and indicates a joyless hierarchical rectitude which largely vanished from the Church (except for occasional and hotly protested eruptions) around the time of the Second Vatican Council. And good riddance.

Nevertheless at least one reason those few Y2K Catholics who have read *Pascendi Dominici Gregis* find it so disagreeable is the nearly idolatrous veneration of individual freedom which prevails in middle class society at our own end of the century. Much as the members of the National Rifle Association reflexively reject even a suggestion that the acquisition of firearms might not be an absolutely private matter, many post-conciliar Catholics tend to regard any assertion of authority as authoritarian. If some Catholic pastors at the beginning of the century were excessively vigilant, even boorish, in their defense of the Church against what one *Catholic Encyclopedia* contributor called "the literary danger," they were also commendably aware, as too many of us seem not to be, that reading, like everything else we Catholics do, is done within and deeply affects our entire community, the Church. If it is reasonable, perhaps even imperative, to question their target selection, it is unfair to characterize them, as too many glib historians nowadays do, as an excitable and anti-literate mob of ecclesiastical skinheads.

That Curious Institution, the Index

The Index of Forbidden Books was the curious institution to which censoriously inclined Catholics liked to appeal in those days. Established in 1557 by Pope Paul IV, this list of titles which Catholics were forbidden to read or even to own without ecclesiastical permission was being assiduously compiled, revised, and updated well into the twentieth century. The penalty for unauthorized reading or owning was excommunication.

The Index generated a cultural atmosphere which understandably spooked the average modern intellectual. There is, for instance, a memorable passage in Thomas Merton's mid-century autobiography, *The Seven Storey Mountain,* in which Merton recounts a pre-conversion close encounter of the first kind with an alien community of Catholic readers. He had just purchased a copy of Etienne Gilson's *The Spirit of Medieval Philosophy* in a Manhattan bookstore and brought it onboard a homebound bus before he noticed the "Nihil obstat" and "imprimatur" on the title page:

Merton wrote:

> The feeling of disgust and deception struck me like a knife in the pit of the stomach. I felt as if I had been cheated! They should have warned me that it was a

Catholic book! Then I would never have bought it. As it was, I was tempted to throw the thing out of the window at the houses of Woodside—to get rid of it as something dangerous and unclean. Such is the terror that is aroused in the enlightened modern mind by a little innocent Latin and the signature of a priest.

But between those days and our own a great abyss is now fixed, much of it excavated in the early 1960s by the assembled Catholic bishops of the Second Vatican Council. The "nihil obstat" and "imprimatur," those seals of episcopal approval so alarming to the pagan undergraduate Merton, are still insisted upon from time to time, especially for theological textbooks. But the mid-century bishops (and their advisors) were less fearful of "the literary danger" than were their *fin de ciecle* confreres. In what seems to be the council's most frequently quoted document, *Gaudium et spes,* the bishops deployed an almost comically clumsy understatement acknowledging that from time to time "there have been difficulties in the way of harmonizing culture with Christian thought, arising out of contingent factors." But they insisted that grace can and does resound through the occasional dissonance arising from the encounter between a disciplined community of believers and an indifferent, even occasionally suspicious culture. "These difficulties do not necessarily harm the life of faith," the bishops wrote, "but can rather stimulate a more precise and deeper understanding of that faith."

"In their own way, literature and art are very important in the life of the Church." The bishops went on, heedless of the offense their non-inclusive language might give to a future and more fastidious generation:

They seek to give expression to man's nature, his problems and his experience in an effort to discover and perfect man himself and the world in which he lives; they try to discover his place in history and in the universe; to throw light on his suffering and joy, his needs and his potentialities, and to outline a happier destiny in store for him.

Accordingly, the bishops concluded, "every effort should be made . . . to make artists feel that they are understood by the Church in their artistic work and to encourage them, while enjoying a reasonable standard of freedom, to enter into happier relations with the Christian community."

While the tone of *Gaudium et spes* is undoubtedly a great improvement on that of *Pascendi Dominici Gregis,* it isn't as if Catholic writers had been imaginatively and expressively hamstrung during those days before 1966, when Pope Paul VI abolished the Index. Evelyn Waugh alluded to this in a querulous and fairly reactionary article which appeared two years earlier on both sides of the Atlantic—the *Spectator* in England and the *National Review* in the United States: "In general," according to Waugh, the Index of Forbidden Books "is not a troublesome document. Sartre's presence on the list provides a convenient excuse for not reading him. But there is an obvious anomaly in preserving a legal act which is generally disregarded."

Among those Catholics who apparently did not so disregard the Index in those pre-conciliar days was the anomalous novelist and short story writer Flannery O'Connor. In her essay "The Church and the Fiction Writer," she sounds even more nonchalant than Waugh about its effects on the arts. She wrote:

> The business of protecting souls from dangerous literature belongs properly to the Church. All fiction, even when it satisfies the requirements of art, will not turn out to be suitable for everyone's consumption, and if in some instance the Church sees fit to forbid the faithful to read a work without permission, the author, if he is a Catholic, will be thankful that the Church is willing to perform this service for him. It means that he can limit himself to the demands of art.

Indeed, O'Connor herself was sufficiently scrupulous to approach a priest friend of hers in 1957, seeking information on how to get permission to read the work of André Gide. She said that she "despised" Gide's writing, but that she had been invited to join a local ecumenical book club whose proposed reading list included works by this proscribed author. Her admission to her friend that she despised Gide invites the question, "How did she know?" unless she had previously violated a Church law she was now attempting to negotiate. At any rate, her friend apparently advised her that there was, in fact, an applicable dispensation, called *epeikia,* which allowed for instances in which a law could be interpreted and obeyed in spirit rather than by the letter. Thanking him for his trouble, O'Connor somewhat impishly replied, "I will use the *epeikia* and also invoke that word, which is very fancy."

O'Connor, who called herself a "hillbilly Thomist," baffled and fascinated literary critics with her simultaneously hilarious and terrifying evocations of the invasion of grace and the inbreaking of God's kingdom. Thomas Merton, whose generous spirit occasionally rendered his literary judgment susceptible to hyperbole, once compared her work to that of Sophocles. But this may have been one instance of Merton's extravagance coinciding with accuracy. Halfway through the twentieth century, this amazing young Georgian had produced a numinous body of fiction—thirty-one short stories and two novels, *Wise Blood* and *The Violent Bear It Away*—marked by an ancient predilection she once described as an artistic imperative "to observe our fierce and fading manners in the light of an ultimate concern."

Scandalous as it appeared and continues to appear to literary sons and daughters of the Enlightenment, the "ultimate concern" in Flannery O'Connor's grotesque and apocalyptic fiction was remembered, retrieved, energized, refreshed, and revivified first and foremost by her membership in a disciplined communion of believers, men and women willing to honor even the sporadically fuddy-duddy assertions of ecclesiastical authority as the cost of that membership. She knew that it was only within that communion that she could draw near to the bush that burns without being consumed, and if communion cost a humility one rarely sees in the literary world nowadays, so be it. In any event, it would require an almost fanatically secularist reading of O'Connor's fiction to argue that the author's advertent intellectual docility had weakened her work, rendered her narrative sentimental, or occluded her imaginative eyesight. She once wrote:

> Henry James said that the morality of a piece of fiction depended on the amount of 'felt life' that was in it. The Catholic writer, insofar as he has the mind of the Church, will feel life from the standpoint of the central Christian mystery: that it has, for all its horror, been found by God to be worth dying for. But this should enlarge, not narrow, his field of vision.

As if to justify her assertion, O'Connor's own unflinching fiction, characterized by that enlarged and challenging scope, has already become an unavoidable presence in American letters.

Dealing with Contemporary Culture

Accommodating the "mind of the Church" is not the sort of thing that the average North American intellectual, academic, journalist, or artist is inclined to do. *Appropriating* the mind of the Church, as Flannery O'-Connor seems to recommend, may be permissible for a celebrated martyr like Archbishop Oscar Romero of San Salvador—whose episcopal motto and mission was "to feel what the Church feels"—but to appropriate the mind of a community, even to assert that a community could have a distinctive mind (or heart or body), is repugnant to contemporary American orthodoxy and First Amendment dogma. But even while surrounded by a culture which fetishizes individual autonomy and unfettered self expression, everything worthwhile that Catholics have communicated to each other and to others, whether by prose, poetry, song, or image, pulsates with Christ's singular account of the world, which cannot be kept secret.

True, the pulse has not always been a strong one. It seemed to weaken precipitously during the second half of the century, as television began to saturate and transfigure the modern world. Another novelist, Walker Percy, alluded to this in January 1988 when he was invited to address a symposium in Rome sponsored by the Vatican's Pontifical Council for Culture. Despite the ethnic and religious diversity of contemporary American (and Western industrial) culture, Percy said, "there is at work a force, extraordinarily powerful but not necessarily beneficent, which makes for a uniformity of sorts. I am speaking, of course, of the mass media, television in particular." He remarked on the cultural revolution ignited by the invention of the printing press and wondered, "but if books, written and read by a few educated people, turned the world upside down, how to calculate the effect of watching images on a small screen, day after day, year after year, on the human mind, especially on the mind of a growing child?" In addition to the conspicuous effects of the new medium on economic, political, and social behavior, Percy noted

> the radical effect on the psyche itself of daily time spent on media and messages approximating the hours devoted to working and sleeping. Surely there has not occurred in all of man's history an event of greater moment both for good and for ill, an event whose import is only beginning to be understood.

The cultural damage inflicted by television is, as Percy admitted in his address, a commonplace of social criticism. One need not be a trained anthropologist to notice how the disintegration of families, the spreading drug befuddlement, the erosion of all interior life, the commodification of sex, the coarsening of appetite, and the triumph of consumerism all seem to flourish in its pale blue deadpan immensity. But Percy, who was, to put it mildly, less than completely at home in the modern age, suggested that the Church might do well to consider the potential benefits of this new, curious, and unsettling medium. "By the very virtue of its technique," he said, "its instant transmission of word and image, its near total access to the entire population of a modern society, it would be difficult to imagine a more perfect instrument through which the Church can teach, inform, indeed evangelize."

Archbishop Fulton J. Sheen, who died nearly ten years before Percy's remarks and who was praised in those remarks as a "Catholic pioneer in TV evangelism," had been more than willing to try out the new instrument. During the 1920s, while serving on the faculty at the Catholic University of America, Sheen became a popular and innovative lecturer and preacher. In 1930 he began to preach regularly on a new radio program, "The Catholic Hour," which attracted a nationwide audience of Catholics and non-Catholics alike. His "Life Is Worth Living" television program went on the air in 1952 and ran for five seasons, eventually attracting a prime-time audience of at least thirty million people, a viewing public scarcely imaginable in those days.

For many historians these events—perhaps even more than the election of President John F. Kennedy—indicate the comfortable "arrival" of Catholics in the cultural mainstream of America. Martin E. Marty, the occasionally astute Protestant observer, has suggested that the diversity and scope of Sheen's audience signaled the end of the tension which had until then prevailed between the Catholic and Protestant churches in the country.

Whatever one thinks about such observations, it's a remarkable thing, this emergence of a mannered, Tridentine, and stoutly ultramontane cleric with graduate degrees from Louvain, the Sorbonne, and Angelicum University in Rome into a competing celebrity with Ernie Kovacs and Sid Caesar. The same priest described in *Time* magazine by an anonymous Vatican official as "our right arm in the U.S." was a welcome guest—or at least a welcome image of a guest—in the blue-lit living rooms of millions of American households, whether Catholic or not. Indeed, Sheen was awarded the American Legion's Gold Medal for "exemplary work on behalf of Americanism," probably in gratitude for his vitriolic, red-white-and-blue denunciations of Communism and Soviet expansion.

It's worth remembering here how strange and un-American Catholic discourse had hitherto seemed. In the earliest experiences of Catholic Americans, the only communications had been intramural experiments within the various and disparate communities of European immigrants. One early, delightful, and, I think, peculiarly American departure from this parochialism took place in Detroit in 1809, when Fr. Gabriel Richard, pastor of St. Anne's parish, published Michigan's first newspaper, the *Michigan Essay*. It was a four-page, bilingual (French and English) publication which accepted articles written by "gentlemen of talent" whether they were Catholic or not, and, despite the fact that it would unapologetically include such essays as "Nine Days Devotion to the Sacred Heart of Jesus," its principal purpose was secular, specifically, to relieve St. Anne's sacristan of his responsibilities as town crier.

But for the most part, the editors and publishers of America's nineteenth-century Catholic periodicals, most of them laypeople, understood their work as a ministry of the Church. So did the bishops, who, in a pastoral letter issuing from their 1837 meeting in Baltimore, urged Catholics "to sustain with better efforts those journals which, though not officially sanctioned by us, still are most useful to explain our tenets, to defend our rights, and to vindicate our conduct." By the beginning of the twentieth century, Catholics in America were sustaining more than 250 such "useful" publications.

The establishment of the Catholic Press Association (CPA) in 1911 greatly improved these publications, whether or not it enhanced the somewhat defensive utility the bishops had praised in their pastoral letter. The formation of a news service for Catholic newspapers, for instance (today called the Catholic News Service), provided Catholic readers with a glimpse of a Church which manifestly transcended and challenged the distinctions among Irish, Polish, German, or Italian communities.

At first, the CPA, like the majority of the Catholic periodicals it served, was formally independent of the Catholic bishops. Several priests and members of religious orders belonged, but lay people generally presided. This began to change shortly after World War I. The government's mobilization of the country to assist in the bloodshed overseas had inflated the national cost of anti-Catholic bigotry and provided the bishops with a dubious opportunity to form their first corporate institution, the National Catholic War Council. In 1919, the bishops reorganized the National Catholic War Council into the National Catholic Welfare Council (NCWC), a body with an arguably more benevolent purpose. The NCWC, which we know today as the National Conference of Catholic Bishops, included a press department. During the reorganization, the CPA agreed to join its news service to the NCWC's press department, thus greatly increasing its members' subscriptions while ceding editorial control to the bishops. Few Catholic News Service readers within or without the Catholic Church would argue that the national hierarchy has been tyrannical in its corporate editorship, and most Catholic journalists seem to regard the CPA as a very useful professional organization. It certainly seems to be flourishing as a new century breaks upon us, with more than three hundred publications in the United States and Canada availing themselves of the services and educational programs the CPA provides.

Along with the CPA, Catholic institutions of higher learning have exerted a benevolent influence on Catholic journalism in America. In 1910, Marquette University established a department of journalism, and two years later the University of Notre Dame established a journalism professorship. College and university graduates in an increasingly educated, increasingly nationwide Catholic community began to find national magazines such as *America,* which the Jesuits founded in 1909, and *Commonweal,* founded by laypeople in 1924. Both magazines survive today, but earlier in the century they were among many others which provided a distinctively Catholic perspective and offered a distinctively Catholic commentary on ecclesial, political, social, literary, and all other aspects of contemporary life. By the middle of the century, the circulation of Catholic periodicals in North America had reached a total of some fifteen million. By the closing of the Second Vatican Council in 1965, that figure had nearly doubled.

For what was probably the most convulsive and transformative event in the Catholic Church since the Reformation, Vatican Council II expressed nothing very wise about journalism and produced no worthwhile or even very interesting document on the subject. The bishops did manage to agree upon a Decree on the Instruments of Social Communication *(Inter mirifica),* which is remarkable principally for its unreadability. When Cardinal John Heenan of Westminister called *Inter mirifica* the "greatest failure" of Vatican II, few bishops or laypeople, and certainly no journalists, could be heard to disagree with him.

Which is not at all to say that Vatican II had no effects on Catholic journalism. The passions aroused by the event itself, and the obvious enthusiasm—expressed generally in *Gaudium et spes* and more specifically in *Communio et progressio* (the 1971 pastoral instruction on the application of *Inter mirifica*)—for an honest and open discourse within the Church galvanized the writers, editors, and publishers of Catholic newspapers and magazines. According to A.E.P. Wall, who in those days worked for the *Catholic Review* in Baltimore, the Second Vatican Council "was a signal to broaden the scope of [diocesan newspaper] coverage of the news and to publish articles exploring such controversial subjects as the role of authority, homosexuality [and] the ordination of women to the priesthood."

Those controversial subjects and abortion, in the wake of the Supreme Court decisions which legalized it, continue to account for miles of column inches in Catholic newspapers and magazines. One effect of this newfound—or perhaps rediscovered—freedom has been that the discussion of the Catholic Church has become difficult to distinguish from the discussion of the American nation. The discourse of the Catholic Church in America seems increasingly to rely on conventional American national political categories, which is why we are tempted to assume that a "liberal" publication like the *National Catholic Reporter* is counterbalanced by a "conservative" publication like *The Wanderer.* We may safely assume that the former will never be able to summon much editorial passion against abortion (because liberals generally seem to agree that the killing of the unborn is a private matter) and that the latter will hesitate to object very loudly to the rapacity of a deliriously free market (because conservatives generally seem to agree that the maximization of profit is an absolute right).

Whether or not these developments in Catholic journalism have been helpful to the Catholic Church in the United States, they have not increased the number of American people reading Catholic publications. In 1965 the CPA reported that the combined circulation of Catholic newspapers, magazines, and newsletters in North America had reached 28,944,724. Slightly more than three decades later, and despite a remarkable growth in the Catholic population, that figure now stands at 27,348,517.

In my gloomier moments, I suspect that those Catholics who drift away from or fail to come to this readership are not really missing much. A *Commonweal* editorial on the recent death of John F. Kennedy Jr. noted how much Catholics in America have changed since his father's election to the presidency in 1960. "Catholics, it turned out, were more like the rest of America than either they or the rest of America imagined. That remains, it seems fair to say, both a blessing and a challenge." I agree, but I fear that

we aren't meeting the challenge all that well. Aside from what we find in
the parish bulletin, it too often seems that what we Catholics have to communicate to each other and to others is little more than a sort of "churchy"
and bowdlerized version of the national discourse—National Public Radio
with an occasional comment from the bishop, "Entertainment Tonight"
with the explicit sex and violence removed, *New York Times* editorials with
occasional quotes from bourgeois theologians and occasional references
to old documents with Latin titles. It sometimes seems that our conversation constitutes an acquiescence in a world that is passing away, an insistence that here we have an abiding city, a refusal to see the incarnation as
a singular, *the* singular event, a passive endorsement of the customary
ways of making do. In other words, it sometimes seem that our discourse
has far too little to do with "the mind of the Church."

Those of us who occasionally lament this apparent truncation are
often admonished about the dangers of sectarianism. We are warned, usually by people who have done rather nicely by modern culture, of the dangers of being countercultural. Our recommendation that the Church refuse
to engage the world on the world's terms is characterized as a recommendation that the Church withdraw from the world. Our insistence that Christ
has a Church is characterized as an insistence that that Church is the exclusive locus of God's activity. Our observation that Original Sin is a fact
of life, and that both we and the world are besieged and in need of rescue,
is characterized as a boorish longing for otherworldly salvation.

Such objections, sincere and well-intended as they often are, strike
me as terribly unfair. They bring to mind Walker Percy's account, in his
novel *The Second Coming,* of "the present-day unbeliever" who

> is crazy because he finds himself born into a world of endless wonders, having
> no notion how he got here, a world in which he eats, sleeps, . . . works, grows
> old, gets sick, and dies, and is quite content to have it so. Not once in his entire
> life does it cross his mind to say to himself that his situation is preposterous, that
> an explanation is due to him and to demand such an explanation and to refuse
> to play out another act of the farce until an explanation is forthcoming.

It seems to me that the best Catholic journalists and artists and theologians
are men and women who share with Percy and Flannery O'Connor and
Evelyn Waugh and Thomas Merton and Annie Dillard and Shusako Endo
and Leon Bloy and Pope John Paul II a rejection of the craziness of modern unbelief and a firm conviction that a self-consciously Catholic worldview, a deliberate appropriation of "the mind of the Church," is the only
sensible, perhaps the only possible response to the preposterous situation
Percy describes.

Such an appropriation is surely what Pope John Paul II had in mind in a Letter to Artists which he published on the last Easter of the millennium. He wrote:

> Sacred Scripture has become a sort of "immense vocabulary" (Paul Claudel) and "iconographic atlas" (Marc Chagall), from which both Christian culture and art have drawn. The Old Testament, read in the light of the New, has provided endless streams of inspiration. From the stories of the Creation and sin, the Flood, the cycle of the Patriarchs, the events of the Exodus to so many other episodes and characters in the history of salvation, the biblical text has fired the imagination of painters, poets, musicians, playwrights and film-makers. A figure like Job, to take but one example, with his searing and ever relevant question of suffering, still arouses an interest which is not just philosophical but literary and artistic as well. And what should we say of the New Testament? From the Nativity to Golgotha, from the Transfiguration to the Resurrection, from the miracles to the teachings of Christ, and on to the events recounted in the Acts of the Apostles or foreseen by the Apocalypse in an eschatological key, on countless occasions the biblical word has become image, music and poetry, evoking the mystery of "the Word made flesh" in the language of art.

Adrift, Deafened, Mesmerized

At the beginning of the millennium, when my grandfather was purchasing his *Catholic Encyclopedia,* the phrase "the mind of the Church" might have suggested very little promise of an "immense vocabulary" or of those "endless streams of inspiration" to which John Paul refers. For most people, whether Catholic or not, the phrase would surely have suggested a spinsterly suspicion of everything beyond clerical control, and perhaps even a predilection for the sorts of censorship and frog-marching intellectual conformity which would be notoriously perfected later on in the century by Josef Stalin. But at the end of the millennium, we are adrift in a sea of increasingly meaningless images, deafened by increasingly insistent and frivolous commercial appeals, mesmerized by media technologies which colonize the inmost reaches of our imaginations and souls. At the end of the millennium, "the mind of the Church" is a phrase that promises to break a lethal spell.

When the theologian Rev. James T. Burtchaell, C.S.C., addressed the 1985 convention of the CPA he gave a memorable account of the mission to which all Catholic journalists (and indeed all Catholic believers) were summoned by baptism to dedicate themselves. They must, he said, insist

> that men and women continue to be heartbroken and exhilarated by the rediscovery of an obstinately gracious God and of a fecklessly selfish world. And also that a Christian people be built up and sustained: as individuals who are mature and generous and truthful to a fault, as was Jesus crucified, who died so recklessly at our hands; and as a community that is intimate and neighborly and

determined—sisters and brothers in faith who are bent upon serving every need that is in the world because, like Jesus, we know no strangers and we refuse to have enemies. And that a Catholic Church rise up in constant celebration of God's grace, of our resurgence to life—and life abundantly—in that grace, and of the imperatives that grace impels us to: to draw every weary, distracted, dutiful fellow human into our exhausting and joyful secret that eternity is under way and whether we perish or flourish depends on how we cherish one another.

It is a paradox, or at least a surprise, that any of us could encounter or express the mind of such a Catholic Church as Father Burtchaell described in the middle of all the noise of media and the chaos of cyberspace. An exhausted web-surfer could wash up on some eccentric website—perhaps the New Advent website—and be arrested by some curiously compelling phrase from Augustine or some passage from the Mass readings of the day or some digitalized reproduction of a painting by El Greco. A treasonous, anarchistic, muckraking, revolutionary journalist named Dorothy Day once included a wonderful celebration of this phenomenon in her regular column in *The Catholic Worker* newspaper:

> The books will always be there. If we give up many other distractions, we can turn to them. We can browse among the millions of words written and often just what we find can nourish us, enlighten us, strengthen us—in fact, be our food just as Christ, the Word, is also our food.

Finding and spreading that Word will be the principal challenge for Catholic artists and journalists in the new millennium, just as it was the principal challenge for Catholic journalists and artists in the millennium just ended. My own suspicion is that their twenty-first–century challenge has been made more formidable by the passivity with which too many of their twentieth-century predecessors have regarded the quiet collapse of Catholic identity into the American mainstream. Perhaps these men and women have been traumatized by a painful collective memory of the bad old days of the Index, or perhaps they have been overeager in accommodating the secular orthodoxies regnant in the academy, studio, and newsroom, or perhaps they have not entered deeply enough into the mystery of faith to forge much of a conviction about it. For whatever reason, they have been reprehensibly bashful about asserting the legitimacy, let alone the indispensability, of the mind of the Church. To the extent that they are unable to overcome that bashfulness, they, and we who look at their pictures, read and listen to their words and music, and share their dreams will continue to be handicapped. We will continue to be the sorts of people we are now, people like the blind beggar sitting outside Jericho, desperately bellowing appeal after appeal to Jesus while voices from the surrounding darkness insist that we pipe down, that we shut the hell up.

Spirituality: Five Twentieth-Century Witnesses of Discipleship

Bishop Robert F. Morneau

Introduction

The late Fr. Raymond E. Brown, s.s., wrote: "To have had a significant past helps to give confidence about the future."[1] If we are to have
hope in the new millennium, it is well for us to reflect back on our recent
past, to reflect on the lives of various individuals who exemplify various
spiritual themes and events that inform us of our age in its relationship to
God. This will be followed by a series of "lessons" that the century just
closed offers for instruction. History is a great teacher. Not to attend her
class can be a fatal mistake.

So who are the individuals of the past century who have helped
shaped the spirituality in North America and beyond? Many come to mind
but I limit myself to five witnesses of discipleship: Thomas Merton, Pope
John XXIII, Dorothy Day, Flannery O'Connor, and John Courtney Murray.
Thomas Merton, living as a Trappist for twenty-seven years, used his gift
as a writer to remind us of the wealth of the contemplative tradition and the
necessity to integrate prayer into one's entire life. Pope John XXIII, calling
the Church to an ecumenical council, began an extensive renewal that continues to unfold in every area of Church life. Dorothy Day, foundress of the
Catholic Worker movement, took the Gospel to the streets and put the cor-
poral and spiritual works of mercy into practice. In unique ways Flannery
O'Connor and John Courtney Murray also made significant contributions
to the spiritual life of the twentieth century.

This approach does not mean to exclude key events over the past
hundred years that have shaped the soul of the century. Again the principle
of selectivity demands that we choose symbolic moments to express
major influences. World War II and the Holocaust have forever changed

---

[1] Raymond E. Brown, *The Churches the Apostles Left Behind* (New York: Paulist
Press, 1984) 69.

the landscape of spirituality in raising the question of divine providence in the midst of such horrendous suffering and pain. Another event lies in the field of science and technology: the reaching out into the heavens through space flights and the invention of such instruments as the Hubble Space Telescope that has expanded our awareness of the vastness of the universe. A third event of major import was the experience of the Vatican Council II and its sixteen documents. This *aggiornamento* ("updating") continues to send spiritual waves around the world challenging us to understand ourselves, the world, and the Church in new and deeper ways.

And then there are lessons to be learned, mistakes to be noted, debates to be continued. Like miners who carefully extract precious minerals from the bowels of the earth, we do well to mine the wisdom of our century lest the lessons be lost. We have learned much in every area of church life: liturgy, evangelization, stewardship, leadership, education. If the new millennium is to be fruitful, we must appropriate the wisdom of the past and allow it to shape our individual collective lives in the here and now.

What Is This Thing Called Spirituality?

Before focusing on individuals, events, and lessons, we need to say something about spirituality, a many leveled concept and reality. Spirituality has to do with our relationship with God. For Christians, that relationship is grounded in the mystery of Christ and his incarnation. God has been made present and manifest in the person of Jesus who calls all people to fullness of life. More, the grace and gift of the Holy Spirit has been given to empower us to know, love, and serve the gracious God who calls us to freedom and new life. At the center of Christian spirituality is the paschal mystery, the life-death-resurrection event that gained us salvation.

Within the Catholic tradition, spirituality is centered on our sacramental life, especially the Eucharist. Through signs and symbols, God continues to enter our lives and draw us ever more deeply into holiness and the works of justice. Further, prayer and asceticism are means that sustain and deepen our relationship with the living God and assist us to become servants of the kingdom. Spirituality is staying awake to God's presence; it is being attentive and responsive to the slightest action of grace.

Spirituality addresses the hungers of the soul for meaning, commitment, and integration. Spirituality presents to all the universal vocation to holiness, the perfection of love. In a sense all our eggs are in one basket (a poor economic practice but the only option for disciples). The basket is one of love: being loved by God and living a loving life in return. The great tragedy, American or otherwise, is not to exercise the virtue of charity.

Over the past one hundred years our understanding and practice of spirituality changed and this evolution will surely impact on the new century, the new millennium. A glance back is just that—a glance. As Tolstoy was told by his mother regarding sketching: the first decision regards what you are going to leave out.

Shapers of Our Spiritual Landscape

Thomas Merton (1915–68)

If spirituality is about searching, struggle, restlessness, Thomas Merton was one deeply engaged in these activities throughout his life. Educated in France, England, and the United States, Merton knew well that life was a pilgrimage and that we have no final home here. His death at age fifty-three in Bangkok gives evidence that right up until his death Merton was on the move externally and interiorly. His trip to Southeast Asia was yet another longing for truth as expressed in a different culture by other religions.

In what lies the good life, the holy life? For Merton and his close friends three things were essential: simplicity, wholeness, love. Merton responded to the call to contemplative life and sought in the radical simplicity of this life his path to God. Closely allied to simplicity is humility, a virtue that Merton often wrote about and which he found difficult to practice given his many talents and strong egotism. Yet throughout his writing and his entire life, he knew the one thing necessary: a union with God and people that overflowed in peace and joy.

Wholeness was another spiritual ingredient that Merton prayed for and made valiant efforts to attain. Integrity was a precious gem that he sought to acquire yet found so illusive. At times he would describe himself as a phony, saying one thing and doing another, writing eloquently while knowing that his present reality was quite different. Though never totally successful, part of the attraction to Merton's life and his writing is that they are "real," they present a flawed human being who found pretense abhorrent. There is an authenticity that allows us to appreciate and accept life as a truly "human" journey.

Merton was absolutely clear about the primacy of love on the spiritual journey. That is why he treasured so profoundly friendship, friendship with God as well as with a variety of men and women. The cost of friendship in terms of time, energy, commitment was high and Merton paid the full price. Mistakes were made, hurts were inflicted, some scars never healed. But the importance of relationships over things and career stands out as a major contribution to spirituality in the last one hundred years.

Merton also contributed much to the role of prayer and contemplation on the spiritual journey. He wrote brilliantly and movingly about the necessity of silence and solitude. He was in full agreement with John of the Cross in holding that contemplation at bottom was essentially loving attention. Merton sought more and more the depth of prayer that led to union. He hungered with a passionate restlessness for "experience," for the immediacy of God that left concepts and images and creedal propositions far behind. Merton witnessed to the contemplative life and a good part of the world paid attention.

One of the constant refrains in Merton's journey was the issue of the false self. Here the Trappist monk had a deep appreciation for modern psychology and its many insights. All of us deal with a variety of selves; our ideal self, our social self, our "real" self, and, yes, our false self. We are capable of constructing an image of who we think we are and what we would like to be, which is not the image that God has of us. Stripping away the false self—the process of conversion—is a life-long process and one senses that right up to his fifty-third and final year, Merton was engaged in a violent warfare against the false self.

So what has Merton left the twentieth century as a legacy? Numerous books describing prayer, solitude, the hungers of the human heart; a life that was "real," filled with successes and failures, graces and sins; an appreciation of friendship as one of the greatest of all God's gifts; the willingness to stay in the process of conversion, turning from our false self to the living and true God; the need to balance our excessive desire for full autonomy with an awareness that some authority and guidance is absolutely necessary; the joy of living and the ecstasy of poetry; an appreciation of the richness of other traditions and the need to glean their wisdom; a love for writing by which we can process our lives.

Although Merton has been dead for over thirty years, his writings continue to be published and read. Let me leave Merton on a personal note. A friend of mine was working as a salesman. He happened one evening to see a copy of Merton's autobiographical piece *The Seven Storey Mountain*. He read it through the night and within a week applied to enter the seminary. He was ordained and served as a priest for twenty-eight years until his death. Many other individuals also attribute to Merton a part of their finding God. No greater legacy could be left.

Pope John XXIII (1881–1963)

Born Angelo Giuseppe Roncalli, this son of a peasant family became pope on October 28, 1958, leading the Church as its pontiff for four and a half years. Rather than fulfill the expectancy of many as an interim, "do-nothing" pope, John XXIII called an ecumenical council and radically challenged the people of God to interface with the modern world. The shock waves continue to impact our world.

Here are five influences on spirituality deriving from the ministry and life of Pope John XXIII: (1) a sense of the importance of history, (2) the need for dialogue, (3) a firm hope in the providence of God, (4) a joy and enthusiasm that was contagious, (5) the centrality of the cross and obedience.

HISTORY

The maxim *historia magistra veritas* ("history is the teacher of truth") was carved deeply into Roncalli's soul. He had a well-developed philosophy of history which supported the claim that to move into the future with maturity and responsibility we must go back and absorb the wisdom and experiences and writings of our ancestors. Our newness and freshness depend upon our roots; our youthfulness and vitality are contingent on the mystery of ancestry. From this point of view tradition is not a musty archive containing old, dead truths but a flourishing garden that must be tended with care and love.

Pope John XXIII insisted that our faith life, our spirituality, be historical and existential. It must be alive to the signs of the time and grounded in a living tradition that provides direction and evaluative markers. The Church is a living, growing organism that must respond to the immediacy of the moment while being keenly aware of its rich background and values. Spirituality is thus an evolutionary and developmental reality, as are all historical entities, and must be wary of any attempt to ossify our imagination and our institutions. John XXIII wrote: "One of my favorite phrases brings me great comfort: we are not on earth as museum-keepers, but to cultivate a flourishing garden of life and to prepare a glorious future."

DIALOGUE

Spirituality is essentially a dialogic relationship: God speaking to us and our responding to God in word and deed. This is what is understood by prayer which, though multiple in form, comes back to the basic: listen and respond. John XXIII was a listener. He was aware of science and its new methodologies, of politics and its complexity, beauties and limitations, of economics and its impact on the totality of human life, of education and the work in the great universities, of culture and the hunger of the human soul for beauty. The Church must be in dialogue with this complex, ambiguous, often dangerous world. No longer can there be an isolationism, an us-against-them mentality, a refusal to talk. This was not happy news for many who were certain that the Church has nothing to gain and everything to lose in entering into a "covenant" with the rest of the world. John XXIII thought otherwise and won.

One of the most often-quoted passages from the Vatican Council II is Pope John's address in October of 1962 at the opening session of the council:

> In the daily exercise of our pastoral office, we sometimes have to listen—much to our regret—to voices of persons who, though burning with religious zeal, are not endowed with too much sense of discretion or measure. In these modern times they can see nothing but prevarication and ruin. . . . We feel we must disagree with these prophets of gloom. In the present order of things, divine providence is leading us to a new order of human relations which, by human effort and even beyond human expectation, are directed toward the fulfillment of God's higher and inscrutable designs; and everything, even human differences, leads to the greater good of the Church.

Central to Pope John's vision was the notion of unity. His zeal of oneness and harmony was grounded in the truth and he maintained that even though there are differences and untruths in the world, there is more that unites us than divides us. This conviction was revolutionary. Now we must find in every field—politics, economics, psychology, science, technology, culture—those values and attitudes that we agree upon while not ignoring what is the cause of disharmony and error. What Pope John XXIII did was get the Church back to the table with the attitude that we have a message to deliver, the good news of Jesus, and we have much to learn about how God has been and is operating in various segments of society.

HOPE

The Church is called to be a community of faith, hope, and love. Deeply ingrained in Pope John's soul was the virtue of the "not-yet," for he had grounded his life on a promise that God was with and for his people and the world. Facing great obstacles in calling the council, the Holy Father knew that God would guide it through the working of the Holy Spirit. He would not live to see the council's final work, but he had the conviction that the seeds planted would germinate and bear fruit, fruit that would last unto eternal life.

Elected pope on October 28, 1959, at the age of seventy-seven, there was little sense of "hope" for major changes. Yet within three months of his election, John XXIII stated his intention to convene an ecumenical council. That announcement contained so many elements of hope: freshness and new possibilities for the Church in the modern world; new energy in promoting the kingdom and doing the work of evangelization; trust that the future would be filled with unexpected graces; the expectation that love and faith would carry the day. If the council called by Giuseppe Roncalli needed a subtitle it would surely be "The Council of Hope." God's promise of being with the Church was taken seriously and the response to that promise was one of hope and trust.

JOY

Someone once wrote that the infallible sign of God's presence is joy. Whether or not it is wise to attribute infallibility of virtues, it is certainly wise and prudent to attribute to Pope John XXIII the grace of joy and enthusiasm. Here was a man who knew himself to be loved and called by God. That knowledge, appropriated through prayer, study, and discipline, expressed itself in a countenance that people found warm and inviting. The twinkle in the eye, the affability toward all, the capacity to laugh, even his "impishness" gave evidence of a rich and tender spirituality. John was not only a mentor but a model for the disciple of Jesus. Christianity is not a dour religion, weighed down by a negative theology and oppressive tradition. It is a jubilant and joy-filled religion flowing from the love of a Triune God who became one of us through the incarnation.

The joy exhibited by Pope John had nothing to do with a superficial understanding of reality. He was aware of evil and pain, suffering and brutality, wars and injustice. He had seen it all and knew, first-hand, the work of evil in the world. Yet facts and experiences could not and would not crush his ideals and dreams. God was still in charge and Christian hope and trust are in God's promises. Thus, Giuseppe Roncalli grounded his spirituality in the cross. As he lay dying, he commented to his priest-secretary that the secret of his ministry could be found in one object: the crucifix hanging on his bedroom wall. Christ's death, embracing with open arms the entire world in his love and forgiveness, was the cause for ultimate joy and provided the energy for a totally committed ministry filled with enthusiasm and unreserved generosity.

OBEDIENCE

Roncalli chose as his episcopal motto the Latin phrase *Obedientia et Pax* (obedience and peace). There was only one road to peace and that was the pathway of obedience. All depended on aligning one's own will with that of God. The sacrifice that was his obedience was total and absolute. Herein is the crisis of spirituality: the disposing of one's freedom into the hands of God. In our time which idolizes freedom as the absolute value, the claim that obedience is the only way to peace is thoroughly countercultural.

Roncalli, like so many other disciples, witnessed to this obedience as the *sine qua non* of discipleship.

Closely allied to obedience is the notion of vulnerability. Placing oneself in the space where one can be injured takes great courage. Calling a council at age seventy-seven is either an eccentric egotistical adventure or a surrendering response to a God who moved this man to begin a renewal that would further the kingdom of God. Pope John refused the immunity game. He was not immune to criticism or attack; he left himself vulnerable, as vulnerable as Jesus on the cross. One senses that the spirituality left us by John XXIII is one centered in the garden of Gethesami and on the hill of Calvary. It is a spiritual life that conforms itself to the simple, demanding statement: "Your will be done," whatever the price.

In the excellent biography *Pope John XIII: Shepherd of the Modern World,* Peter Hebblethwaite quotes this passage from John Milton's "Areopagitica" as a truth that Pope John had assimilated and lived: "I cannot praise a fugitive and cloistered virtue, unexercised and unbreathed, that never sallies out and sees her adversary, but slinks out of the race."[2] This pope sallied forth not so much to engage in a war but to foster the virtues of unity and harmony among nations, religions, and the Roman Catholic Church. Pope John has taught us so many lessons of spirituality that we will need several centuries to appropriate them.

Dorothy Day (1897–1980)

Spirituality has always struggled with a series of dialectics: prayer and action, freedom and obedience, solitude and community, time and eternity. The tendency is to construct an either/or dichotomy rather than a both/and integration. Dorothy Day, born in Brooklyn in 1897, became a person who developed an amazing ability of integration. She refused to compartmentalize life and fought to ensure that faith permeated every segment of one's Christian existence. Her contribution to the spirituality of the twentieth century was one of reconciling faith and justice.

Her vision of the kingdom called for more than a hands-on ministry, important as that is. There is a need to clothe the naked, feed the hungry, visit the imprisoned. But more is demanded of the follower of Christ. The question must be asked regarding the causes of nakedness, the system that leads to worldwide starvation, a society in which crime has become rampant and more and more prisons are being built. Christians must do upstream ministry in eradicating the causes and systems and philosophies

---

[2] Peter Hebblethwaite, *Pope John XIII: Shepherd of the Modern World* (Garden City, N.Y.: Doubleday, 1985) 34.

that throw bodies into the water. The down-stream ministry of pulling the bodies out of the water is certainly necessary but it is not sufficient.

Dorothy Day believed in education. In 1933 she started a newspaper that would criticize whatever was not of the gospel in our society and the world. This paper would take up the cause of the worker and the poor and promote their rights. She was calling for a new social order in which the dignity of every person would be honored and protected. No small wonder that she met so much opposition from those in authority whose power was being threatened. Two things mattered in her ministry: fostering the love that alone brings peace and justice, and embracing the lowly in a marvelous solidarity.

FAITH AND SOCIAL JUSTICE

Spirituality involves a double vocation of union with God and unity with our brothers and sisters. An integral faith which lives with the conviction of God's redeeming love that embraces us also extends itself to a radical concern for the welfare of humankind. The Scriptures constantly remind us that we cannot claim that we love God while neglecting the needy. Dorothy Day knew that holiness has a social and political dimension. The call to love must find expression in works of justice and peace.

As part of the Catholic tradition, Day appropriated the basic principle of human dignity. Every person has intrinsic worth and deserves our respect and help. In a special way those most disadvantaged have a claim on our ministry. Her discipleship emulated the servanthood of Jesus who went where the suffering was. Grounded in a graced empathy and compassion, Dorothy Day identified with the oppressed and fought for their liberation. It simply was not sufficient to pray for the poor or even provide for their immediate needs. The social systems of injustice had to be changed.

Reconciling faith and social justice is highlighted in the twenty-fifth chapter of the gospel of St. Matthew wherein the last judgment scene presents the ultimate criterion for salvation. It is what we do for the hungry and thirsty, the stranger and alienated that really matters. Dorothy Day realized that it was in proximity to the poor that she would encounter Jesus, with the gospel awareness that what she did or did not do for them she did or did not do for the Lord. This "mystery of the poor" was central to her spirituality and remains a central part of her legacy to the world.

FAITH AND NONVIOLENCE

The twentieth century was marked by an astounding amount of violence. The millions slain in the world wars, the countless victims of the holocaust, the random violence in our civilized country stain our times as the most brutal in all of recorded history. With the growth of science and technology we have now developed the capacity to many times over destroy our small planet Earth. The voices protesting the increase in violence have not been as numerous as one would hope.

Dorothy Day was committed to nonviolence, protesting wars and the nuclear build-up around the world. She knew and practiced the doctrine of civil disobedience knowing that there is a higher authority than that of the state. This stance cost her dearly but she paid the price. It was the support of her community and her personal prayer life that sustained her in this struggle to be a peacemaker. Spirituality, as lived by Dorothy Day, had a place for social protest.

One dimension of faith is submissive obedience to the lordship of Jesus. In the Beatitudes Jesus spoke of the blest as hungering and thirsting for justice as well as being peacemakers. Certain individuals have been graced to committing themselves to witnessing to nonviolence so as to challenge the rest of us to reconsider our stance of seeing the use of force as the ordinary way of handling conflict. While it is extremely difficult to justify an absolute pacifism, nonviolence is the model that comes to us from the Gospel and from most of our tradition.

FAITH AND HOSPITALITY

When Dorothy Day began the *Catholic Worker* newspaper in 1933, our country was in the midst of the Depression. Thousands upon thousands of individuals were without food and shelter. Day responded by converting her newspaper office into a space of hospitality. The poor were welcome and received nourishment, shelter, and love.

There is a haunting segment in Willa Cather's novel *My Antonia* in which a Bohemian family immigrates to the prairies. Destitute and forlorn they receive food and support from a family living at a neighboring farm. This hospitality and outreach was more than an act of kindness; it was a matter of life and death. And when the father of the Bohemian family was driven by despair to commit suicide, the young boy in the American family blames his grandparents for not doing more. This example is pertinent to our century because so many people have come to our lands. Far too many have received a limited hospitality, if any at all. It is people like Dorothy Day and the Catholic Worker movement who challenge us to live a gospel inclusivity and a generous hospitality.

What makes social hospitality possible and consistent is the presence of a spiritual hospitality in which the soul opens itself to the gift of the Holy Spirit. For Dorothy Day this was accomplished by means of a traditional and somewhat conservative devotional life. She turned to the Little Flower, Thérèse of Lisieux, for Thérèse's "little way" was a model of spirituality of simplicity and great profundity. Her legacy of hospitality began in prayer and ended in opening her heart and soul to the Christ she saw in the poor and abandoned.

Flannery O'Connor (1925–64)

She died at the age of thirty-nine from the painful disease of lupus. She spent most of her life in Georgia living with her mother on the family dairy farm. She traveled little and read much. Her name was Mary Flannery O'Connor, writer, disciple, prophet of the good news.

The twentieth century was in need of hope, and prophets are those individuals who not only criticize what is wrong with the times but offer new possibilities and new directions that lead to peace. Flannery O'Connor was given a creative imagination and she expressed her deep and abiding faith through narrative—and strange narratives they were. Characters who were eccentric and often self-absorbed, violence that was shocking as it was abhorrent, betrayals and deceptions that tore their souls apart. Yet in all this "realism" and messiness of life, the mystery of God's light and love was active and transformative. So often the image of the sun appears in her stories as a reminder of transcendence. So often it is confrontation and seemingly destructive actions that open the road to truth and redemption.

Flannery O'Connor wrote as a believer, as a Catholic. It was her faith that informed her vision. Her vision of mystery and sacraments colored her creative writings and shaped her rich imagination. Liturgy, study (especially the writing of St. Thomas Aquinas, Teilhard de Chardin, and Romano Guardini), and personal prayer fostered her faith development as she lived out her "narrow" vocation as a southern regional writer. Her thought captured many aspects of our past century and prophetically has prepared us to embrace the new gift of time.

In selecting Flannery O'Connor as a representative figure of the twentieth century in the field of literature I see three major contributions from her writings and life: the "violence" of grace and its incredible realness; the power of writing and the use of story as an evangelizing instrument; the challenge to embrace the human condition with its radical poverty and suffering.

GRACE

Grace is about change and change is painful, causing disorientation and a letting go of the darkness of sin. O'Connor had little patience for sentimental piety and none for romanticism. Life is messy and ambiguous;

the devil is active and effective. She saw grace as "almost imperceptible intrusions" that the modern eye finds hard to discern. Few people have much "feeling for the nature of the violences which precede and follow them [graces]." Her challenge to our century was to understand faith as operating in some of the darkest characters possible. O'Connor believed the Gospel message that the violent will bear it away. In the end all depends upon the acceptance or rejection of grace, upon the exercise of our free will.

Grace must be understood in the context of one's concept of God. Here Flannery O'Connor has a double vision. God, from one point of view, is unlimited, infinite, almighty. With the other eye she sees a God revealed specifically in the person of Jesus who became one of us, entered into the violence of our world, rose from the dead, and calls us home. The mysteries of incarnation and redemption confound us. Yet it is precisely the operation of God's gratuitous love in the violence of the paschal mystery that enables us to reach the faith conviction that God cares. Ultimately we come to know this God through charity, being loved, and living lives of generosity. Here is the grace that conquers violence and leads to the peace that all prophets, including the prophet O'Connor, see and proclaim. The charity that is grace has a hardness and endurance that precludes a sentimental view of life.

WRITING/STORY

Like Pope John Paul II, Flannery O'Connor realized the significance of truth. As a writer and story-teller she was concerned about the truth of things, the telling of life the way it is. Hers was a narrative theology, a telling of truth through story even though at times the narrative was repulsive and deeply disturbing. Her mother once suggested that her daughter should write about "nice" people. "Niceness" was not part of O'Connor's vocabulary. Her steely combativeness in being a servant of the truth sometimes startles and confuses the reader. Paradoxically she believed that sometimes truth is comprehended by readers only when it is distorted because of contemporary blindness and deafness.

O'Connor offers several lessons for our spiritual life. One is discipline, the other is patience. Any vocation to be fully activated demands constant effort. Gifts given must be cherished, nurtured, and developed by constant discipline. In her own life, severely limited because of lupus and therefore a lack of energy, she could only devote two hours a day to her writing. But, she was there at the writing table day after day. The discipline was supplemented by patience, that awful waiting for the creative impulse to stir words into life. Again O'Connor's realism came to her aid in that she did not allow expectation to become neurotic. Writing is painstaking work and she embraced her vocation as a calling from God and felt a deep responsibility to God and her audience for the proper use of her gift. For Flannery, "routine is a condition of survival."

The writer's problem is to find that "peculiar crossroads where time and place and eternity somehow meet." That is O'Connor's gift to our times: pointing out in narrative how God and the human person (community) intersect in the ordinary and extraordinary events of human life. Faith sees all as sacramental; grace is mediated through the senses and in history. In her novels and short stories there is an existential and historical approach to the Christian life. It's real, concrete, dynamic, transformative.

Poverty/Suffering

Thirty-nine years of life is both a long and a short time. The gift of writing is a responsibility and a limitation. Participating in the suffering of Christ is a formidable vocation. Flannery O'Connor was keenly aware of her own intrinsic poverty, her radical indigence. This is part of the human condition and relates to the first beatitude describing those blest who are "poor in spirit." O'Connor saw her gift to write and the inspiration she received as a miracle, as sheer grace. One senses in her letters and essays a profound gratitude for the blessings bestowed upon her. Humility drove her to recognize the source of her gift.

Suffering takes many forms: poor health, emotional turmoil, intellectual deprivation, spiritual darkness, the list goes on. Flannery knew suffering and pain; she drank deep at the well of the cross. But this was central to her faith life and to her work. Faith is not an "electric blanket" bringing comfort and an easy life. Faith is the participation in the fullness of Christ and she struggled to embrace the full cost of discipleship. Prayer sustained her. Not mystical prayer or even Ignatian spirituality but the simple prayer of presence and attentiveness. She would write in a letter: "You will have found Christ when you are concerned with other people's sufferings and not your own."

Another word here, one important to O'Connor's vocabulary, is limitation. Poverty and suffering are constant reminders of our limitation. Yet, and here is the insight, limitation is "a gateway to reality." This passion for living in reality, of being an authentic person, is O'Connor's great legacy. She ranks with some of the great prophets, like Ezekiel and Isaiah, in being a voice in the wilderness crying the truth of our human dignity, our fallenness and disgrace, our restoration through the power of the Holy Spirit.

John Courtney Murray (1904–67)

Two powerful markings of the twentieth century are pluralism and relativism. These terms have multiple meanings, but essentially they refer to the human search for truth and goodness. Pluralism approaches truth from many angles holding that no one tradition or intellectual school of thought has a monopoly on truth. Pushed to its extreme, pluralism appears to some as a vast cafateria line and truth is for one's subjective picking. Relativism says the same about "the good," holding that Shakespearean proposition that something is good or bad by thinking it so. Standards and criteria for morality are abandoned, if not blatantly denied.

A Jesuit priest, Fr. John Courtney Murray, felt a calling to address the complex issue of American pluralism as it interfaced with his own tradition of Roman Catholicism. Working as a scholar and political analyst, he articulated the thesis that the American principle of democracy and freedom was not incompatible with Christian discipleship but that, in fact, it freed the Church to do its proper work of evangelization. This new understanding and insight achieved the effect of helping many Catholics, especially in the political world, to feel confident that their work as politicians did not compromise their life as Catholic Christians.

John Courtney Murray taught theology, edited the very important periodical *Theological Studies,* and participated in the Vatican Council II. Though censored for a time from publishing in the area of Church-state issues, Murray eventually was vindicated when asked to draft the document on religious freedom for the council. The theme of the document stressed that faith must be freely chosen. Any coercion as to choice of religion is a violation of human dignity and is to be repudiated. We tend to take such a proposition for granted, but for centuries religious freedom was not extended as an intrinsic right. John Courtney Murray's gifts have enriched the life of the Church in our times.

I had the privilege of hearing Father Murray give a theological paper in 1965. At the end of the eloquent discourse I had a single thought: he could have documented every paragraph with titles of scholarly works. His brilliance and his love for scholarship were obvious. Here are three brief comments on Murray's legacy to us impacting on our spiritual lives.

HISTORICAL PERSPECTIVE

Following the insights of John Henry Cardinal Newman and others, Father Murray fostered an immense historical perspective as he did his theological work. Thus there is an evolutionary process in thought as there is in nature that draws us more deeply into the truth of things. Sometimes development makes wrong turns and must be corrected, but on the whole we are growing in our understanding of the mystery of God, of ourselves, of our Church, and of our society. Serious and sustained research is mandatory in the acquisition of a historical point of view. Father Murray is such a scholar and took his work with extreme seriousness.

BEING PROACTIVE

There is a reciprocity of influences in life. Culture influences us and we have the potential of influencing the culture. Thus both being reactive and proactive are qualities essential to human development. During the 1940s and 1950s there was considerable negativity regarding Catholicism. Father Murray did more than react to the charge that one could not be a good Catholic and a good American simultaneously. In a proactive way he began a series of articles demonstrating with eloquence and clarity and rigor of thought that there is a compatibility between the democracy of our land and our lives as Catholic disciples. He went further: the relationship between Church and state need not be antagonistic. We each have something significant to contribute to the common good and, indeed, to each other. So influential was Murray's work that he appeared on the cover of *Time* magazine, a periodical not noted for its love of Catholicism. This proactive and energetic stance demonstrated the importance of taking the initiative in bringing the Gospel message to the public.

FAITH AND REASON

The United States is a relatively young nation. A considerable amount of energy in our first two hundred years of existence has been devoted to pragmatic and utilitarian concerns, and rightly so. But in the midst of these survival and development patterns, there has been an implicit down-playing of the intrinsic value and importance of the intellectual life. More, so central has been the technological and rational pursuits that the faith component has often been relegated to the private sector of one's own conscience. Faith as a source of authentic truth and knowledge has fallen upon hard times.

Father Murray, in his life and ministry, valued both faith and reason as a means of coming into contact with the fullness of reality. Sensing his call to the priesthood already at the age of sixteen, he spent his entire life in the service of the Gospel and the person of Christ. As a scholar, he took upon himself the rigors of research and argued his case with clarity and great enthusiasm. His competence won the respect of scholars both within the Church and within society.

Spirituality needs both faith and reason; spirituality needs people who know how and when to be proactive; spirituality needs a vision arising from a broad historical perspective. Fr. John Courtney Murray's legacy is a cherished gift. The reading of his classic *We Hold These Truths* should be mandatory for anyone desirous of understanding the context of Catholicism in America.

Lessons

Every decade, every century, every millennium has its lessons. Here are ten lessons from the past one hundred years that speak to me of spirituality. Whether or not we have learned these lessons and are living them is another matter.

(1) Growth demands participation. In the Vatican II document on the liturgy, every worshiper is challenged to full, conscious, active participation. This principle cuts across every segment of life: we do not grow as spectators. Life is not a sport of observers but for participants.

(2) "No more war! No more war!" This lesson has not been learned. Pope Paul VI's plea forces us to ponder again the horrors of our centuries: world wars, the Holocaust, genocide. Becoming peace-makers and reconcilers is our urgent task.

(3) Discipleship demands stewardship. Stewards are people who know that all is gift and comes from God. Our claim to be followers of Christ requires that we nurture and share our gifts of time, talent, and treasures with others. Stewardship is not an option.

(4) Dialogue is the name of the game. With modern technology we have the tremendous capacity of entering into communication with the entire world. Mutual understanding is now a real possibility, and understanding, if graced, can lead to peace.

(5) "Take only what ye need!" This adage, if lived, would mean that we would have a world in which goods would be distributed among all nations. We must reclaim the ability to know and live the distinction between need and want, between what is necessary and what is useful.

(6) *In omnibus respice finem!* ("In all things, look to the end.") A renewed sense of eschatology helps us to put things in proper perspective. Spirituality keeps teaching us that we came from God, live in his love, and are destined to return home one day.

(7) Empowerment of gifts. Ministry is grounded in two realities: needs and gifts. In recent times we have sensed a rich development in using the gifts of more and more people. We still have a ways to go, aware that God will hold us accountable for not using our personal gifts and for inhibiting others from using their gifts in proper ways.

(8) A growing sense of interdependence. For many decades a type of absolute freedom and autonomy has led to a devastating individualism.

There are now signs indicating that only through mutuality and cooperation can we achieve full personhood.

(9) Call to liberation. Throughout the world there have been strong movements to thwart oppressive regimes. Some of the means used have been violent; others, respectful of human dignity. The gospel call to liberation is reaching more and more people.

(10) Banner: "The main thing is to know the main thing and to keep the main thing the main thing." Of course, the main thing in our spiritual life is to be loved and to be loving. Augustine describes grace in those terms: *Quia amasti me, Domine, fecisti me amabilem.* ("Because you have loved me, O Lord, you have made me lovable.")

Contributors

JOHN C. CORT, long-time social activist, joined the Catholic Worker in New York City in 1936, a year after graduating *cum laude* from Harvard. He was a founder of the Association of Catholic Trade Unionists (ACTU) and its first executive secretary. After a bout with tuberculosis, Cort returned to ACTU in 1946 as managing editor of *The Labor Leader.* He served as labor editor for *Commonweal* magazine for more than ten years, business agent of the Newspaper Guild of Boston, AFL-CIO, for twelve years, and from 1962 until 1964 was associate director of the Peace Corps in the Philippines. He was director of the Commonwealth Service Corps of Massachusetts from 1964 until 1970, and from 1970 until 1973 director of the Lynn (Massachusetts) Model Cities Program. Cort is the author of *Christian Socialism: A History* (Maryknoll, N.Y.: Orbis Books, 1964), and publisher and co-editor of *Christian Socialism: An Informal History* (Maryknoll, N.Y.: Orbis Books, 1988). Among other journals, his work has appeared in *The Progressive, The Nation, New Oxford Review,* and *Dissent.*

SALLY CUNNEEN is professor emeritus at Rockland Community College (SUNY), Suffern, New York, where she teaches courses in creative writing, African and Caribbean literature, and an interdisciplinary, cross-cultural course called "People in Families," which she designed and taught with an anthropologist. A native of Providence, Rhode Island, she is an honors graduate of the University of Toronto, holds a master's degree from Fordham University, New York City, and a doctorate in philosophy of education from Columbia University, New York City. In 1950 she became founding co-editor (with husband Joseph Cunneen) of *Cross Currents,* a scholarly interreligious quarterly, and she continues as an active associate editor. She has published widely in the religious and general press, and is the author of four books exploring the positive implications of women's religious experience. *In Search of Mary: The Woman and the Symbol* (New York: Ballantine Books, 1996), a book tracing the changing understanding of the God-Bearer who is also "the daughter of humanity," won the 1997 College Theology Book Award.

JOHN DEEDY is the author of a number of books, ranging from biography to ecology to Catholic commentary and history. *The Catholic Fact Book* (Chicago: Thomas More Press, 1986) won a 1987 national Catholic book award of the Catholic Press Association of the United States and Canada. Deedy holds a bachelor's degree from the College of the Holy Cross, Worcester, Massachusetts, a master's degree from Trinity College Dublin, and a certificate from the Institut du Pantheon in Paris. He worked in daily journalism in Worcester and Boston before becoming founding editor of *The Catholic Free Press,* newspaper of the Diocese of Worcester, in 1951. He was editor of *The Pittsburgh Catholic* from 1959 until 1967, and managing editor of *Commonweal* from 1969 to 1978, thereupon becoming an independent writer. His work has appeared in numerous American and European journals, among them *The New York Times, The Nation, The New Republic,* and *The Tablet* of London.

JAMES FINN was an associate editor of *Commonweal* from 1955 until 1961, and subsequently served as editor of *Worldview,* published by the Council on Religion and International Affairs, and of *Freedom Review,* published by Freedom House. He has written, edited, and contributed to a number of books, and written hundreds of essays for leading periodicals on the relation of religious, political, and cultural issues. He was the United States representative to the first international United Nations conference on the resolution on discrimination and intolerance concerning matters of religion and belief. He lives in New York City.

GERALD P. FOGARTY, S.J., is a professor of history and the William R. Kenan, Jr., professor of religious studies at the University of Virginia. A native of Baltimore, he holds bachelor and master degrees from Fordham University, New York City, and master and doctoral degrees from Yale, where in 1969 he won the Theron Rockwell Field Prize for the best dissertation in religious literature and poetry. That year he was also awarded the George Washington Egleston Prize for the best essay in American history. His books include *The Vatican and the Americanist Crisis* (Rome: Universita Gregoriana, 1974), winner of the Brewer Prize of the American Society of Church History; *The Vatican and the American Hierarchy from 1870–1965* (Wilmington, Del.: Michael Glazier, 1985); and *American Catholic Biblical Scholarship: A History from the Early Republic to Vatican II* (San Francisco: Harper & Row, 1989). Forthcoming is *Commonwealth Catholicism: A History of the Catholic Church in Virginia.* Fogarty has taught at Fordham University, Woodstock Theological Center (Washington, D.C.), Union Theological Seminary (New York City), Boston College, and the Catholic University of America (Washington, D.C.). Since 1971 he has been archivist for the Maryland Province of the Society of Jesus.

MICHAEL O. GARVEY, a native of Springfield, Illinois, is a 1974 graduate of the University of Notre Dame, Indiana, and since 1981 has been a member of the university's public-relations staff. Before returning to Notre Dame he spent several years at a Catholic Worker House in Davenport, Iowa, where he met Margaret Quigley, who became his wife. A former columnist for the *National Catholic Reporter,* Garvey has written essays and reviews for *Commonweal, America,* and *U.S. Catholic,* among other newspapers and journals. He contributed articles to the *HarperCollins Encyclopedia of Catholicism* (San Francisco: HarperSanFrancisco, 1995) and the *Encyclopedia of American Catholic History* (Collegeville: The Liturgical Press, 1997), and is the author of *Finding Fault* (Chicago: Thomas More Press, 1990), *Confessions of a Catholic Worker* (Chicago: Thomas More Press, 1978), and *State O'Chassis: An Earful of Ireland* (Chicago: Thomas More Press, 1980). With Margaret Quigley Garvey he is co-editor of *The Dorothy Day Book* (Springfield, Ill.: Templegate, 1982).

HOWARD J. GRAY, S.J., is director of the Boston College Center for Ignatian Spirituality in Chestnut Hill, Massachusetts. A native of Cleveland, Ohio, he entered the Society of Jesus in 1948 and was ordained in 1961. He spent 1962 through 1963 in tertianship at St. Beuno's, North Wales. Gray holds graduate degrees in theology and English literature, completing his doctoral studies at the University of Wisconsin. He has served within the Jesuit order as director of formation for the order's Detroit Province, rector of the Jesuit community at Weston Jesuit School of Theology, Cambridge, Massachusetts, and provincial superior of the Detroit Province. From 1989 to 1990 he was a special consultant to Jesuits of the East Asia Assistancy. Gray has written and lectured widely on Ignatian spirituality, priesthood, lay leadership, and ministry, in the United States as well as in Asia, Africa, the United Kingdom, and Ireland. He was a delegate to Jesuit General Congregations 33 and 34 [1983 and 1995, respectively], and from 1985 to 1988 was vice-president of the Conference of Major Superiors of Men. He has served on a number of university boards, and was on the papal-mandated teams that studied American religious life and assessed seminary life and training in the United States.

JEFFERY GROS, F.S.C., is associate director of the Secretariat for Ecumenical and Interreligious Affairs of the National Conference of Catholic Bishops/U.S. Catholic Conference. A native of Memphis, Tennessee, he holds degrees from St. Mary's University, Winona, Minnesota, Marquette University, Wisconsin, and a doctorate in systematic theology from Fordham University, New York City. He taught from high-school through graduate-school levels prior to becoming director in 1981 of the Commission on Faith and Order of the National Conference of Churches in the USA, a post he held for ten years. In 1986 he received the James Fitzgerald Award for Ecumenism from the National Association of Diocesan (R.C.) Ecumenical Officers, and in 1995 Manhattan College declared him an honorary doctor of pedagogy. He is the editor of several books dealing with ecumenical issues, and a writer for leading theological periodicals.

JOHN C. HAUGHEY, S.J., has been a professor of Christian ethics in Loyola University's graduate program (Illinois) since 1991. He has published numerous articles in national journals, and is the author of nine books, most recently *Virtue and Affluence* (Kansas City, Mo.: Sheed & Ward, 1997). Father Haughey has served as an associate editor of *America,* the national Jesuit journal of opinion, as pastor of St. Peter's Church in Charlotte, North Carolina, and as a senior research fellow at the Woodstock Theological Center at Georgetown University in Washington, D.C. He has also been a visiting professor at Weston School of Theology in Massachusetts and at Seton Hall University in New Jersey, and from 1985 to 1998 was a member of the Pontifical Council for Promoting Christian Unity, specifically in connection with its dialogue with World Pentecostalism. In 1988 he held the Touhy Chair at John Carroll University in Ohio.

JEANNE KNOERLE, S.P., is a Sister of Providence of St. Mary-of-the-Woods, Indiana. She taught in schools in Chicago, Washington, D.C., and Taiwan. From 1968 to 1983 she was president of St. Mary-of-the-Woods College in Indiana. Thereupon, for ten years she was a program officer in the Religion Division of the Lilly Endowment in Indianapolis. She is now retired, but continues to serve as a consultant to the Lilly Endowment.

BARBARA KRAEMER, O.S.F., is director of the Center for the Study of Religious Life. Located at Catholic Theological Union in Chicago, the center promotes interdisciplinary reflection and action on the life of Catholic religious sisters, brothers, and priests in the United States, and serves as a resource to religious leadership. Most recently Kraemer was on the faculty of the graduate program in public services at DePaul University, Chicago. Previously she was associate dean of faculty at St. Augustine College, a nondenominational, bilingual college for Hispanics in Chicago. From 1980 to 1988 she served on the generalate team of the School Sisters of St. Francis, Milwaukee. She holds a doctorate in public policy analysis from the University of Illinois at Chicago, master's degrees from DePaul University and Washington University in St. Louis, and a bachelor's degree from Alverno College in Milwaukee.

CATHERINE LUPORI, associate professor emeritus at the College of St. Catherine in St. Paul, Minnesota, joined the English department there in 1951 and served as its chair from 1977 to 1986. When the Abigail Quigley McCarthy Center for Women's Research, Resources and Scholarship was established at St. Catherine's in 1985, Lupori became its founding director. She was coordinator of women's studies at the college and taught courses in that field before retiring in 1994. A member of St. Joan of Arc parish in Minneapolis, Lupori has served on the drafting committee for a St. Paul–Minneapolis archdiocesan paper on women and the Church, on a Catholic interracial council scholarship program, and, most recently, on the planning program for an ecumenical women's spirituality group.

PATRICIA M. MCDONALD, S.H.C.J., an English-born religious of the Society of the Holy Child Jesus, is in her ninth year of teaching of Mount St. Mary's College, Emmitsburg, Maryland. She is currently an associate professor in the college's theology department, and has been department chair since January 1999. She holds bachelor's and master's degrees from Cambridge University in England and Heythrop College, University of London, a licentiate from the Pontifical Biblical Institute in Rome, and a doctor of philosophy degree from the Catholic University of America, Washington, D.C. She has lectured and published widely on biblical themes, including in the *Journal for the Study of the New Testament* and *Horizons.* Her current book project is tentatively titled *The Peaceable Bible.*

BISHOP ROBERT F. MORNEAU was ordained auxiliary bishop of Green Bay, Wisconsin, in 1979, previously serving as diocesan director for religious and as an instructor of philosophy at Silver Lake College in Manitowoc, Wisconsin. He has also taught at the Summer Theological Institute of St. Nobert Abbey in De Pere, Wisconsin. A priest since 1966, Bishop Morneau holds a master of arts degree from the Catholic University of America and is the author of many books, among them studies of the poet Jessica Powers. He is in wide demand as a retreat master and lecturer throughout the United States. His writings have appeared in such periodicals as *Contemplative Review, Review for Religious, Sisters Today, Spiritual Life, Pastoral Life Magazine,* and *U.S. Catholic.*

DAVID J. O'BRIEN is Loyola Professor of Roman Catholic Studies and professor of history at the College of the Holy Cross in Worcester, Massachusetts. He is also director of the college's Peace and Conflict Studies Program. A 1960 graduate of the University of Notre Dame, Indiana, O'Brien holds a doctor of philosophy degree from the University of Rochester and has been awarded a number of honorary doctorates. Among his several books are a history of the Diocese of Syracuse, New York, and a biography of Isaac Hecker, founder of the Paulists, titled *Isaac Hecker: An American Catholic* (Mahwah, N.J.: Paulist Press, 1992). The Hecker book won the John Gilmary Shea Prize of the American Catholic Historical Association, and the Alpha Sigma Nu Award as the best book in the humanities published that year by a professor in an American Jesuit college or university. His latest book is *From the Heart of the American Church: Catholic Higher Education and American Culture* (Maryknoll, N.Y.: Orbis Books, 1994). In 1998–99, O'Brien served as president of the American Catholic Historical Association.

MARY JO RICHARDSON, a consultant specializing in evaluation of educational programs, holds a doctorate in education from the University of St. Thomas, St. Paul, Minnesota. She served as executive director of the Minneapolis Commission on National and Community Service from its inception in 1993 through 1997, and in that position was responsible for launching the AmeriCorps programs for the state of Minnesota. Previously she established the youth development/youth service network that exists in more than three hundred school districts of the state. She has served as assistant commissioner in the Department of Economic Security and as a senior planner at Minnesota Planning. Prior to her work in state government, Richardson taught in both Catholic and public high schools and was executive director of the Minnesota Association for Children with Learning Disabilities. She likewise has served as chair of the Urban Affairs Commission of the Archdiocese of St. Paul–Minneapolis, and as a member of the Archdiocesan Pastoral Council. Currently she is a member of the social justice committee of St. Odilia's Church in Shoreview, Minnesota.

Selected Index

Abortion
    Roe v. Wade, Supreme Court
      decision, 198ff
"Americanism" controversy, 117–18
Association of Catholic Trade
    Unionists (ACTU) 159,
    160, 164–5

Ball, William Bentley, 183–4
Benedict XV, pope
    and World War I, 3–4
Biblical Scholarship, 113ff
    climate of suspicion, 120–1
    and Pius XII's *Divino afflante*
      Spiritu, 121, 124–6
    and Vatican II's *Dei Verbum,*
      125–6
    and ecumenical interaction, 130
Brownson, Orestes, 103
Buckley, William F., Jr., 150, 161
Burtchaell, James T., 214–15

Capitalism, Catholic attitudes, 150
Catechism of the Catholic Church
    (1994), 129
Catholic Biblical Association of
    America, 122–4
Catholic Press Association, 210–11
Catholic Worker Movement, 163, 173
    see also Dorothy Day
Christian Family Movement, 62–3, 94

Church and state, 183ff
    and Oregon School Law, 186–7
    and Vatican II, 196
    and presidential race of Alfred E.
      Smith, 187–9
    and presidential race of John
      Fitzgerald Kennedy, 195ff
    and aid to parochial schools
      (busing, released time, etc.), 189ff
    and saluting the flag, 188–9
Communications and the Arts, 203ff
    John Paul II and communications,
      203, 213, 214
    Pius X and communications,
      204–5
    U.S. Bishops and communications,
      210–11
    Vatican II and communications,
      211–12
Crowley, Pat and Patty, 62, 65–6
Curran, Charles E., 66

Day, Dorothy, 58, 78–9, 94, 163–4,
    173, 215
    influence after death, 165
    spiritual legacy, 224–7
Democratic Socialism, 149ff

Economic Justice
    and U.S. bishops, 172ff
    and Vatican II, 173–4

Ecumenism, 131ff
stirrings in Protestantism, 133–4
Catholic ambivalence, 134
mid-century shift in Catholic attitudes, 137–40
non-Catholic observers at Vatican II, 138
post-Vatican II developments, 140–6
sacramental sharing, 142–4
challenges, 146–7
Education, Catholic, 101ff
Catholic school system, 106–7
role of religion in schools, 103–4
and Third Plenary Council (1884), 104
Supreme Court rulings, 104–5
and *Ex corde ecclesiae,* 110–11, 201

Family, Catholic, 57–71
contraception, 59–60, 64–6
birth control pill, 63
rhythm method, 63
Papal Birth Control Commission, 65
post-World War II, 61–6
divorce rates, 71
Fenton, Joseph C., 125

Gay Catholics, 27–9
Globalization, challenges of, 178–81
Greeley, Andrew, 65, 71, 89, 96, 176

Hecker, Isaac, 103
Higgins, George G., 163, 166
Humanae vitae, xv, 66–7
see also Paul VI
Hutchins, Robert M.
on federal aid to education, 196–7

Index of Forbidden Books, 205, 206, 207

Jewish people
repudiation of notion of Deicide, xii–xiii

John XXIII on Jewish people, 10
John XXIII, pope
election as pontiff, 8
calls Vatican II, 9–10
and interior life of Church, 10
encyclicals, 10–11
Cuban missile crisis, 10
on socialism, 154
spiritual legacy, 220–4
and Jewish people, 10
John Paul I, pope, 15
John Paul II, pope, x
election as pontiff, 15–16
encyclicals, 17
and internal life of Church, 17–18
and the Orthodox, 18
and social encyclical, *Centesimus annus,* 149ff
critique of capitalism, 149ff

Kennedy, Joseph P., 59
Kennedy, John Fitzgerald, 14, 41, 110, 195ff
Küng, Hans, 17

Las Hermanas (1971), 45
Lateran Treaty (1929), x, 4
see also Roman Question
Leo XIII, pope
intellectual legacy, 1
and *Providentissimus Deus* (1895 encyclical), 114–15, 118, 124, 126
and Church and State, 185, 186
and Pontifical Biblical Commission, 115

Maurin, Peter, 78, 94, 163, 173
Merton, Thomas, 205–6, 207, 213
spiritual legacy, 219, 220
Murray, John Courtney, x, 1, 8, 193–6, 202
spiritual legacy, 229–32
Mystical Body of Christ, 7

National Black Catholic Clergy
Conference, 45
National Black Catholic Sisters
Conference, 45
National Catholic Welfare Conference
Pius XI's condemnation, 6
forerunner of U.S. Catholic Con-
ference, 160
Neuhaus, Richard, 151, 161
Noonan, John T., Jr., 64, 65, 202
Novak, Michael, 150, 155–6,
160–1, 177

O'Connor, Flannery, 207–8, 213
spiritual legacy, 227–9
O'Connor, John Cardinal, 165–6
Oxford Movement, 134

Padres (1969), 45
Paul VI, pope, 11–15
election as pontiff, 11–12
and Vatican II, 12, 13
Humanae vitae, 13, 66
Pentacostal Movement, 145
Percy, Walker, 208–09, 213
Pius X, pope
policies of pontificate, 2–3
and Pontifical Biblical Institute,
115, 121
Pius XI, pope
encyclicals, 5, 6
condemnations of totalitarian
regimes, 5
and interior life of the Church,
5–6
Pius XII, pope
background and election, 6
the Holocaust and World War II, 7
and internal life of the Church, 7–8
and rhythm method of birth regulation, 63
and *Divino afflante Spiritu,* 121
Priesthood, Catholic, 21–36
decline in vocations, 24

acceptance of priests from other
denominations, 33
identity and mission, 22–6
relationship with the people of
God, 26–30, 35
role in secular society, 30–2
pedophilia problem, 32–3
sexual identity, 27–9

Religious Sisters and Brothers, 37–55
response to Vatican II, 41ff
and the civil-rights movement,
45, 47
conferences of religious men and
women, 40–1, 45, 82–4
new ministries, 47–8
retirement needs, 48–9
challenges to authority, 44
and U.S. culture, 44–9
associate memberships, 49–50
vocations and the future, 51–2
and feminism, 47
Roman Question, 1–2, 3–4
see also Lateran Treaty
Ryan, John A., 162–3, 173

Salvation outside the Church, xiv
and *Lumen gentium,* xiv–xv
Scharper, Philip and Sally, 65–6, 71
Social Justice, 149ff
Catholic teaching, 149–50
right to work, 155
right to organize, 166
U.S. Bishops' pastoral on the
economy, 150–1, 174–5
Socialism
softening of Caholic position, 150
Spellman, Francis J., cardinal, 196
Stewardship, 175–8

Taylor, Myron C., 6
Teilhard de Chardin, Pierre, x, 10

Unam sanctam, xiv

Vatican Council II, *passim*
Virgin Mary, 7

Waugh, Eveyln, 206–7, 213
Women, Catholic, 73ff
    Doctors of the Church, xi, 81
    and Vatican II, xi–xii, 73, 80–1
    question of female ordination, xii,
        18, 27–9, 33, 146
    women's movement, 73, 79
    and the ERA, 79–80

and U.S. Bishops, 75–6, 87–8
and Catholic education, 76, 102
role as educators, 102, 107–8
inclusive language, 87

Youth, Catholic, 89ff
    as pawns in culture wars, 90–2
    and religious literacy, 90–1, 98
    and education, 92–3
    youth ministries, 94, 96, 99